THE WORL… ATEST SUPE… ERO!

The AMAZING SPIDER-MAN

Amazing Grace

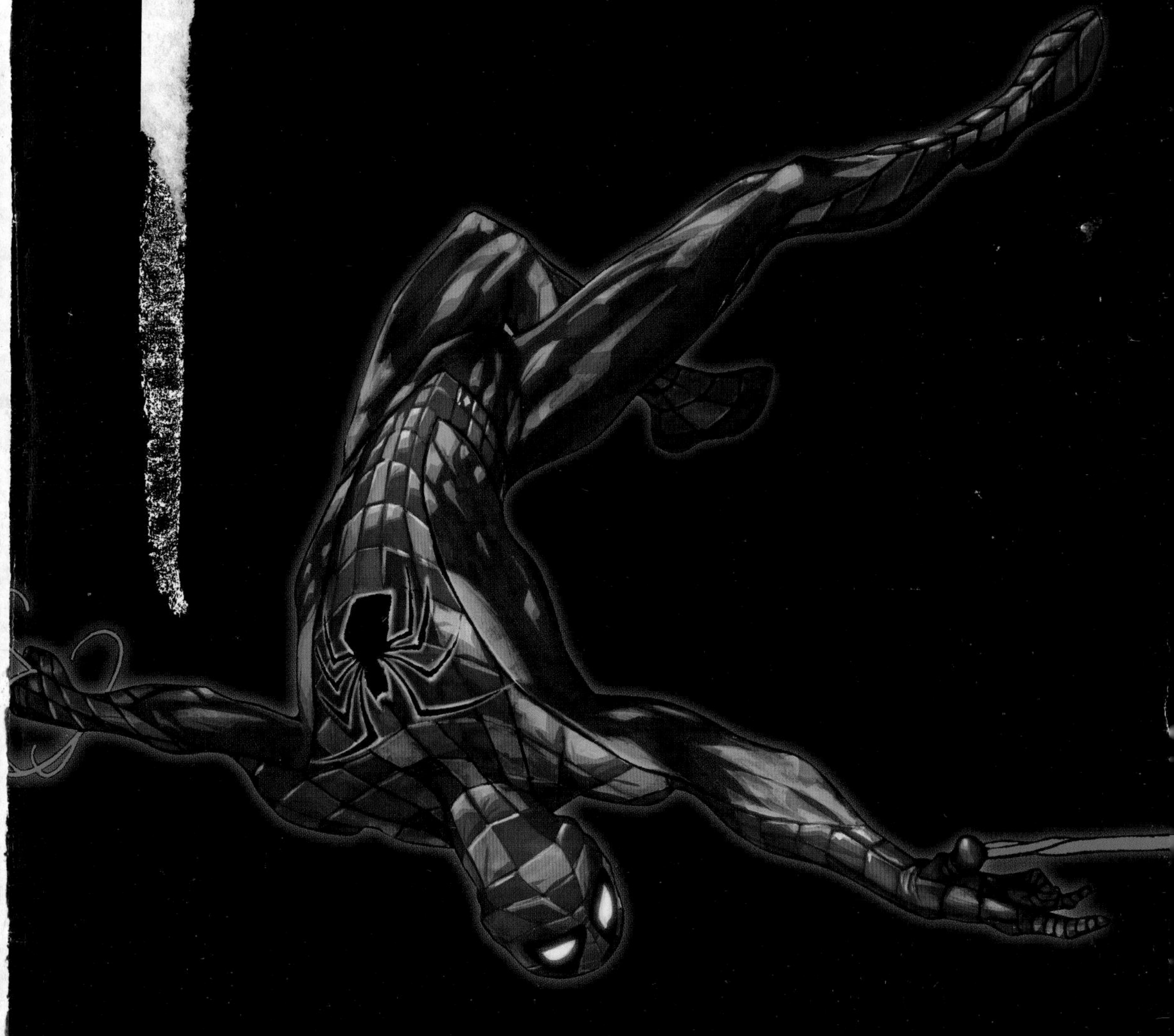

THE WORLD'S GREATEST SUPER HERO!

The AMAZING SPIDER-MAN

Amazing Grace

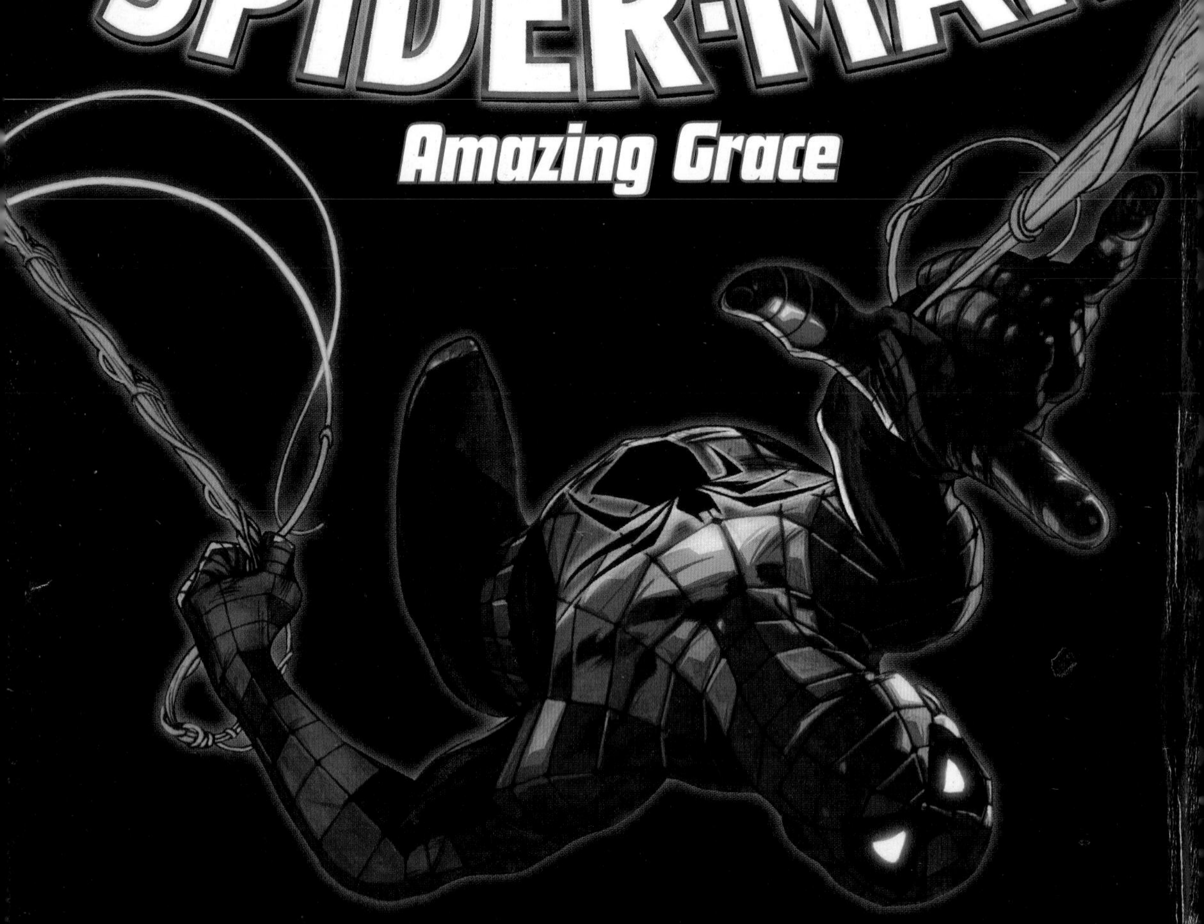

WRITER: JOSE MOLINA
ARTISTS: SIMONE BIANCHI with ANDREA BROCCARDO (ISSUES #1.4-1.6)
COLOURISTS: ISRAEL SILVA, MARTE GRACIA, ANDRES MOSSA, JAVA TARTAGLIA & DAVID CURIEL
LETTERER: VC'S JOE CARAMAGNA

ASSISTANT EDITOR: DEVIN LEWIS
EDITOR: NICK LOWE
EDITOR-IN-CHIEF: AXEL ALONSO

CHIEF CREATIVE OFFICER: JOE QUESADA
EXECUTIVE PRODUCER: ALAN FINE
PUBLISHER: DAN BUCKLEY

COVER ART: SIMONE BIANCHI

Do you have any comments or queries about Amazing Spider-Man: Amazing Grace? Email us at graphicnovels@panini.co.uk
Join us on Facebook at Panini/Marvel Graphic Novels

TM & © 2016 Marvel & Subs. Licensed by Marvel Characters B.V. through Panini S.p.A., Italy. All Rights Reserved. First impression 2016. Published by Panini Publishing, a division of Panini UK Limited. Mike Riddell, Managing Director. Alan O'Keefe, Managing Editor. Mark Irvine, Production Manager. Marco M. Lupoi, Publishing Director Europe. Brady Webb, Reprint Editor. Charlotte Harvey, Designer. Office of publication: Brockbourne House, 77 Mount Ephraim, Tunbridge Wells, Kent TN4 8BS. This publication may not be sold, except by authorised dealers, and is sold subject to the condition that it shall not be sold or distributed with any part of its cover or markings removed, nor in a mutilated condition. Printed in Italy by Lito Terrazzi. ISBN: 978-1-84653-730-1

MARVEL GRAPHIC NOVEL AMAZING SPIDER-MAN VOL 5 #1.1

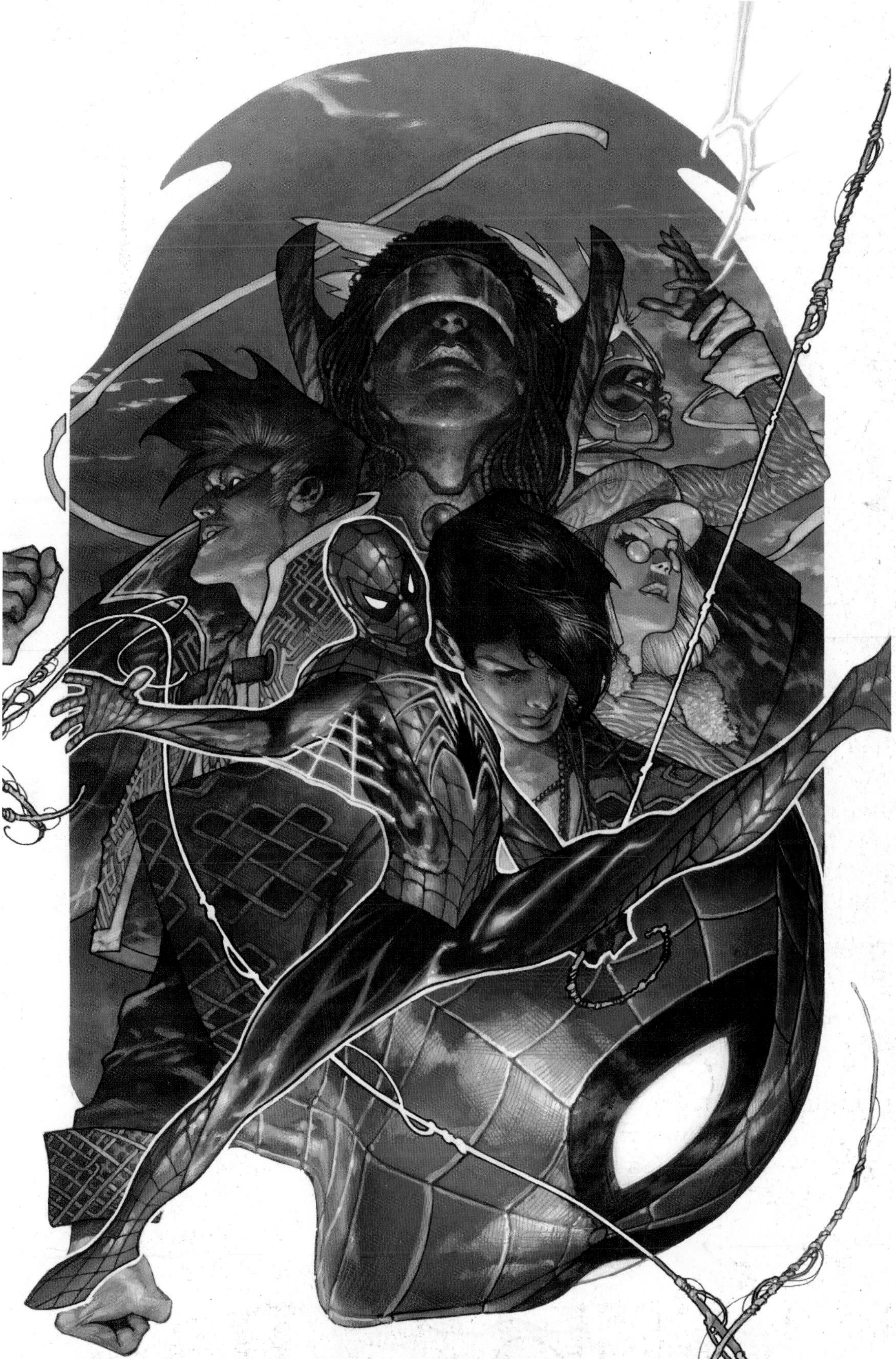

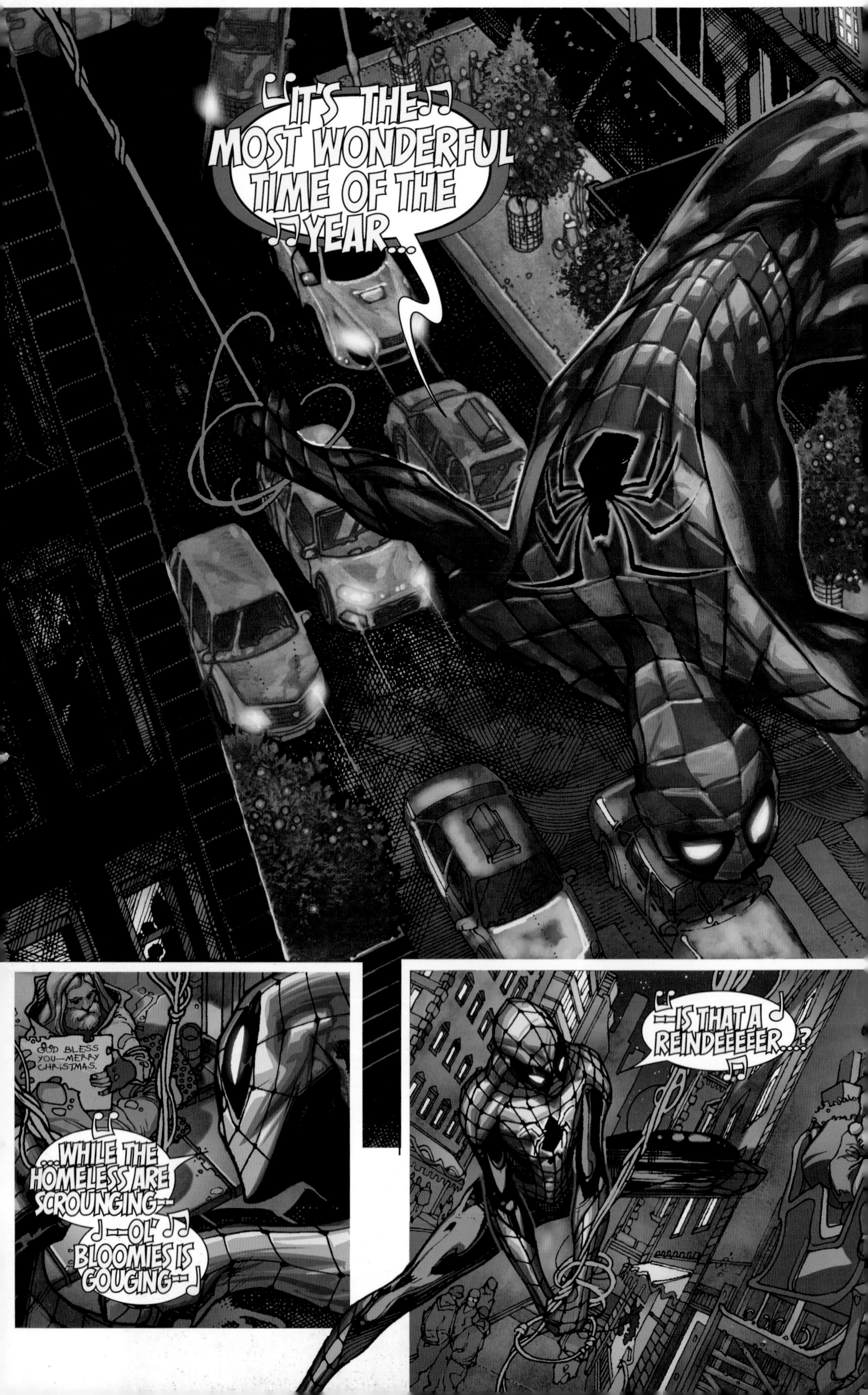
IT'S THE MOST WONDERFUL TIME OF THE YEAR...
GOD BLESS YOU—MERRY CHRISTMAS.
...WHILE THE HOMELESS ARE SCROUNGING--
--OL' BLOOMIES IS GOUGING--
--IS THAT A REINDEEEEEER...?

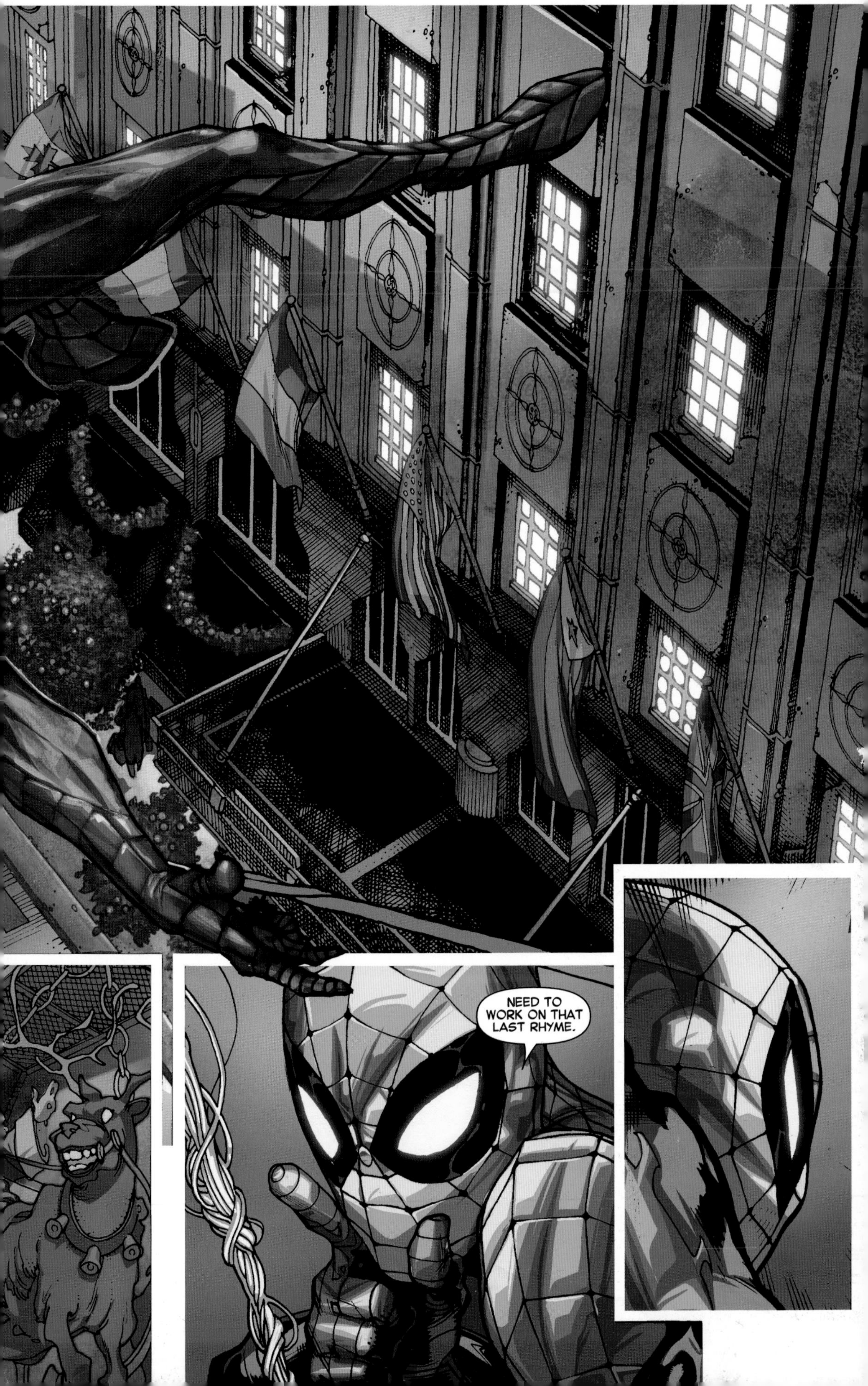
NEED TO
WORK ON THAT
LAST RHYME.

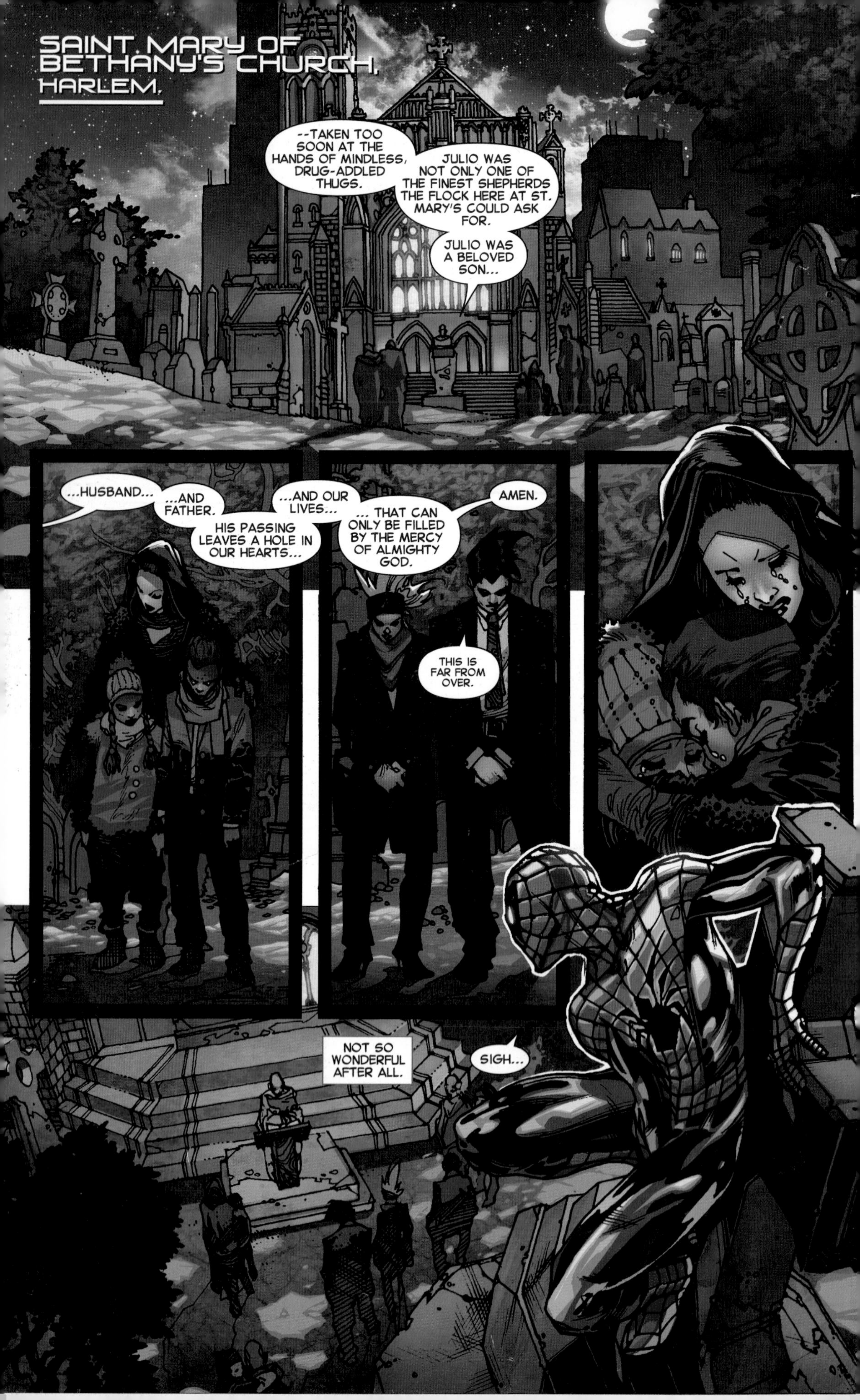
SAINT MARY OF BETHANY'S CHURCH, HARLEM.
--TAKEN TOO SOON AT THE HANDS OF MINDLESS, DRUG-ADDLED THUGS.
JULIO WAS NOT ONLY ONE OF THE FINEST SHEPHERDS THE FLOCK HERE AT ST. MARY'S COULD ASK FOR.
JULIO WAS A BELOVED SON...
...HUSBAND...
...AND FATHER.
HIS PASSING LEAVES A HOLE IN OUR HEARTS...
...AND OUR LIVES...
... THAT CAN ONLY BE FILLED BY THE MERCY OF ALMIGHTY GOD.
AMEN.
THIS IS FAR FROM OVER.
NOT SO WONDERFUL AFTER ALL.
SIGH...

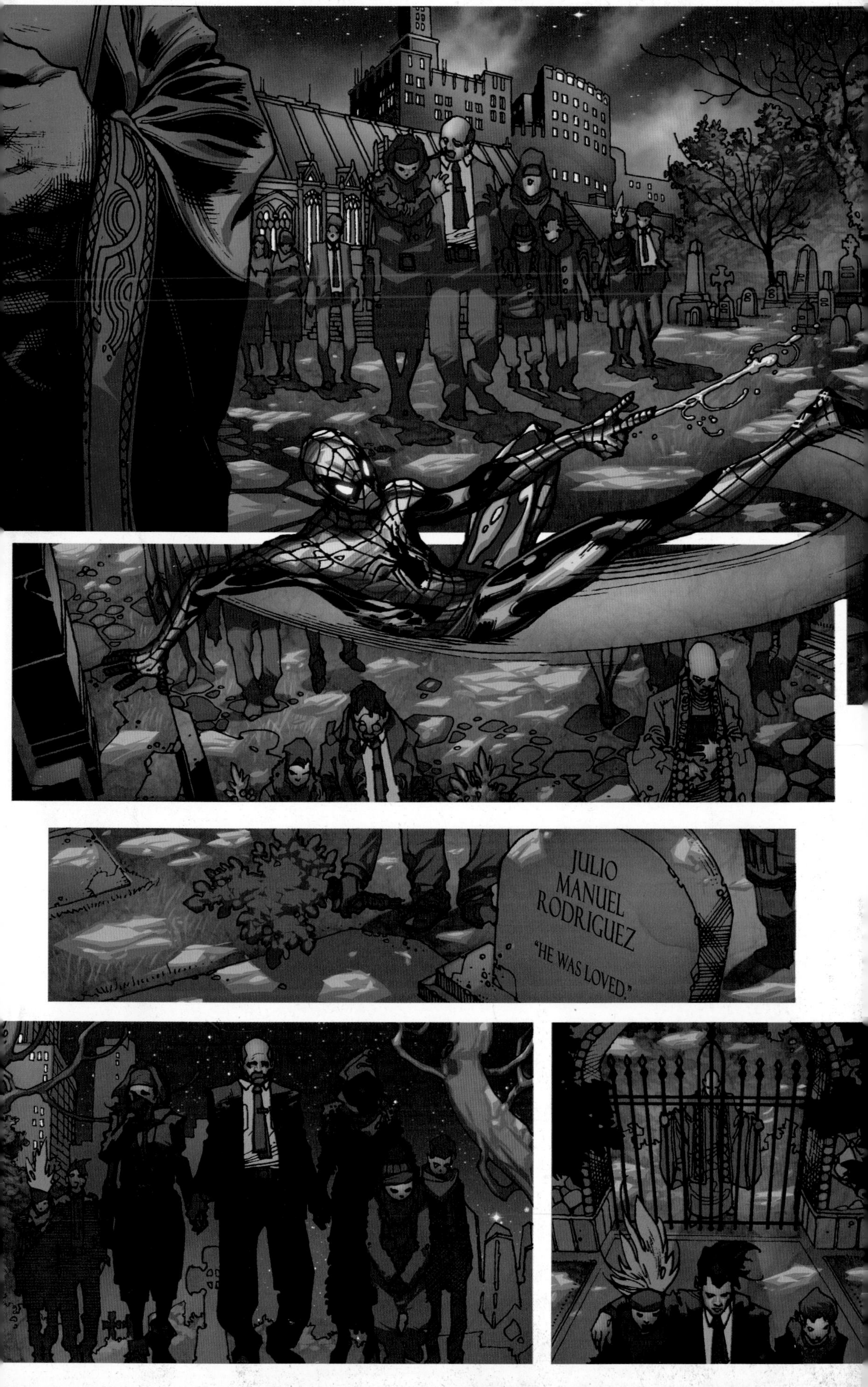
JULIO
MANUEL
RODRIGUEZ
"HE WAS LOVED."

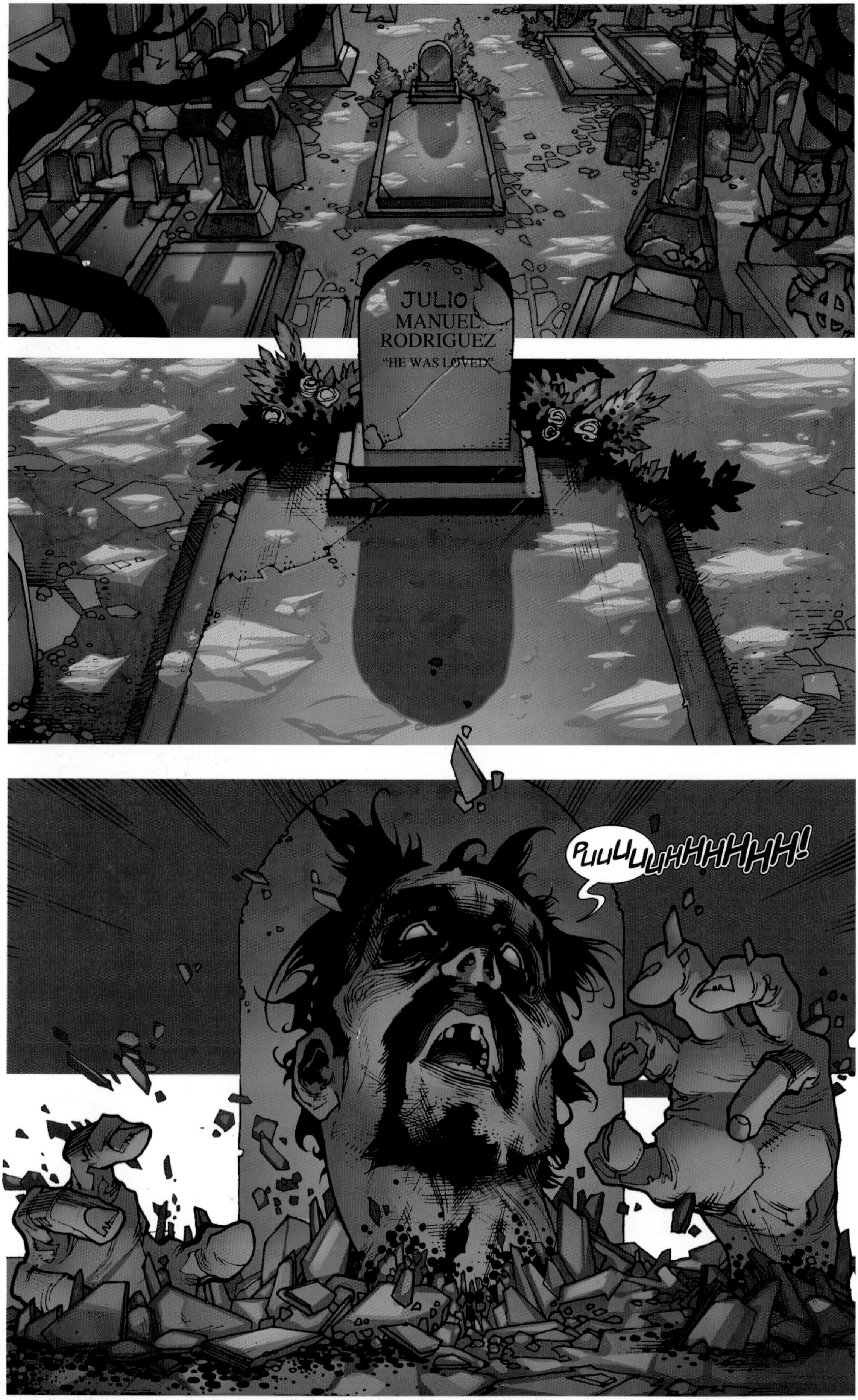
JULIO
MANUEL
RODRIGUEZ
"HE WAS LOVED"
PUUUUUHHHHHH!

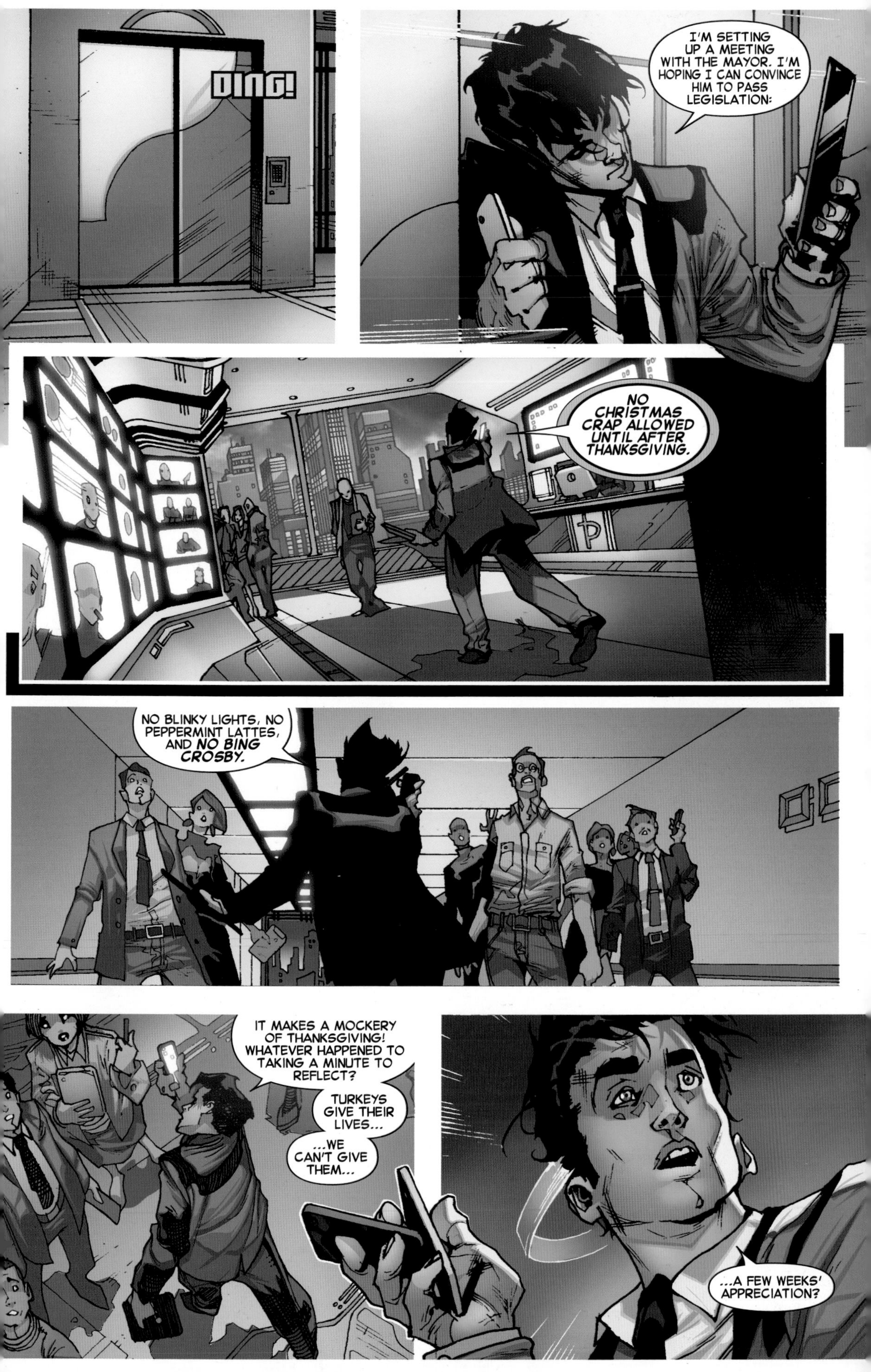
DING!
I'M SETTING UP A MEETING WITH THE MAYOR. I'M HOPING I CAN CONVINCE HIM TO PASS LEGISLATION:
NO CHRISTMAS CRAP ALLOWED UNTIL AFTER THANKSGIVING.
NO BLINKY LIGHTS, NO PEPPERMINT LATTES, AND NO BING CROSBY.
IT MAKES A MOCKERY OF THANKSGIVING! WHATEVER HAPPENED TO TAKING A MINUTE TO REFLECT?
TURKEYS GIVE THEIR LIVES...
...WE CAN'T GIVE THEM...
...A FEW WEEKS' APPRECIATION?

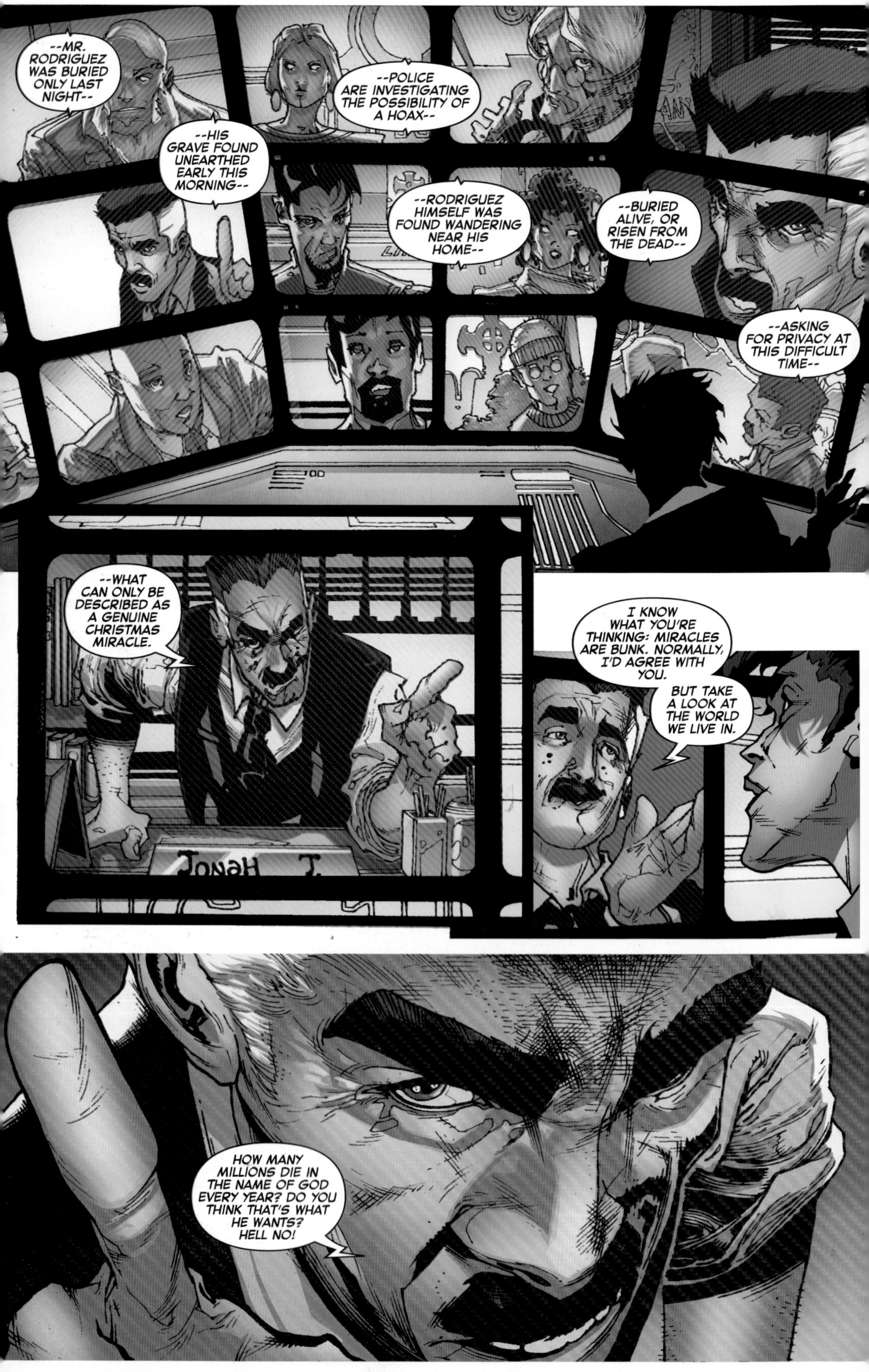
--MR. RODRIGUEZ WAS BURIED ONLY LAST NIGHT--
--POLICE ARE INVESTIGATING THE POSSIBILITY OF A HOAX--
--HIS GRAVE FOUND UNEARTHED EARLY THIS MORNING--
--RODRIGUEZ HIMSELF WAS FOUND WANDERING NEAR HIS HOME--
--BURIED ALIVE, OR RISEN FROM THE DEAD--
--ASKING FOR PRIVACY AT THIS DIFFICULT TIME--
--WHAT CAN ONLY BE DESCRIBED AS A GENUINE CHRISTMAS MIRACLE.
JONAH J.
I KNOW WHAT YOU'RE THINKING: MIRACLES ARE BUNK. NORMALLY, I'D AGREE WITH YOU.
BUT TAKE A LOOK AT THE WORLD WE LIVE IN.
HOW MANY MILLIONS DIE IN THE NAME OF GOD EVERY YEAR? DO YOU THINK THAT'S WHAT HE WANTS? HELL NO!

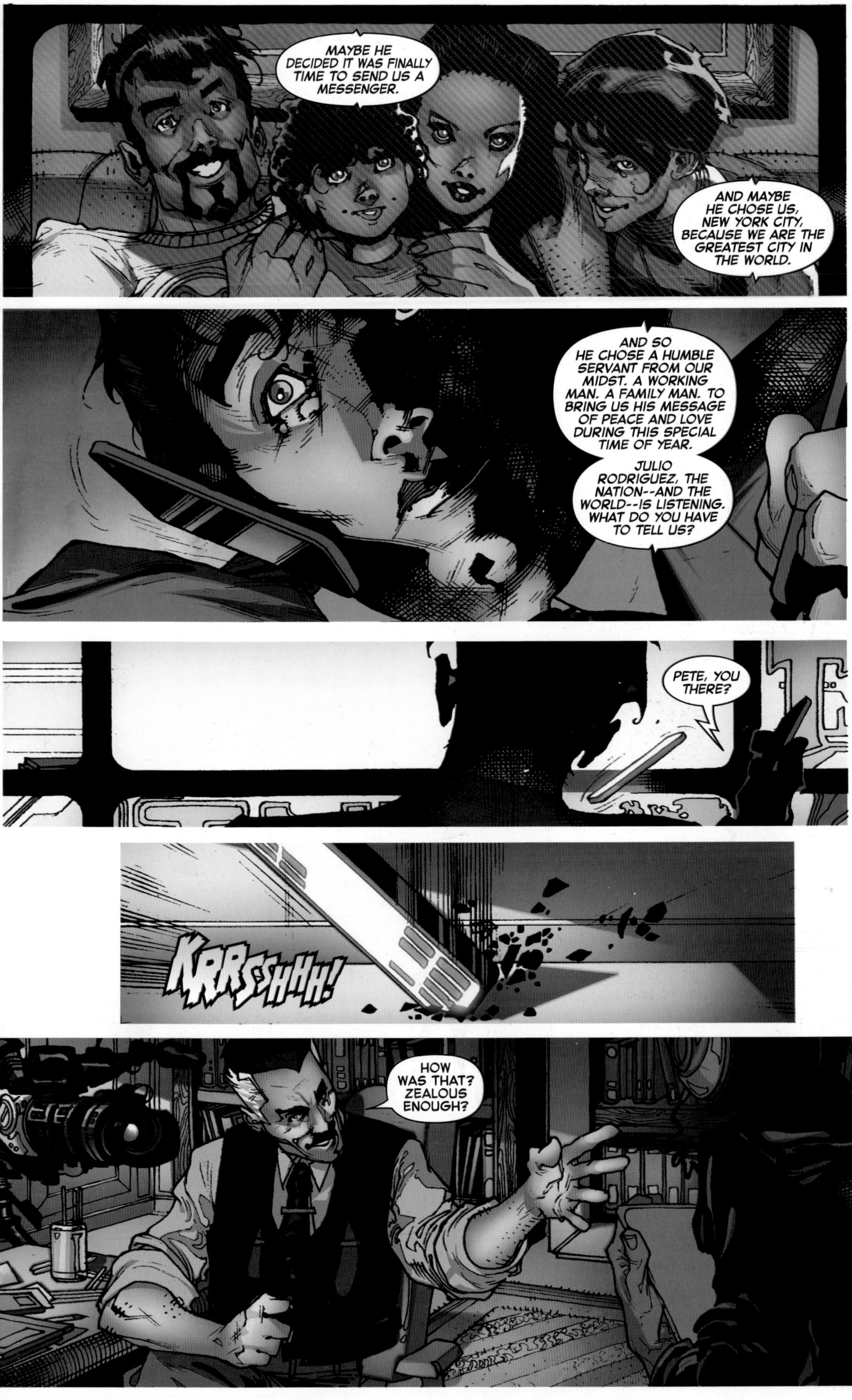
MAYBE HE DECIDED IT WAS FINALLY TIME TO SEND US A MESSENGER.
AND MAYBE HE CHOSE US, NEW YORK CITY, BECAUSE WE ARE THE GREATEST CITY IN THE WORLD.
AND SO HE CHOSE A HUMBLE SERVANT FROM OUR MIDST. A WORKING MAN. A FAMILY MAN. TO BRING US HIS MESSAGE OF PEACE AND LOVE DURING THIS SPECIAL TIME OF YEAR.
JULIO RODRIGUEZ, THE NATION--AND THE WORLD--IS LISTENING. WHAT DO YOU HAVE TO TELL US?
PETE, YOU THERE?
KRRSSHHH!
HOW WAS THAT? ZEALOUS ENOUGH?

O.C.M.E. MANHATTAN.

(THAT'S OFFICE OF THE CHIEF MEDICAL EXAMINER TO YOU AND ME.)

KNOCK KNOCK KNOCK

DR. TEMPLETON, YOU HAVE A VISITOR.

WHAT #$%& PART OF NO #$%& VISITORS DO YOU NOT #$%& UNDERSTAND?!

DR. KEVIN TEMPLETON
...AL EXAMINER

DR. TEMPLETON, I CALLED AHEAD. I WAS TOLD YOU'D BE EXPECTING ME.

OH. IT'S YOU.

HI.

SORRY TO DISTURB YOU, DR. TEMP--

#$%& OFF.

SORRY IF I CAME OFF A LITTLE GRUFF JUST NOW.

NOT GRUFF, JUST... NAUTICAL.

IT'S BEEN A MADHOUSE ALL MORNING. EVERY REPORTER IN THE CITY HAS BEEN CALLING ASKING THE SAME DUMB QUESTION: "IS IT POSSIBLE YOU BURIED A MAN WHO WAS STILL ALIVE?"

UM...IT'S NOT POSSIBLE... RIGHT?

RELAX, PARKER. YOUR DUMBNESS I'LL HUMOR. ANY FRIEND OF ANNA MARIA'S IS OKAY IN MY BOOK.

THIS IS WHAT A DOCTOR LOOKS LIKE

HOW IS MY FUN-SIZE BEARCAT?

SHE'S... WHAT'S A BEARCAT?

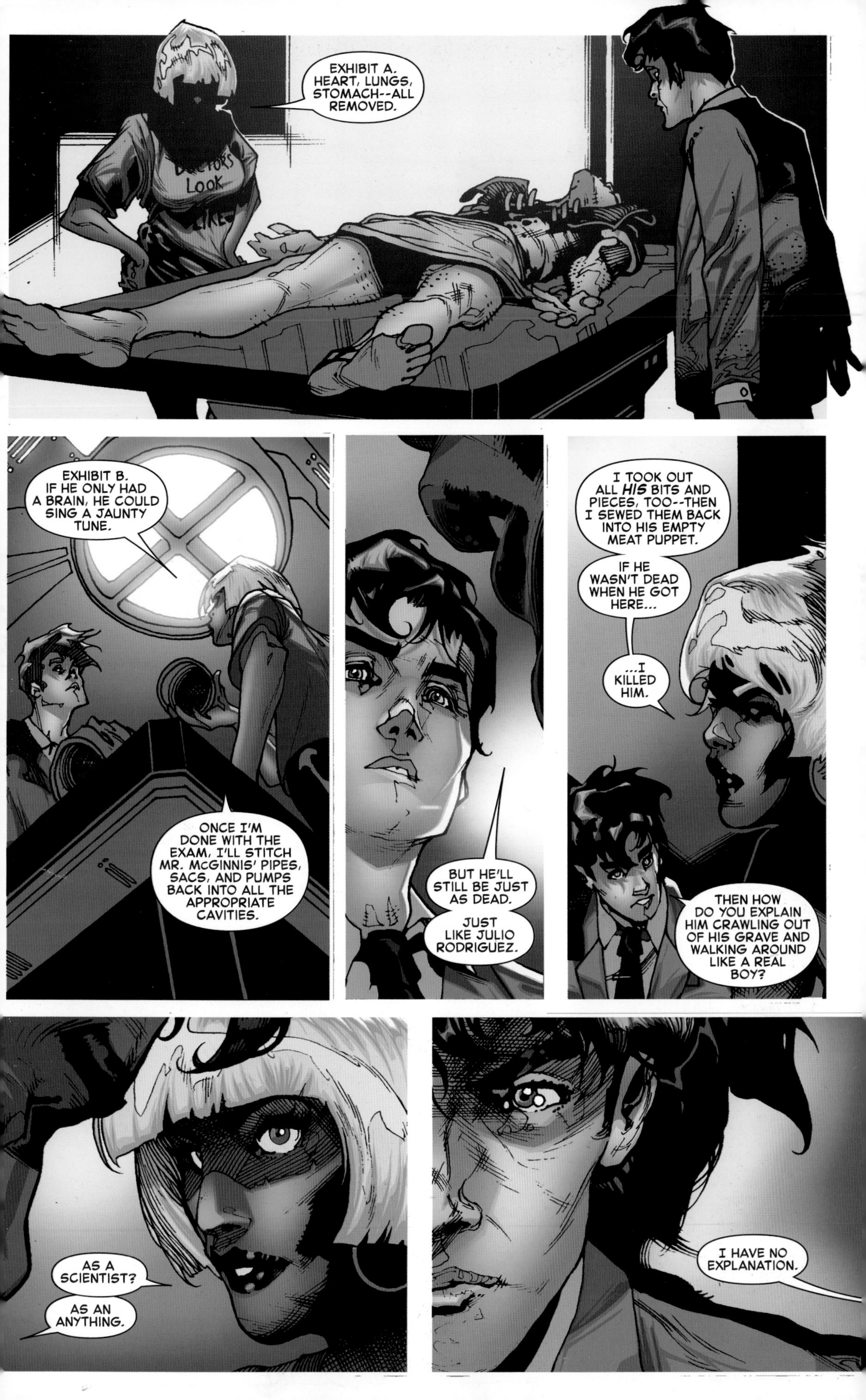
EXHIBIT A. HEART, LUNGS, STOMACH--ALL REMOVED.
DOCTORS LOOK LIKE
EXHIBIT B. IF HE ONLY HAD A BRAIN, HE COULD SING A JAUNTY TUNE.
ONCE I'M DONE WITH THE EXAM, I'LL STITCH MR. McGINNIS' PIPES, SACS, AND PUMPS BACK INTO ALL THE APPROPRIATE CAVITIES.
BUT HE'LL STILL BE JUST AS DEAD.
JUST LIKE JULIO RODRIGUEZ.
I TOOK OUT ALL *HIS* BITS AND PIECES, TOO--THEN I SEWED THEM BACK INTO HIS EMPTY MEAT PUPPET.
IF HE WASN'T DEAD WHEN HE GOT HERE...
...I KILLED HIM.
THEN HOW DO YOU EXPLAIN HIM CRAWLING OUT OF HIS GRAVE AND WALKING AROUND LIKE A REAL BOY?
AS A SCIENTIST?
AS AN ANYTHING.
I HAVE NO EXPLANATION.

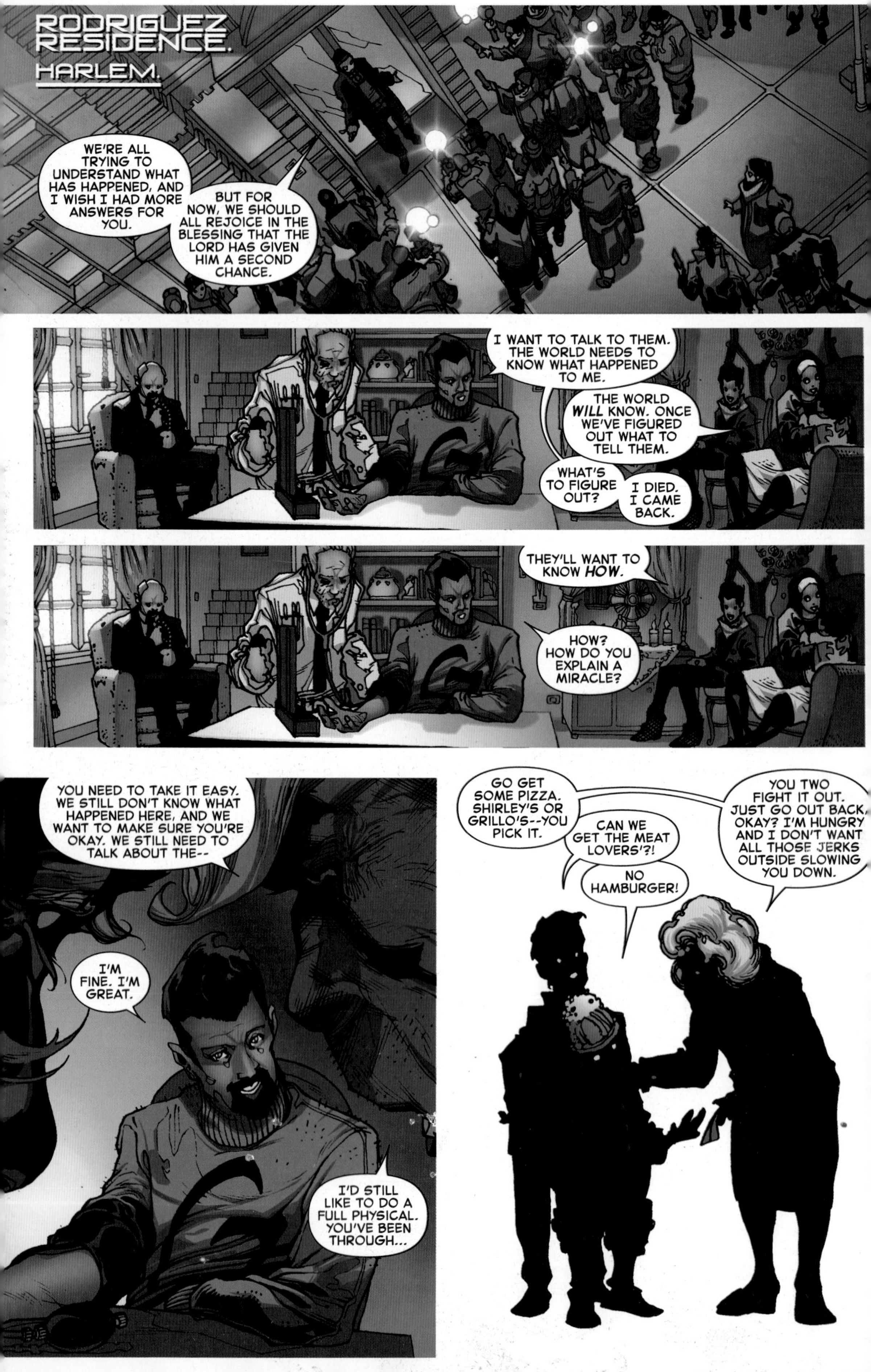
RODRIGUEZ RESIDENCE.
HARLEM.
WE'RE ALL TRYING TO UNDERSTAND WHAT HAS HAPPENED, AND I WISH I HAD MORE ANSWERS FOR YOU.
BUT FOR NOW, WE SHOULD ALL REJOICE IN THE BLESSING THAT THE LORD HAS GIVEN HIM A SECOND CHANCE.
I WANT TO TALK TO THEM. THE WORLD NEEDS TO KNOW WHAT HAPPENED TO ME.
THE WORLD WILL KNOW. ONCE WE'VE FIGURED OUT WHAT TO TELL THEM.
WHAT'S TO FIGURE OUT?
I DIED. I CAME BACK.
THEY'LL WANT TO KNOW HOW.
HOW? HOW DO YOU EXPLAIN A MIRACLE?
YOU NEED TO TAKE IT EASY. WE STILL DON'T KNOW WHAT HAPPENED HERE, AND WE WANT TO MAKE SURE YOU'RE OKAY. WE STILL NEED TO TALK ABOUT THE--
I'M FINE. I'M GREAT.
I'D STILL LIKE TO DO A FULL PHYSICAL. YOU'VE BEEN THROUGH...
GO GET SOME PIZZA. SHIRLEY'S OR GRILLO'S--YOU PICK IT.
YOU TWO FIGHT IT OUT. JUST GO OUT BACK, OKAY? I'M HUNGRY AND I DON'T WANT ALL THOSE JERKS OUTSIDE SLOWING YOU DOWN.
CAN WE GET THE MEAT LOVERS'?!
NO HAMBURGER!

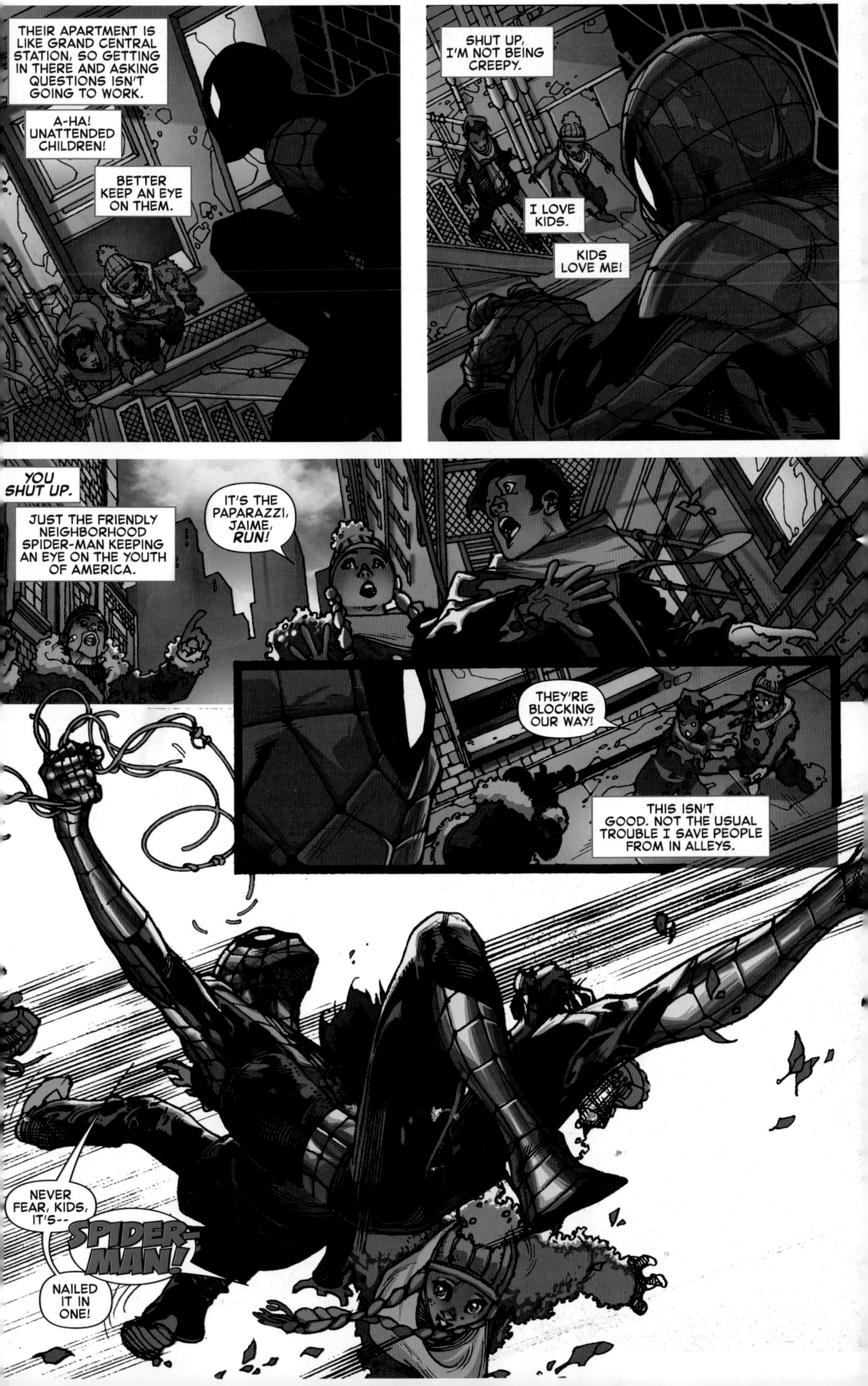
THEIR APARTMENT IS LIKE GRAND CENTRAL STATION, SO GETTING IN THERE AND ASKING QUESTIONS ISN'T GOING TO WORK.
A-HA! UNATTENDED CHILDREN!
BETTER KEEP AN EYE ON THEM.
SHUT UP, I'M NOT BEING CREEPY.
I LOVE KIDS.
KIDS LOVE ME!
YOU SHUT UP.
JUST THE FRIENDLY NEIGHBORHOOD SPIDER-MAN KEEPING AN EYE ON THE YOUTH OF AMERICA.
IT'S THE PAPARAZZI, JAIME, RUN!
THEY'RE BLOCKING OUR WAY!
THIS ISN'T GOOD. NOT THE USUAL TROUBLE I SAVE PEOPLE FROM IN ALLEYS.
NEVER FEAR, KIDS, IT'S--
SPIDER-MAN!
NAILED IT IN ONE!

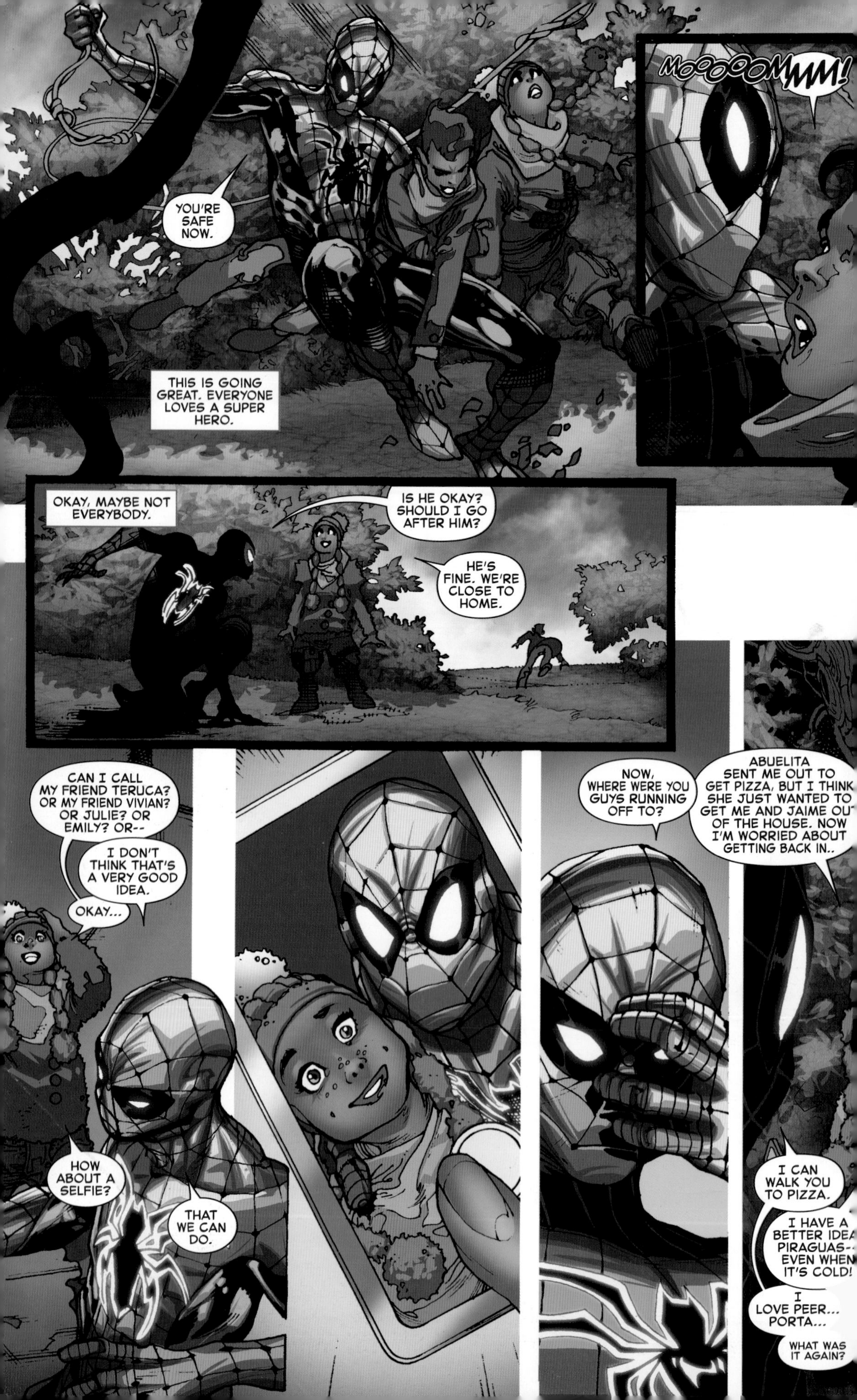
YOU'RE SAFE NOW.
THIS IS GOING GREAT. EVERYONE LOVES A SUPER HERO.
MOOOOOOMMM!
OKAY, MAYBE NOT EVERYBODY.
IS HE OKAY? SHOULD I GO AFTER HIM?
HE'S FINE. WE'RE CLOSE TO HOME.
CAN I CALL MY FRIEND TERUCA? OR MY FRIEND VIVIAN? OR JULIE? OR EMILY? OR--
I DON'T THINK THAT'S A VERY GOOD IDEA.
OKAY...
HOW ABOUT A SELFIE?
THAT WE CAN DO.
NOW, WHERE WERE YOU GUYS RUNNING OFF TO?
ABUELITA SENT ME OUT TO GET PIZZA, BUT I THINK SHE JUST WANTED TO GET ME AND JAIME OUT OF THE HOUSE. NOW I'M WORRIED ABOUT GETTING BACK IN..
I CAN WALK YOU TO PIZZA.
I HAVE A BETTER IDEA. PIRAGUAS-- EVEN WHEN IT'S COLD!
I LOVE PEER... PORTA...
WHAT WAS IT AGAIN?

I PROMISE I'LL PAY YOU BACK. THIS SUIT'S A LITTLE TIGHT FOR POCKETS.

SO, WHY DID ABUELITA WANT TO GET YOU OUT OF THE HOUSE? TOO MUCH CRAZINESS WITH THE REPORTERS?

THANKS, CHARLIE. MERRY CHRISTMAS.

PIRAGUA: A PUERTO RICAN SHAVED ICE DESSERT SHAPED LIKE A PYRAMID, CONSISTING OF SHAVED ICE AND COVERED WITH FRUIT-FLAVORED SYRUP. YOU HAVE TO TRY ONE! --NICK

IT'S BEEN CRAZY FOR A WHILE. EVER SINCE DAD GOT SICK.

I DIDN'T KNOW YOUR DAD WAS SICK.

SOME KIND OF CANCER. THEY TRIED NOT TELLING US ANYTHING AT FIRST BUT SOMETIMES THEY THINK WE CAN'T HEAR THEM IF THEY'RE NOT TALKING TO US.

LAST YEAR.

"I DON'T REALLY KNOW EVERY-THING THAT WAS HAPPENING."

--HE NEEDS TO RUN MORE TESTS, BUT HE'S AFRAID IT MIGHT HAVE SPREAD TO THE LYMPH NODES. IF IT HAS... LET'S JUST HOPE IT HASN'T.

WHAT ARE WE GONNA DO, JULIO?

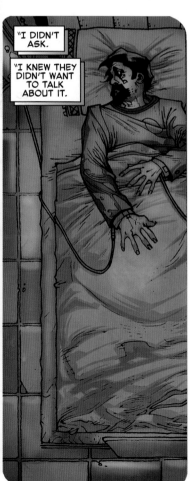

"I DIDN'T ASK.

"I KNEW THEY DIDN'T WANT TO TALK ABOUT IT.

"BUT I KNEW IT WAS BAD."

I'M SORRY.

THANKS.

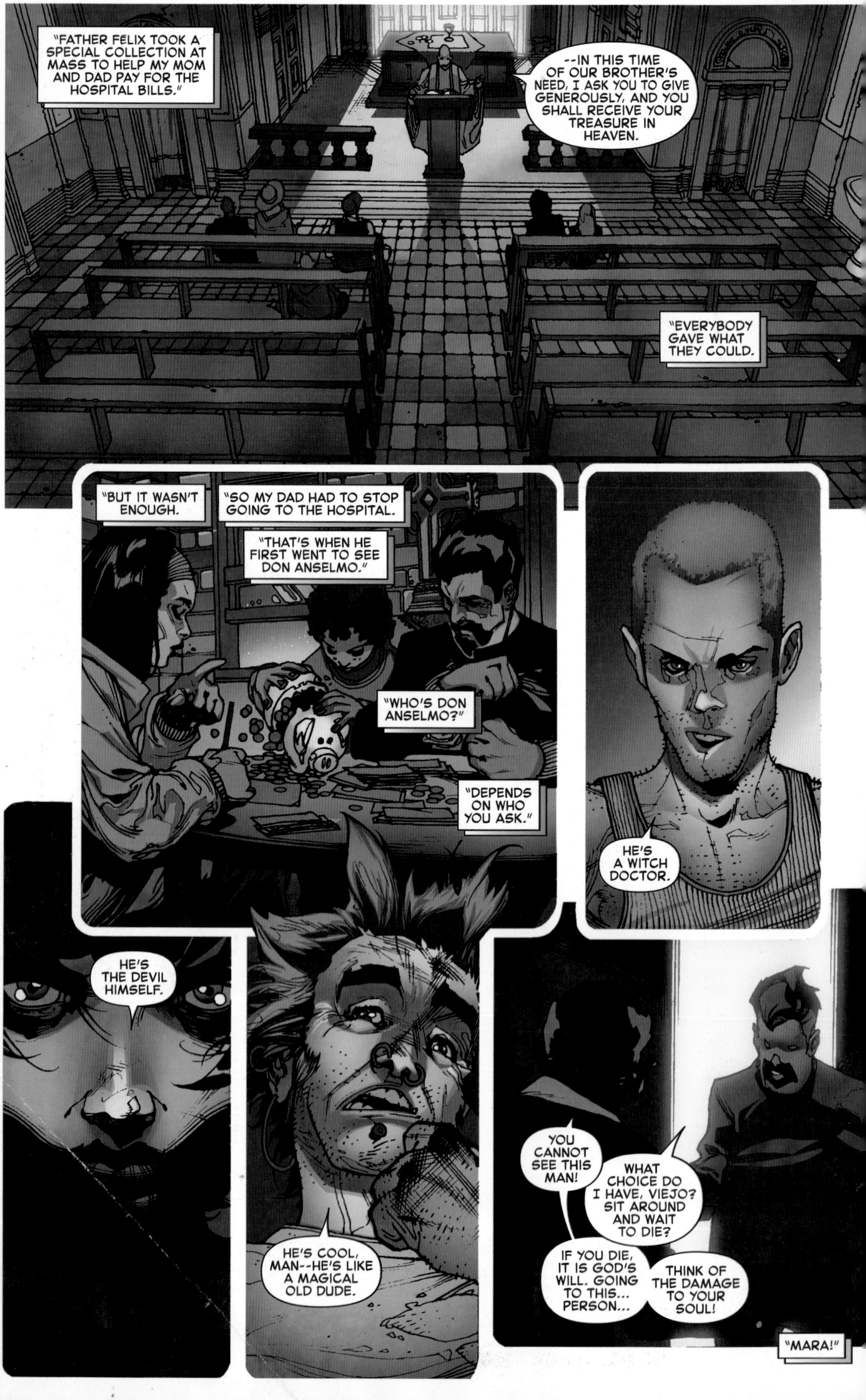
"FATHER FELIX TOOK A SPECIAL COLLECTION AT MASS TO HELP MY MOM AND DAD PAY FOR THE HOSPITAL BILLS."
--IN THIS TIME OF OUR BROTHER'S NEED, I ASK YOU TO GIVE GENEROUSLY, AND YOU SHALL RECEIVE YOUR TREASURE IN HEAVEN.
"EVERYBODY GAVE WHAT THEY COULD.
"BUT IT WASN'T ENOUGH.
"SO MY DAD HAD TO STOP GOING TO THE HOSPITAL.
"THAT'S WHEN HE FIRST WENT TO SEE DON ANSELMO."
"WHO'S DON ANSELMO?"
"DEPENDS ON WHO YOU ASK."
HE'S A WITCH DOCTOR.
HE'S THE DEVIL HIMSELF.
HE'S COOL, MAN--HE'S LIKE A MAGICAL OLD DUDE.
YOU CANNOT SEE THIS MAN!
WHAT CHOICE DO I HAVE, VIEJO? SIT AROUND AND WAIT TO DIE?
IF YOU DIE, IT IS GOD'S WILL. GOING TO THIS... PERSON...
THINK OF THE DAMAGE TO YOUR SOUL!
"MARA!"

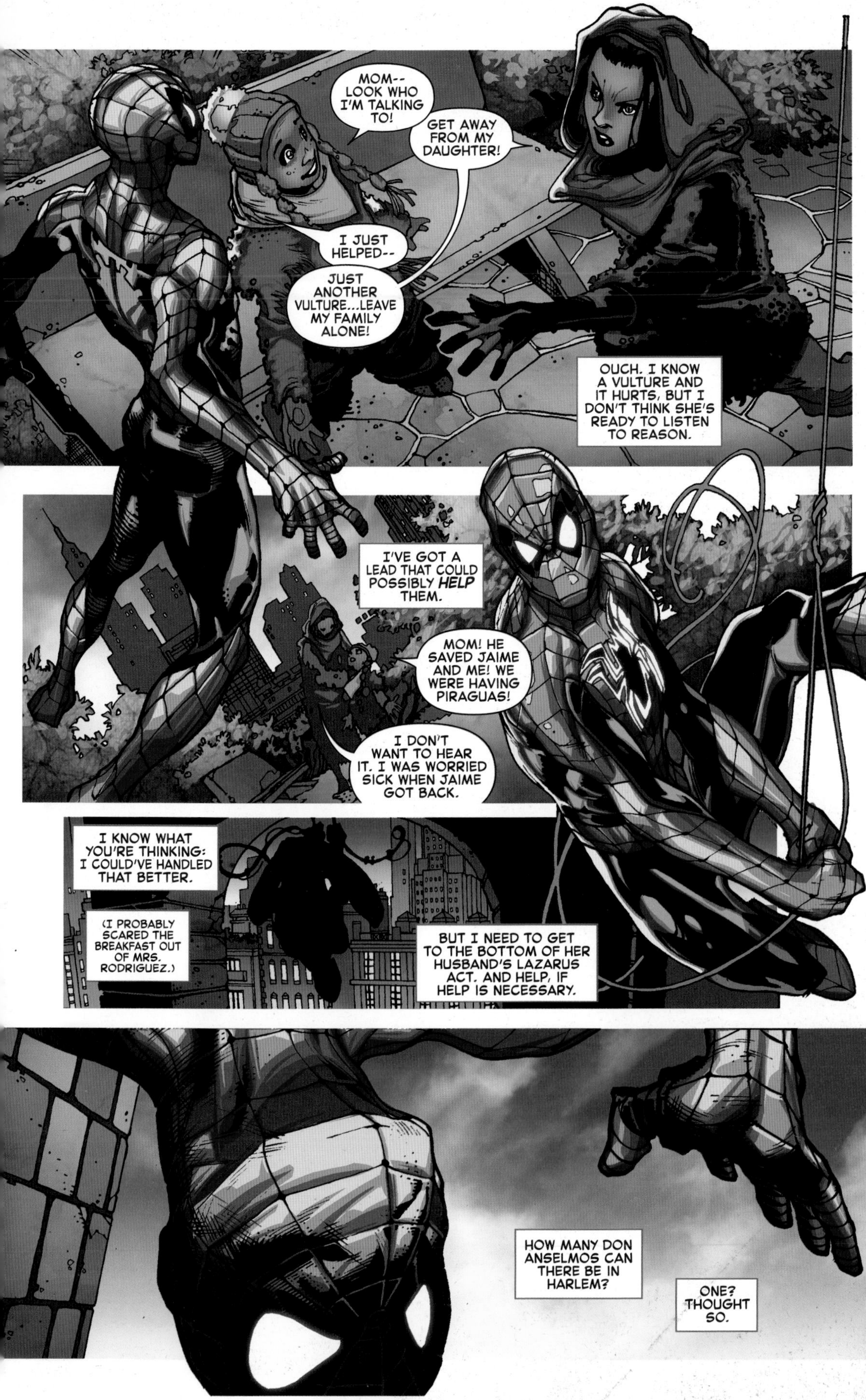
MOM--
LOOK WHO I'M TALKING TO!
GET AWAY FROM MY DAUGHTER!
I JUST HELPED--
JUST ANOTHER VULTURE...LEAVE MY FAMILY ALONE!
OUCH. I KNOW A VULTURE AND IT HURTS, BUT I DON'T THINK SHE'S READY TO LISTEN TO REASON.
I'VE GOT A LEAD THAT COULD POSSIBLY HELP THEM.
MOM! HE SAVED JAIME AND ME! WE WERE HAVING PIRAGUAS!
I DON'T WANT TO HEAR IT. I WAS WORRIED SICK WHEN JAIME GOT BACK.
I KNOW WHAT YOU'RE THINKING: I COULD'VE HANDLED THAT BETTER.
(I PROBABLY SCARED THE BREAKFAST OUT OF MRS. RODRIGUEZ.)
BUT I NEED TO GET TO THE BOTTOM OF HER HUSBAND'S LAZARUS ACT. AND HELP, IF HELP IS NECESSARY.
HOW MANY DON ANSELMOS CAN THERE BE IN HARLEM?
ONE? THOUGHT SO.

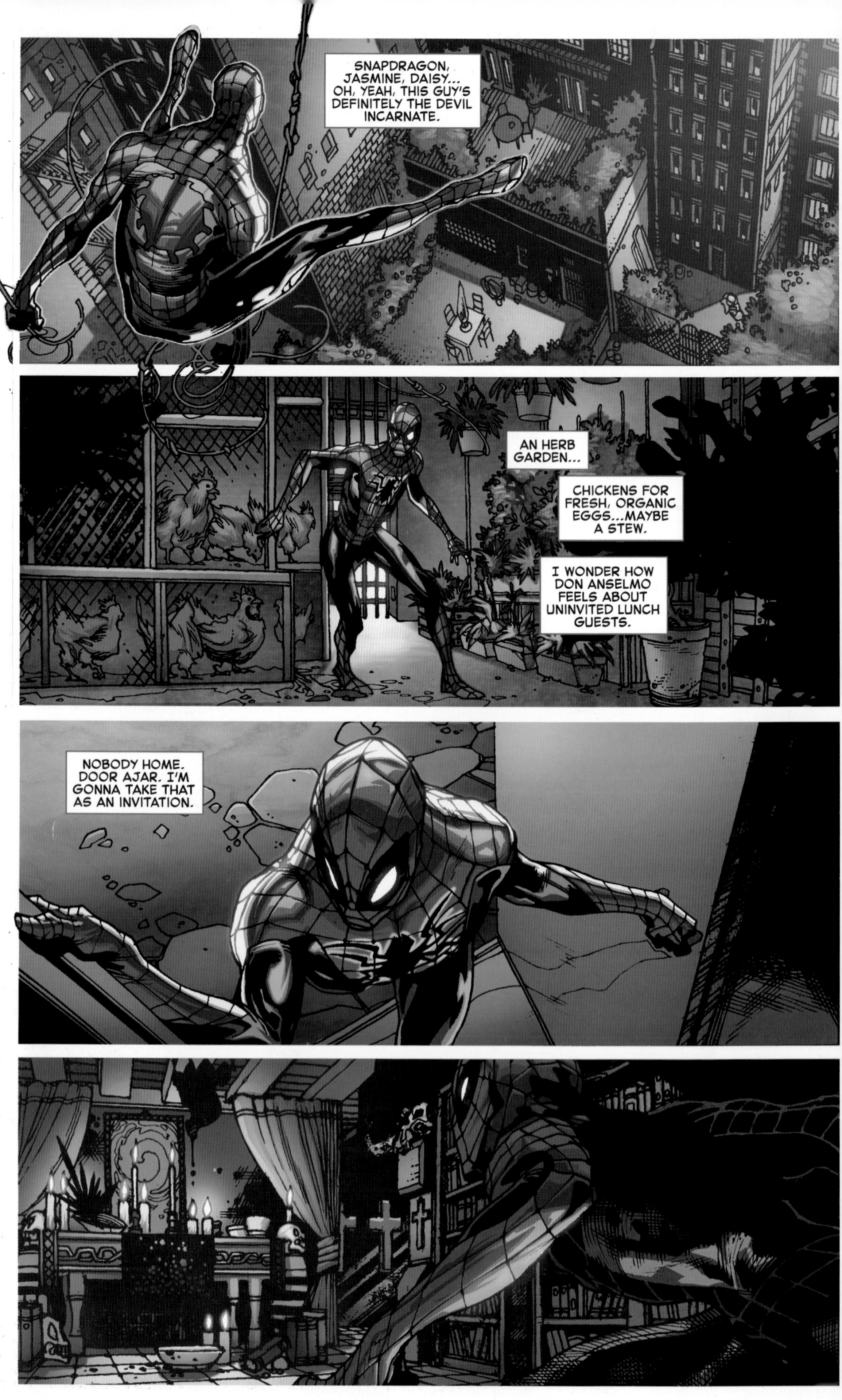
SNAPDRAGON, JASMINE, DAISY... OH, YEAH, THIS GUY'S DEFINITELY THE DEVIL INCARNATE.
AN HERB GARDEN...
CHICKENS FOR FRESH, ORGANIC EGGS...MAYBE A STEW.
I WONDER HOW DON ANSELMO FEELS ABOUT UNINVITED LUNCH GUESTS.
NOBODY HOME. DOOR AJAR. I'M GONNA TAKE THAT AS AN INVITATION.

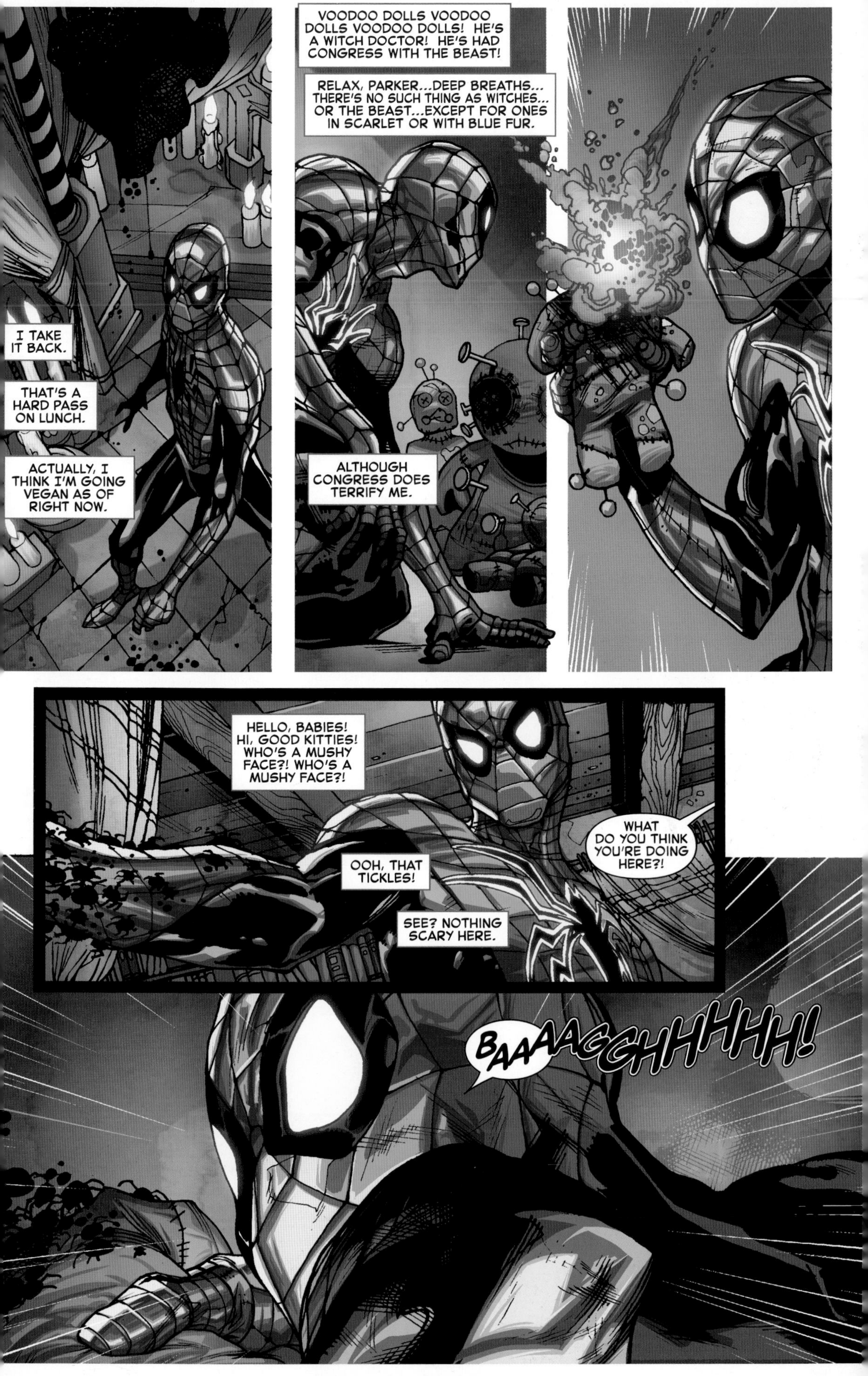

I TAKE IT BACK.
THAT'S A HARD PASS ON LUNCH.
ACTUALLY, I THINK I'M GOING VEGAN AS OF RIGHT NOW.
VOODOO DOLLS VOODOO DOLLS VOODOO DOLLS! HE'S A WITCH DOCTOR! HE'S HAD CONGRESS WITH THE BEAST!
RELAX, PARKER...DEEP BREATHS... THERE'S NO SUCH THING AS WITCHES... OR THE BEAST...EXCEPT FOR ONES IN SCARLET OR WITH BLUE FUR.
ALTHOUGH CONGRESS DOES TERRIFY ME.
HELLO, BABIES! HI, GOOD KITTIES! WHO'S A MUSHY FACE?! WHO'S A MUSHY FACE?!
OOH, THAT TICKLES!
SEE? NOTHING SCARY HERE.
WHAT DO YOU THINK YOU'RE DOING HERE?!
BAAAAGGHHHHH!

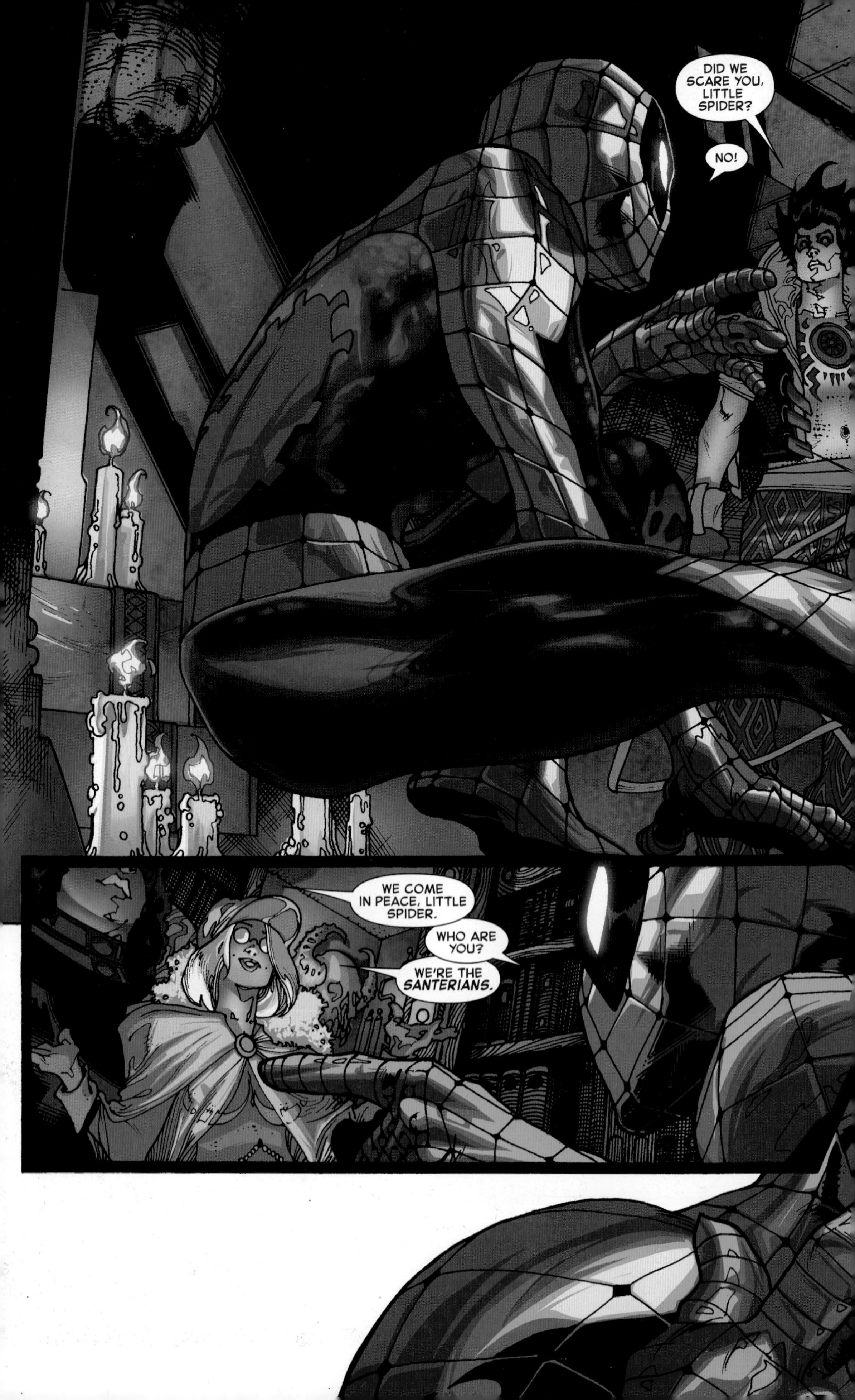
DID WE SCARE YOU, LITTLE SPIDER?
NO!
WE COME IN PEACE, LITTLE SPIDER.
WHO ARE YOU?
WE'RE THE SANTERIANS.

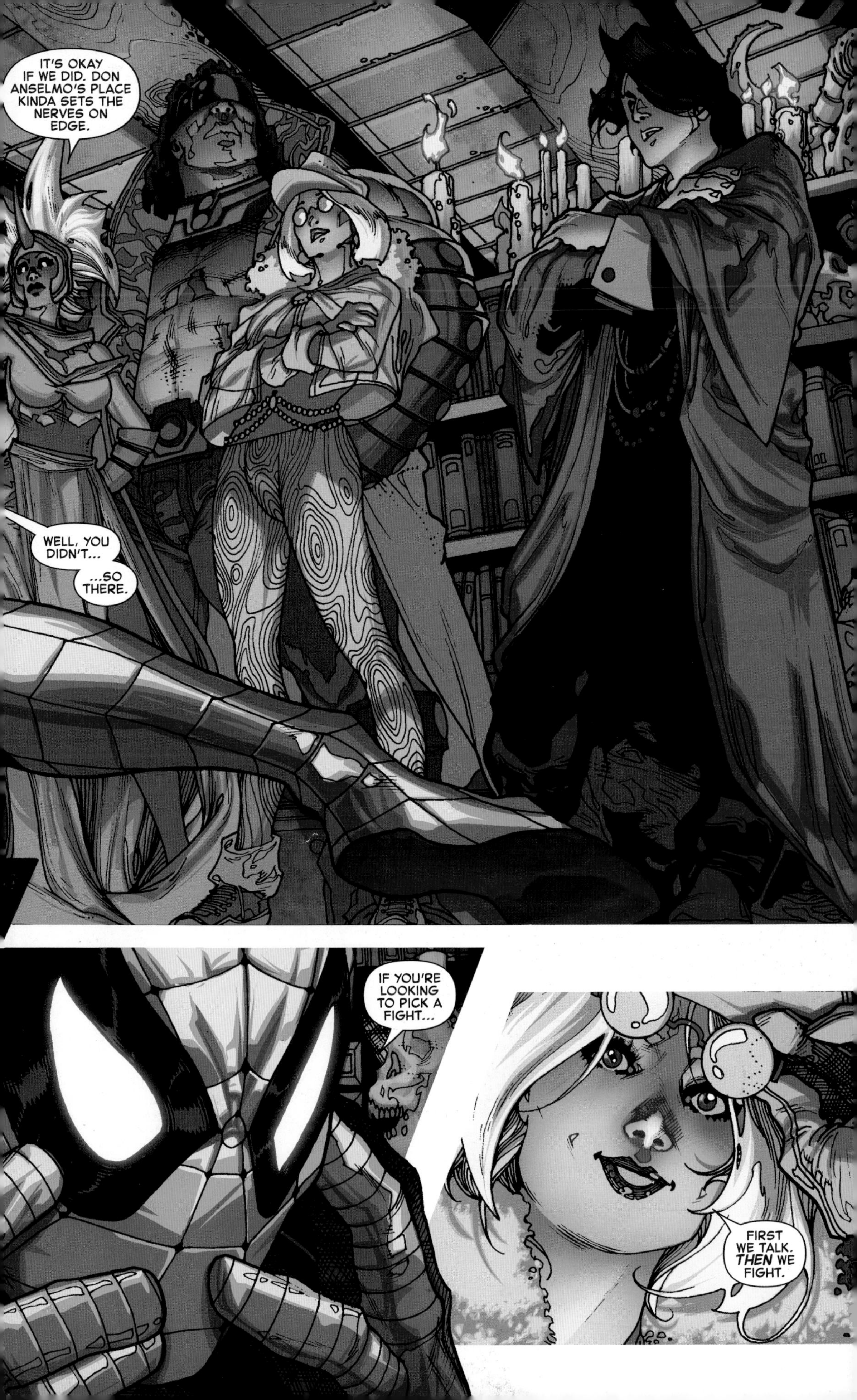
IT'S OKAY IF WE DID. DON ANSELMO'S PLACE KINDA SETS THE NERVES ON EDGE.
WELL, YOU DIDN'T...
...SO THERE.
IF YOU'RE LOOKING TO PICK A FIGHT...
FIRST WE TALK. THEN WE FIGHT.

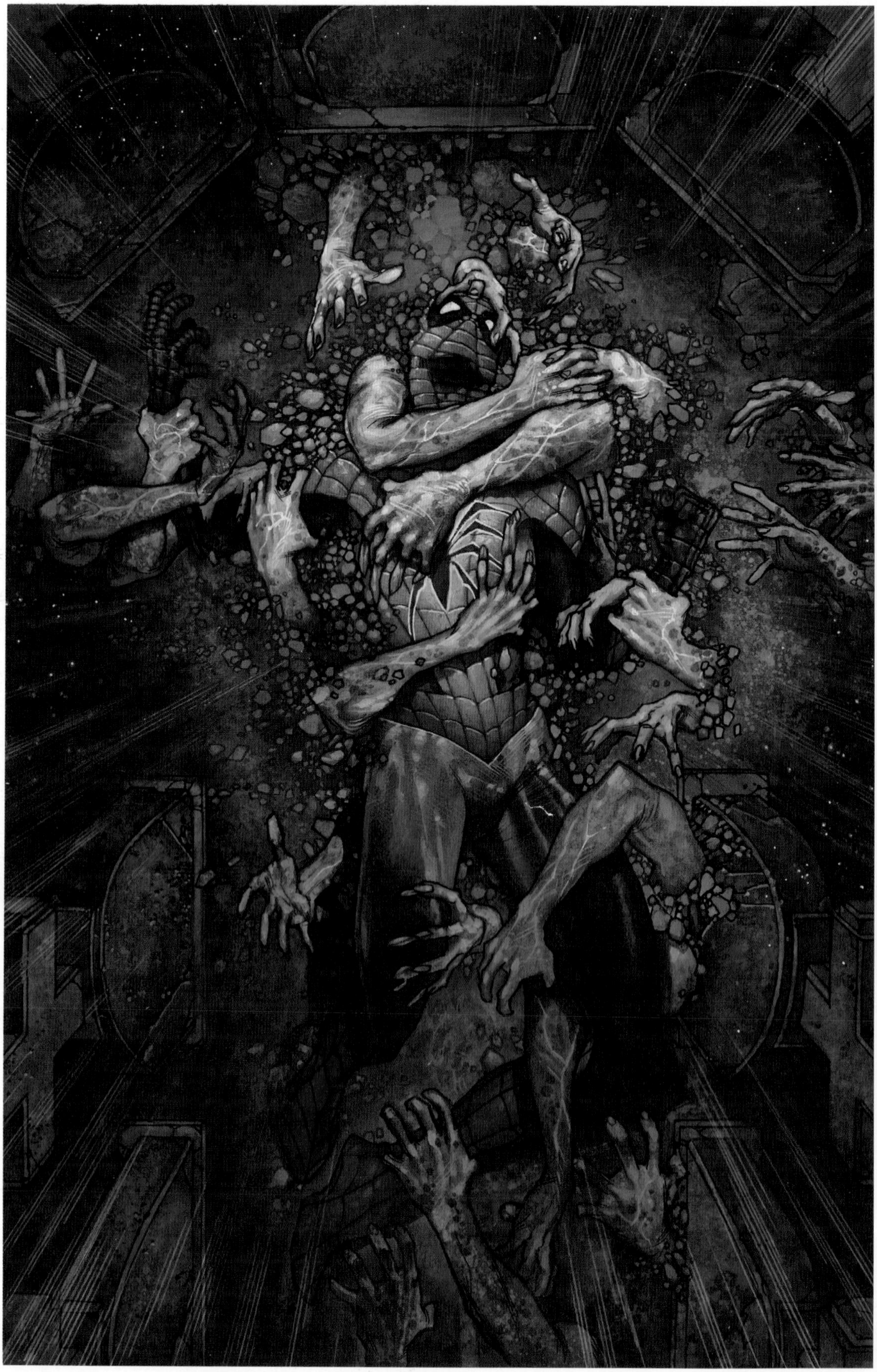

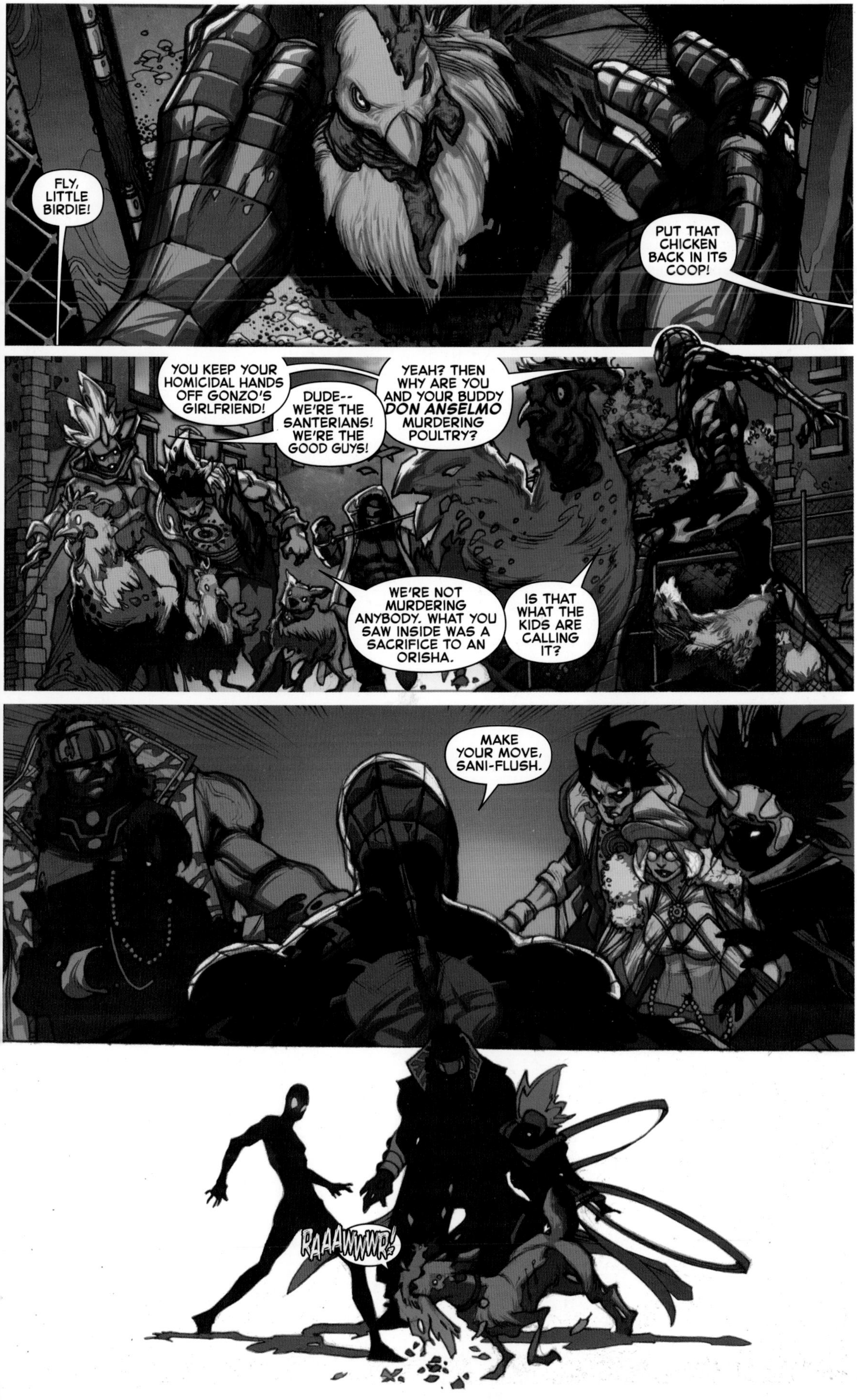
FLY, LITTLE BIRDIE!
PUT THAT CHICKEN BACK IN ITS COOP!
YOU KEEP YOUR HOMICIDAL HANDS OFF GONZO'S GIRLFRIEND!
DUDE-- WE'RE THE SANTERIANS! WE'RE THE GOOD GUYS!
YEAH? THEN WHY ARE YOU AND YOUR BUDDY DON ANSELMO MURDERING POULTRY?
WE'RE NOT MURDERING ANYBODY. WHAT YOU SAW INSIDE WAS A SACRIFICE TO AN ORISHA.
IS THAT WHAT THE KIDS ARE CALLING IT?
MAKE YOUR MOVE, SANI-FLUSH.
RAAAWWWR!

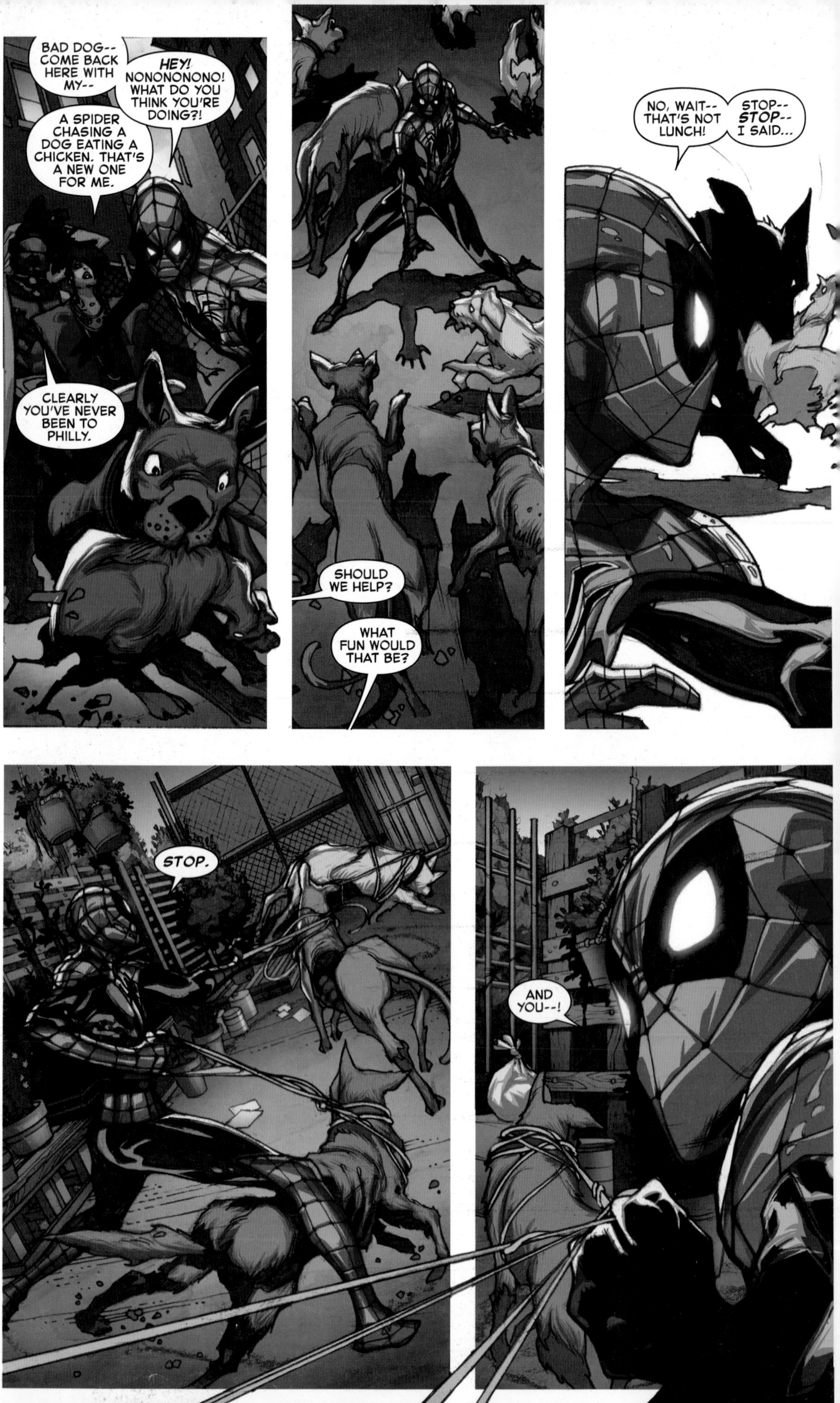
BAD DOG-- COME BACK HERE WITH MY--
HEY! NONONONONO! WHAT DO YOU THINK YOU'RE DOING?!
A SPIDER CHASING A DOG EATING A CHICKEN. THAT'S A NEW ONE FOR ME.
CLEARLY YOU'VE NEVER BEEN TO PHILLY.
SHOULD WE HELP?
WHAT FUN WOULD THAT BE?
NO, WAIT-- THAT'S NOT LUNCH!
STOP-- STOP-- I SAID...
STOP.
AND YOU--!

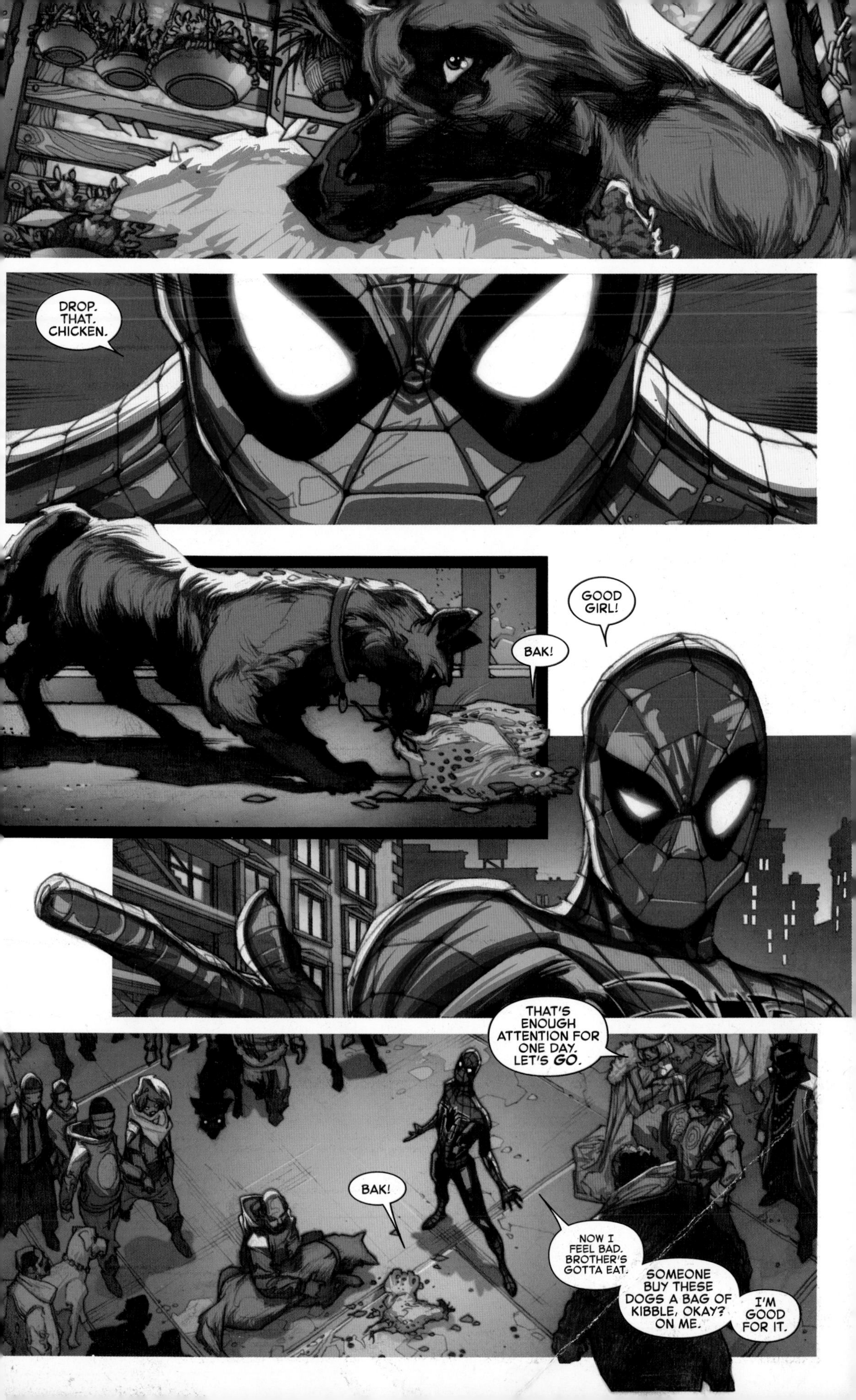
DROP. THAT. CHICKEN.
BAK!
GOOD GIRL!
THAT'S ENOUGH ATTENTION FOR ONE DAY. LET'S *GO*.
BAK!
NOW I FEEL BAD. BROTHER'S GOTTA EAT.
SOMEONE BUY THESE DOGS A BAG OF KIBBLE, OKAY? ON ME.
I'M GOOD FOR IT.

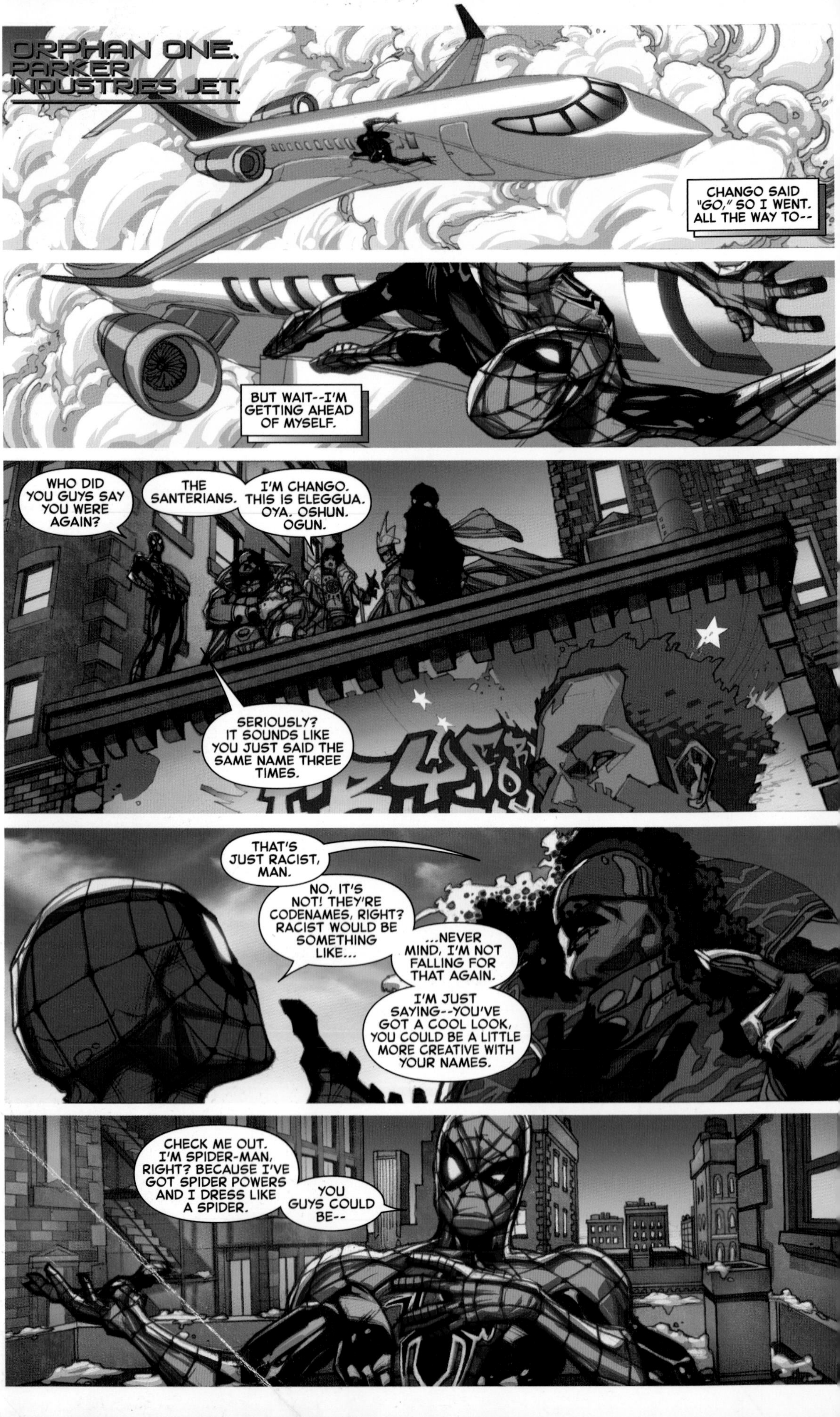
ORPHAN ONE. PARKER INDUSTRIES JET.
CHANGO SAID "GO," SO I WENT. ALL THE WAY TO--
BUT WAIT--I'M GETTING AHEAD OF MYSELF.
WHO DID YOU GUYS SAY YOU WERE AGAIN?
THE SANTERIANS.
I'M CHANGO. THIS IS ELEGGUA. OYA. OSHUN. OGUN.
SERIOUSLY? IT SOUNDS LIKE YOU JUST SAID THE SAME NAME THREE TIMES.
THAT'S JUST RACIST, MAN.
NO, IT'S NOT! THEY'RE CODENAMES, RIGHT? RACIST WOULD BE SOMETHING LIKE...
...NEVER MIND, I'M NOT FALLING FOR THAT AGAIN.
I'M JUST SAYING--YOU'VE GOT A COOL LOOK, YOU COULD BE A LITTLE MORE CREATIVE WITH YOUR NAMES.
CHECK ME OUT. I'M SPIDER-MAN, RIGHT? BECAUSE I'VE GOT SPIDER POWERS AND I DRESS LIKE A SPIDER.
YOU GUYS COULD BE--

ELEGGUA.

KID EMO.

OYA.

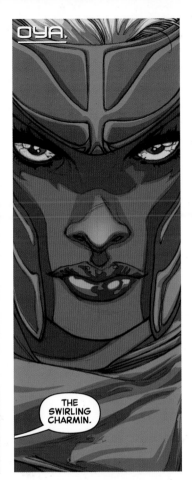

THE SWIRLING CHARMIN.

CHANGO.

THE PUCE POMADE.

I'M NOT EVEN WEARING PUCE.

SHUT UP, MAN, I'M WORKING.

OGUN.

DREADLOCK GEORDI...

OSHUN.

...AND COLDPLAY.

YOU KNOW, BECAUSE "YELLOW."

YOU CAN PLAY WITH THESE, I'M JUST BRAINSTORMING HERE.

I'M GONNA HIT HIM NOW, CHANGO.

WAIT. I WANT DIBS.

I'M A BIG FAN OF TERRIBLE FIRST IMPRESSIONS.

MAKES IT DIFFICULT FOR ANYONE TO THINK LESS OF YOU AFTERWARDS.

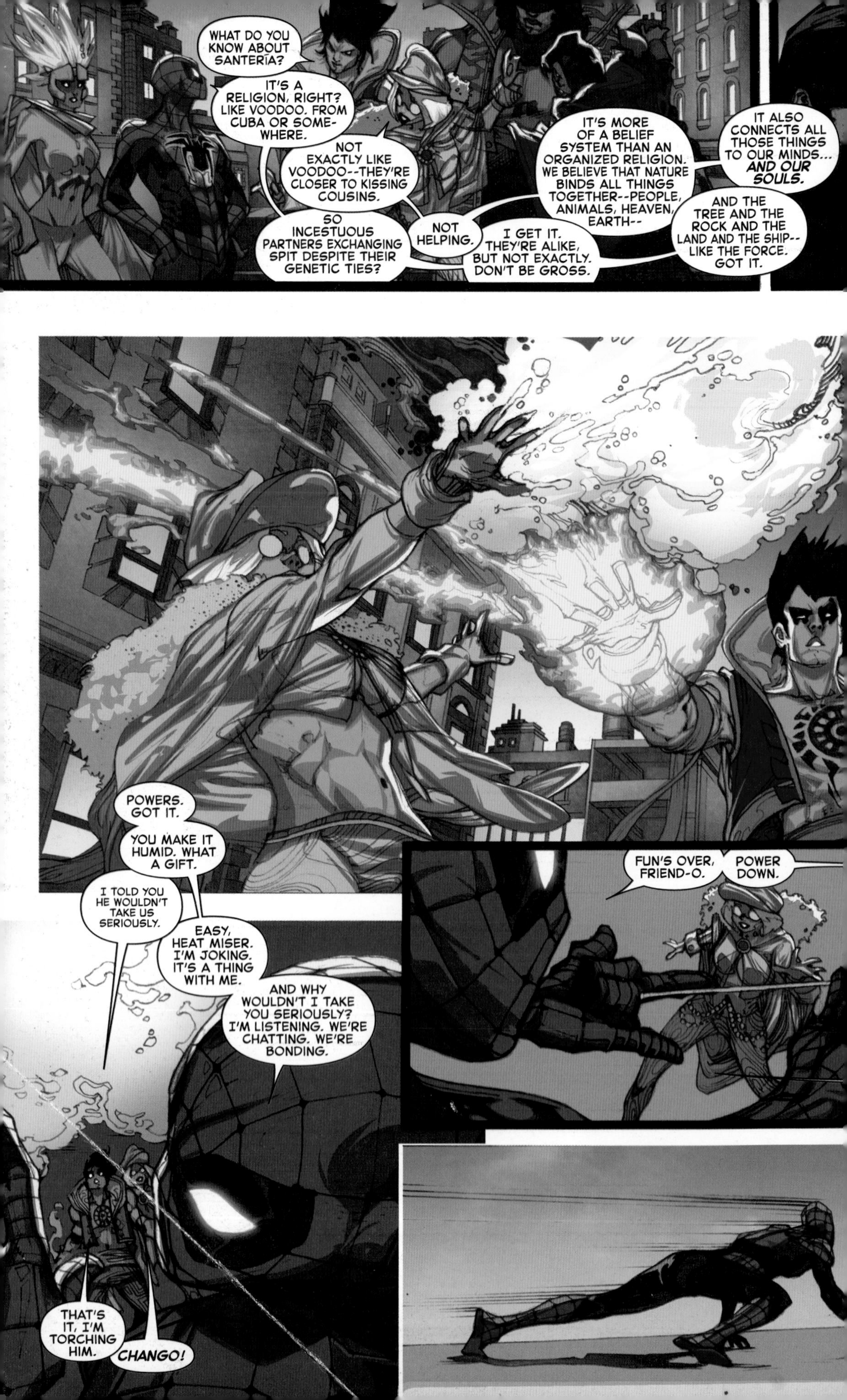
WHAT DO YOU KNOW ABOUT SANTERÍA?
IT'S A RELIGION, RIGHT? LIKE VOODOO. FROM CUBA OR SOME-WHERE.
NOT EXACTLY LIKE VOODOO--THEY'RE CLOSER TO KISSING COUSINS.
SO INCESTUOUS PARTNERS EXCHANGING SPIT DESPITE THEIR GENETIC TIES?
NOT HELPING.
I GET IT. THEY'RE ALIKE, BUT NOT EXACTLY. DON'T BE GROSS.
IT'S MORE OF A BELIEF SYSTEM THAN AN ORGANIZED RELIGION. WE BELIEVE THAT NATURE BINDS ALL THINGS TOGETHER--PEOPLE, ANIMALS, HEAVEN, EARTH--
IT ALSO CONNECTS ALL THOSE THINGS TO OUR MINDS... AND OUR SOULS.
AND THE TREE AND THE ROCK AND THE LAND AND THE SHIP--LIKE THE FORCE. GOT IT.
POWERS. GOT IT.
YOU MAKE IT HUMID. WHAT A GIFT.
I TOLD YOU HE WOULDN'T TAKE US SERIOUSLY.
EASY, HEAT MISER. I'M JOKING. IT'S A THING WITH ME.
AND WHY WOULDN'T I TAKE YOU SERIOUSLY? I'M LISTENING. WE'RE CHATTING. WE'RE BONDING.
THAT'S IT, I'M TORCHING HIM.
CHANGO!
FUN'S OVER, FRIEND-O.
POWER DOWN.

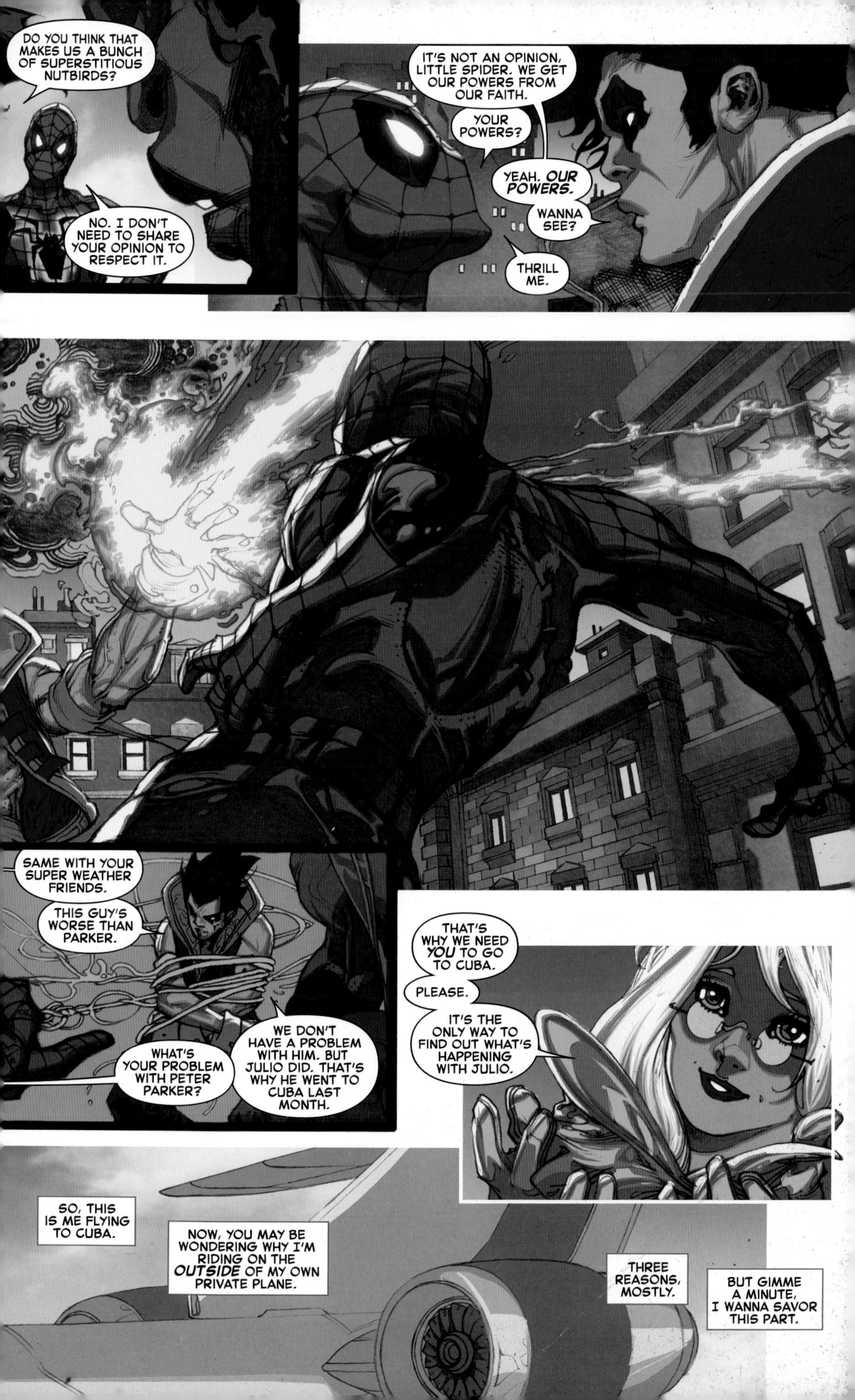
DO YOU THINK THAT MAKES US A BUNCH OF SUPERSTITIOUS NUTBIRDS?
NO. I DON'T NEED TO SHARE YOUR OPINION TO RESPECT IT.
IT'S NOT AN OPINION, LITTLE SPIDER. WE GET OUR POWERS FROM OUR FAITH.
YOUR POWERS?
YEAH. OUR POWERS.
WANNA SEE?
THRILL ME.
SAME WITH YOUR SUPER WEATHER FRIENDS.
THIS GUY'S WORSE THAN PARKER.
WHAT'S YOUR PROBLEM WITH PETER PARKER?
WE DON'T HAVE A PROBLEM WITH HIM. BUT JULIO DID. THAT'S WHY HE WENT TO CUBA LAST MONTH.
THAT'S WHY WE NEED YOU TO GO TO CUBA.
PLEASE.
IT'S THE ONLY WAY TO FIND OUT WHAT'S HAPPENING WITH JULIO.
SO, THIS IS ME FLYING TO CUBA.
NOW, YOU MAY BE WONDERING WHY I'M RIDING ON THE OUTSIDE OF MY OWN PRIVATE PLANE.
THREE REASONS, MOSTLY.
BUT GIMME A MINUTE, I WANNA SAVOR THIS PART.

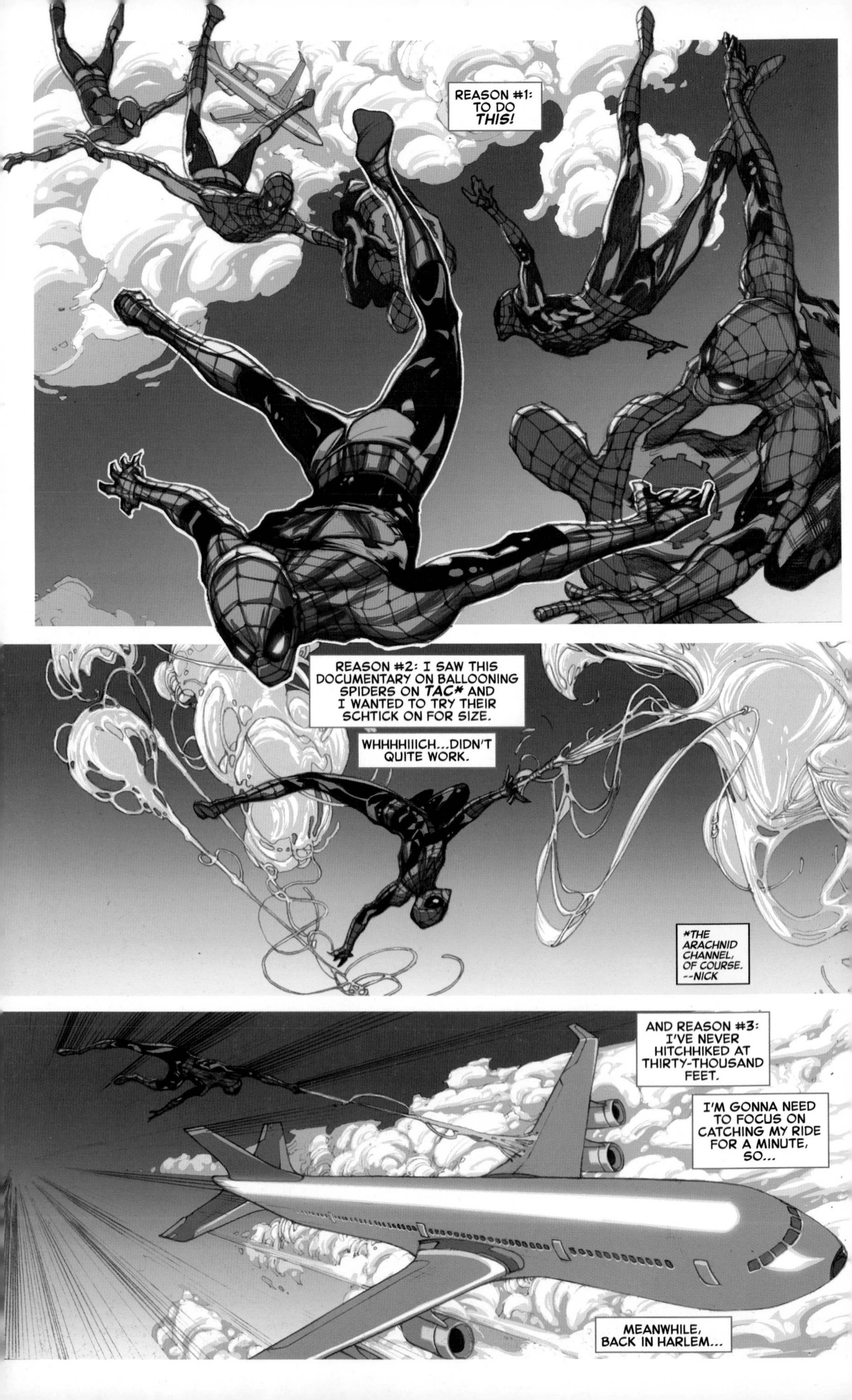
REASON #1: TO DO *THIS!*
REASON #2: I SAW THIS DOCUMENTARY ON BALLOONING SPIDERS ON *TAC** AND I WANTED TO TRY THEIR SCHTICK ON FOR SIZE.
WHHHHIIICH...DIDN'T QUITE WORK.
*THE ARACHNID CHANNEL, OF COURSE. --NICK
AND REASON #3: I'VE NEVER HITCHHIKED AT THIRTY-THOUSAND FEET.
I'M GONNA NEED TO FOCUS ON CATCHING MY RIDE FOR A MINUTE, SO...
MEANWHILE, BACK IN HARLEM...

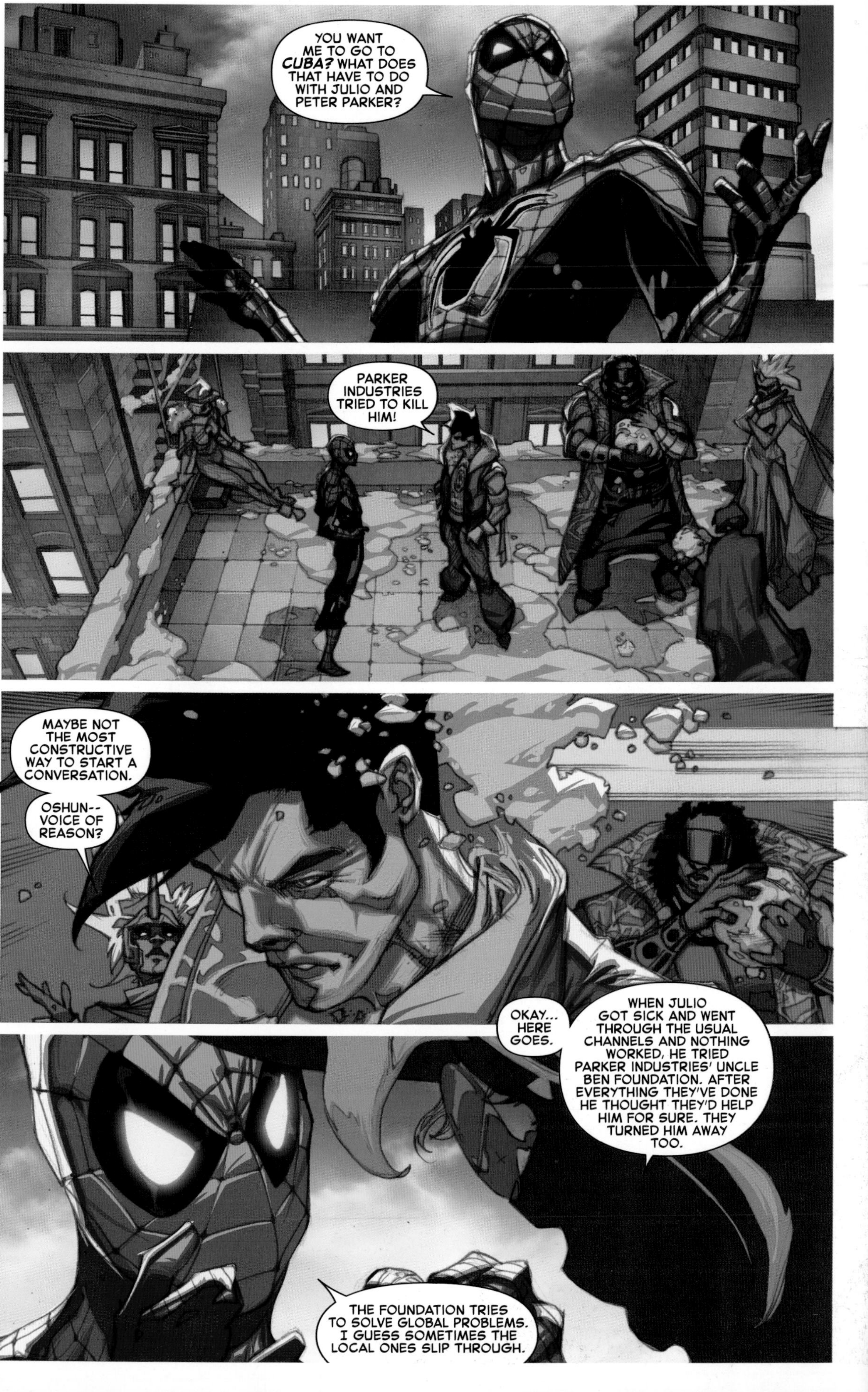
YOU WANT ME TO GO TO CUBA? WHAT DOES THAT HAVE TO DO WITH JULIO AND PETER PARKER?
PARKER INDUSTRIES TRIED TO KILL HIM!
MAYBE NOT THE MOST CONSTRUCTIVE WAY TO START A CONVERSATION.
OSHUN-- VOICE OF REASON?
OKAY... HERE GOES.
WHEN JULIO GOT SICK AND WENT THROUGH THE USUAL CHANNELS AND NOTHING WORKED, HE TRIED PARKER INDUSTRIES' UNCLE BEN FOUNDATION. AFTER EVERYTHING THEY'VE DONE HE THOUGHT THEY'D HELP HIM FOR SURE. THEY TURNED HIM AWAY TOO.
THE FOUNDATION TRIES TO SOLVE GLOBAL PROBLEMS. I GUESS SOMETIMES THE LOCAL ONES SLIP THROUGH.

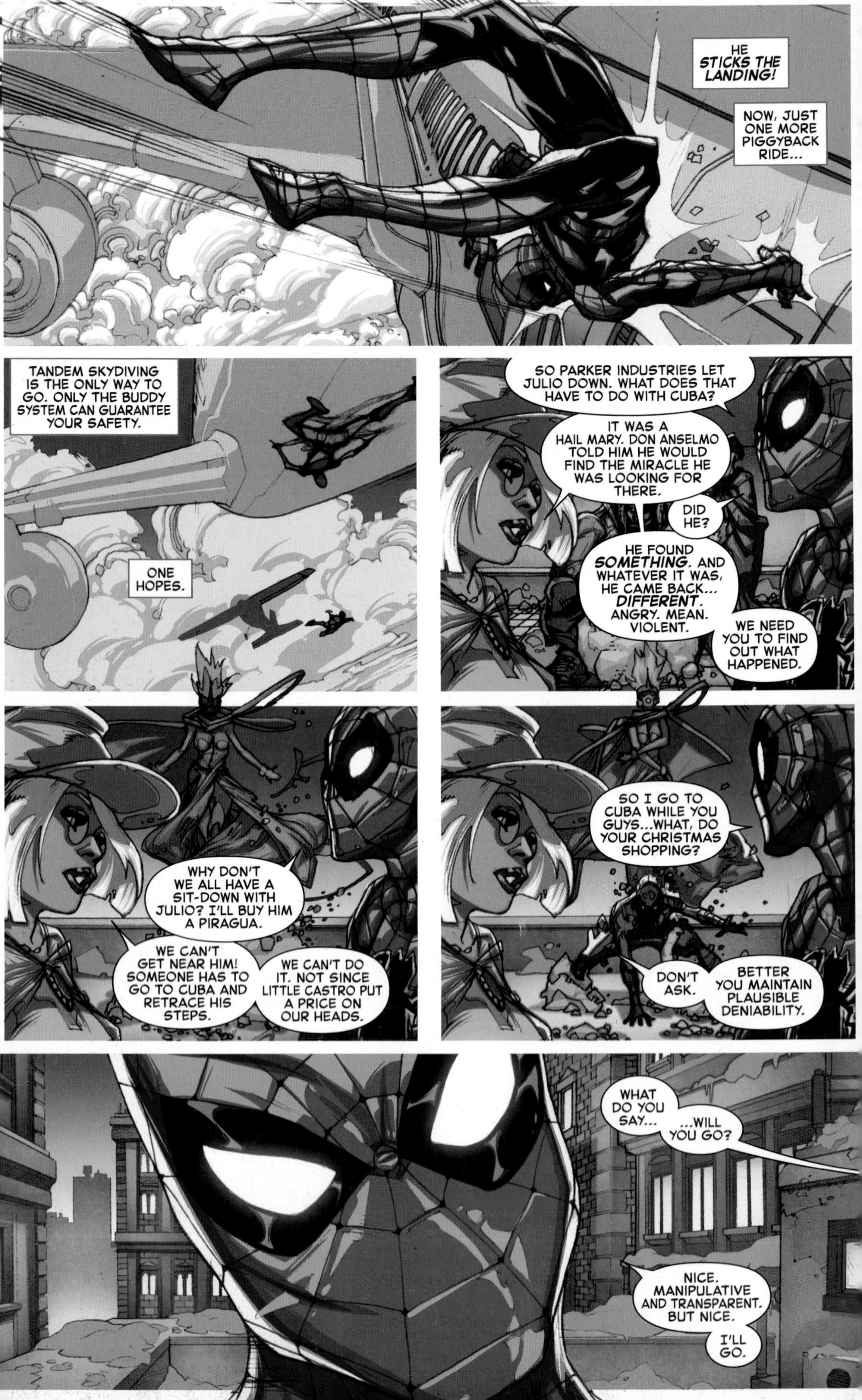
HE STICKS THE LANDING!
NOW, JUST ONE MORE PIGGYBACK RIDE...
TANDEM SKYDIVING IS THE ONLY WAY TO GO. ONLY THE BUDDY SYSTEM CAN GUARANTEE YOUR SAFETY.
ONE HOPES.
SO PARKER INDUSTRIES LET JULIO DOWN. WHAT DOES THAT HAVE TO DO WITH CUBA?
IT WAS A HAIL MARY. DON ANSELMO TOLD HIM HE WOULD FIND THE MIRACLE HE WAS LOOKING FOR THERE.
DID HE?
HE FOUND SOMETHING. AND WHATEVER IT WAS, HE CAME BACK... DIFFERENT. ANGRY. MEAN. VIOLENT.
WE NEED YOU TO FIND OUT WHAT HAPPENED.
WHY DON'T WE ALL HAVE A SIT-DOWN WITH JULIO? I'LL BUY HIM A PIRAGUA.
WE CAN'T GET NEAR HIM! SOMEONE HAS TO GO TO CUBA AND RETRACE HIS STEPS.
WE CAN'T DO IT. NOT SINCE LITTLE CASTRO PUT A PRICE ON OUR HEADS.
SO I GO TO CUBA WHILE YOU GUYS...WHAT, DO YOUR CHRISTMAS SHOPPING?
DON'T ASK.
BETTER YOU MAINTAIN PLAUSIBLE DENIABILITY.
WHAT DO YOU SAY...
...WILL YOU GO?
NICE. MANIPULATIVE AND TRANSPARENT. BUT NICE.
I'LL GO.

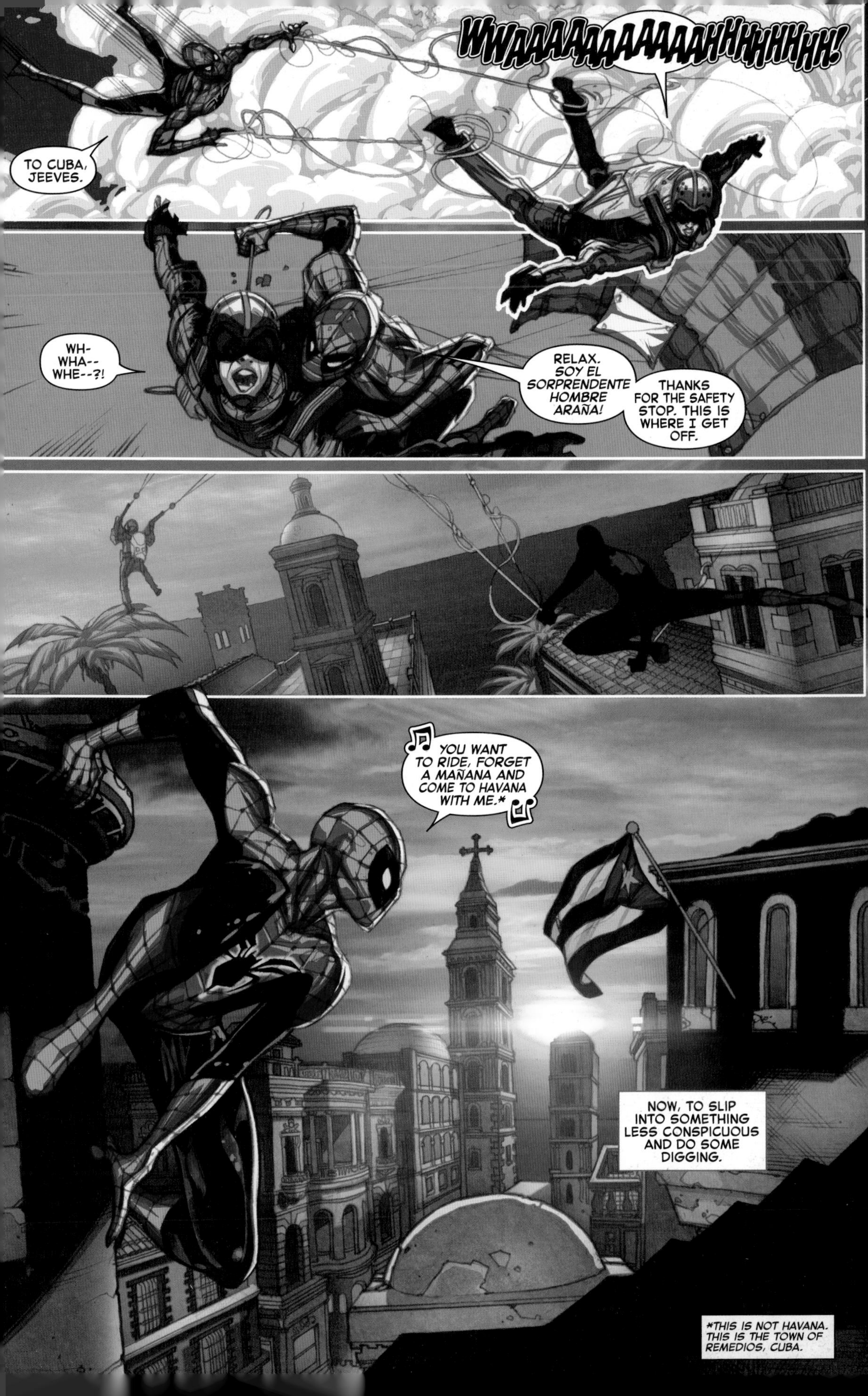
WWAAAAAAAAAAAAHHHHHHHH!
TO CUBA, JEEVES.
WH- WHA-- WHE--?!
RELAX. SOY EL SORPRENDENTE HOMBRE ARAÑA!
THANKS FOR THE SAFETY STOP. THIS IS WHERE I GET OFF.
YOU WANT TO RIDE, FORGET A MAÑANA AND COME TO HAVANA WITH ME.*
NOW, TO SLIP INTO SOMETHING LESS CONSPICUOUS AND DO SOME DIGGING.
*THIS IS NOT HAVANA. THIS IS THE TOWN OF REMEDIOS, CUBA.

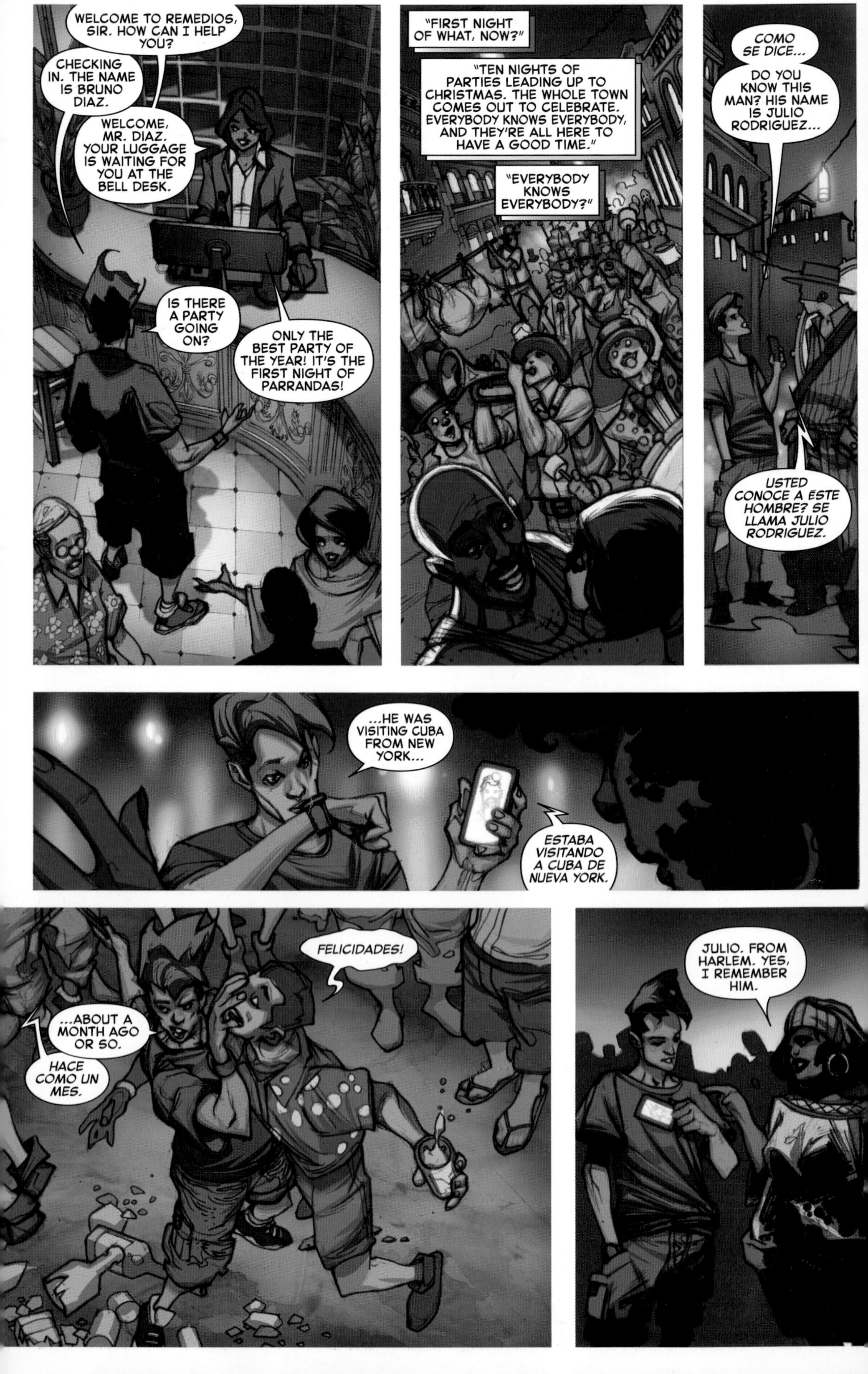
WELCOME TO REMEDIOS, SIR. HOW CAN I HELP YOU?
CHECKING IN. THE NAME IS BRUNO DIAZ.
WELCOME, MR. DIAZ. YOUR LUGGAGE IS WAITING FOR YOU AT THE BELL DESK.
IS THERE A PARTY GOING ON?
ONLY THE BEST PARTY OF THE YEAR! IT'S THE FIRST NIGHT OF PARRANDAS!
"FIRST NIGHT OF WHAT, NOW?"
"TEN NIGHTS OF PARTIES LEADING UP TO CHRISTMAS. THE WHOLE TOWN COMES OUT TO CELEBRATE. EVERYBODY KNOWS EVERYBODY, AND THEY'RE ALL HERE TO HAVE A GOOD TIME."
"EVERYBODY KNOWS EVERYBODY?"
COMO SE DICE...
DO YOU KNOW THIS MAN? HIS NAME IS JULIO RODRIGUEZ...
USTED CONOCE A ESTE HOMBRE? SE LLAMA JULIO RODRIGUEZ.
...HE WAS VISITING CUBA FROM NEW YORK...
ESTABA VISITANDO A CUBA DE NUEVA YORK.
FELICIDADES!
...ABOUT A MONTH AGO OR SO.
HACE COMO UN MES.
JULIO. FROM HARLEM. YES, I REMEMBER HIM.

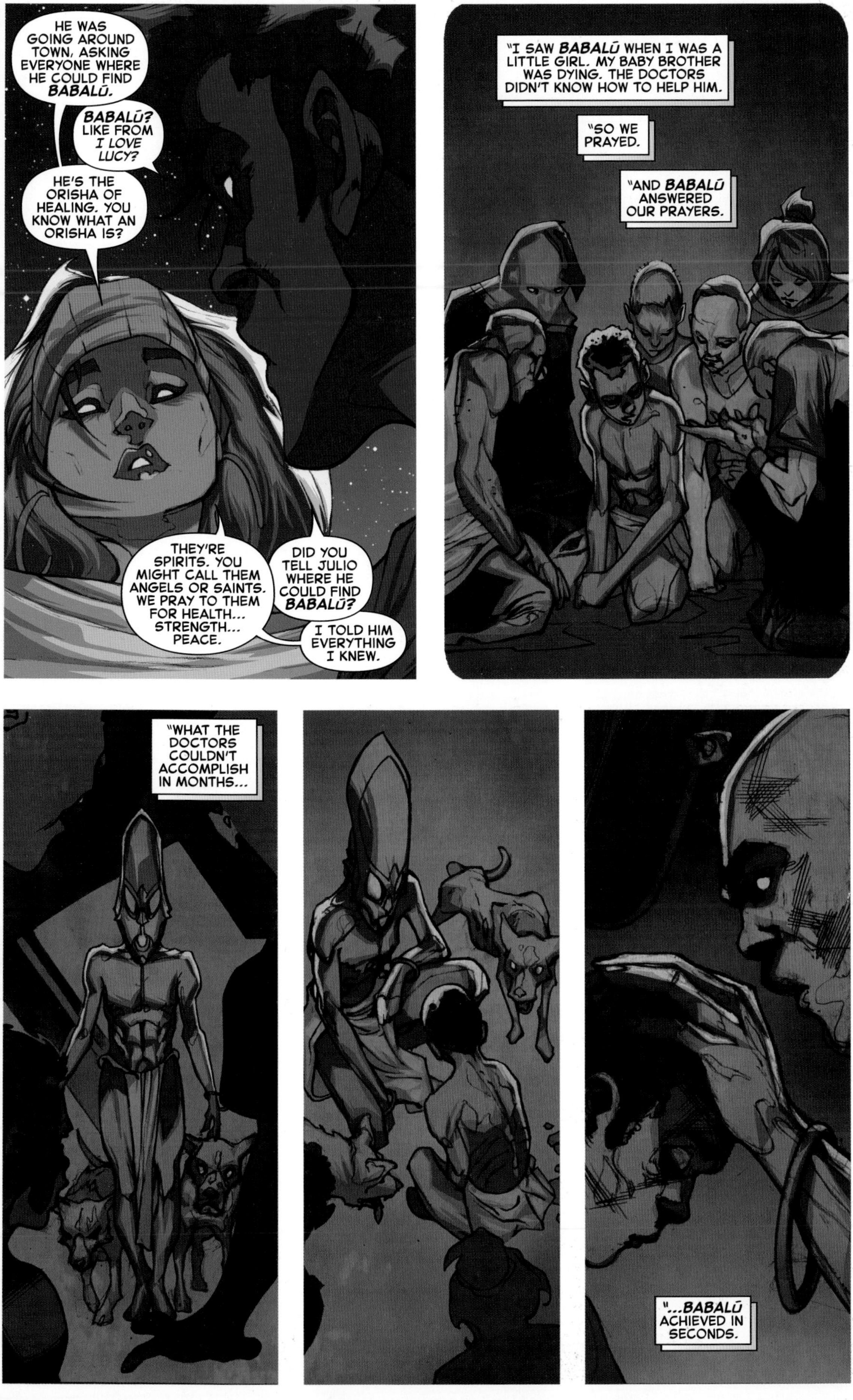

HE WAS GOING AROUND TOWN, ASKING EVERYONE WHERE HE COULD FIND **BABALŪ.**
BABALŪ? LIKE FROM *I LOVE LUCY?*
HE'S THE ORISHA OF HEALING. YOU KNOW WHAT AN ORISHA IS?
THEY'RE SPIRITS. YOU MIGHT CALL THEM ANGELS OR SAINTS. WE PRAY TO THEM FOR HEALTH... STRENGTH... PEACE.
DID YOU TELL JULIO WHERE HE COULD FIND **BABALŪ?**
I TOLD HIM EVERYTHING I KNEW.
"I SAW **BABALŪ** WHEN I WAS A LITTLE GIRL. MY BABY BROTHER WAS DYING. THE DOCTORS DIDN'T KNOW HOW TO HELP HIM.
"SO WE PRAYED.
"AND **BABALŪ** ANSWERED OUR PRAYERS.
"WHAT THE DOCTORS COULDN'T ACCOMPLISH IN MONTHS...
"...**BABALŪ** ACHIEVED IN SECONDS.

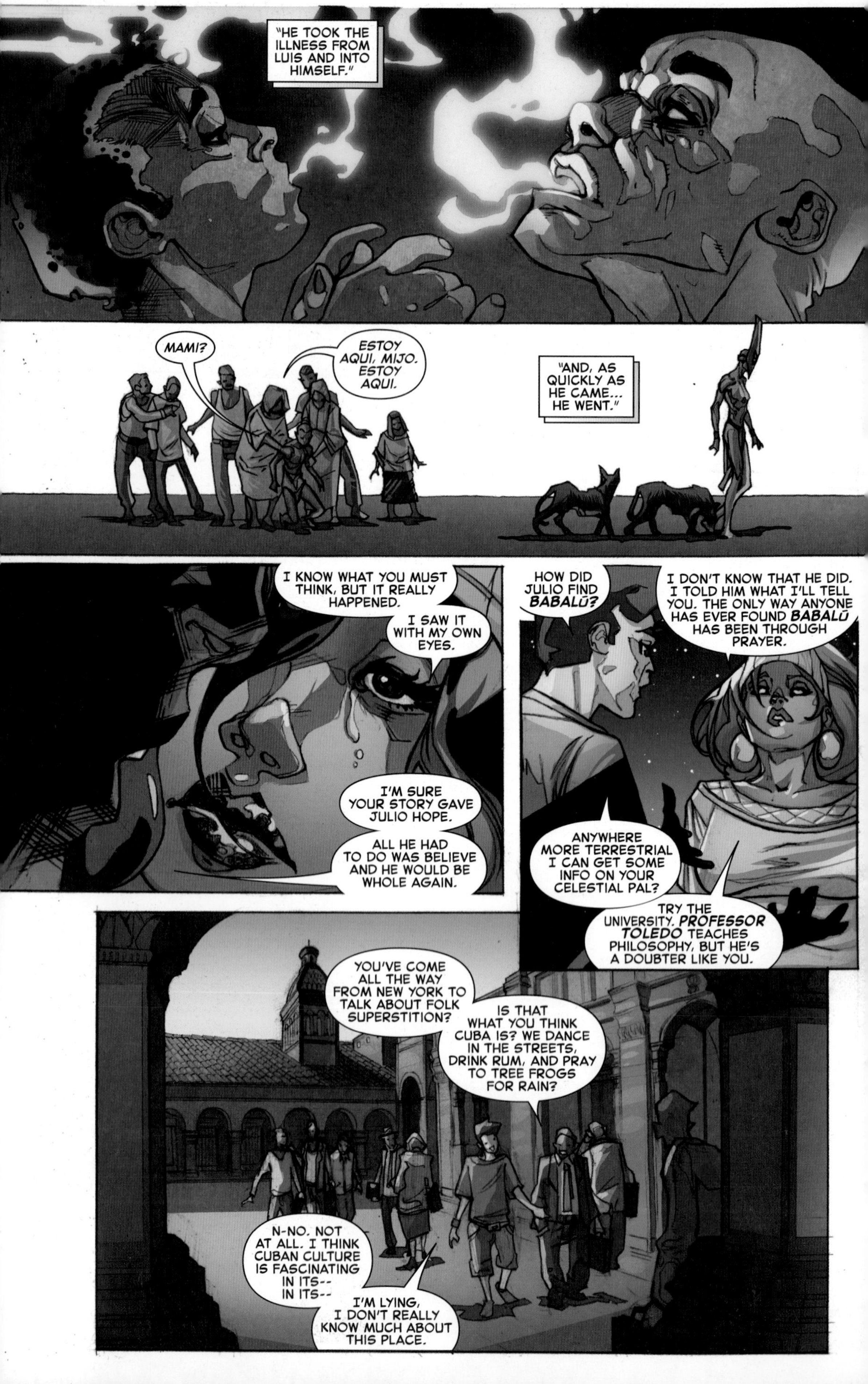
"HE TOOK THE ILLNESS FROM LUIS AND INTO HIMSELF."
MAMI?
ESTOY AQUI, MIJO. ESTOY AQUI.
"AND, AS QUICKLY AS HE CAME... HE WENT."
I KNOW WHAT YOU MUST THINK, BUT IT REALLY HAPPENED.
I SAW IT WITH MY OWN EYES.
I'M SURE YOUR STORY GAVE JULIO HOPE.
ALL HE HAD TO DO WAS BELIEVE AND HE WOULD BE WHOLE AGAIN.
HOW DID JULIO FIND BABALÚ?
I DON'T KNOW THAT HE DID. I TOLD HIM WHAT I'LL TELL YOU. THE ONLY WAY ANYONE HAS EVER FOUND BABALÚ HAS BEEN THROUGH PRAYER.
ANYWHERE MORE TERRESTRIAL I CAN GET SOME INFO ON YOUR CELESTIAL PAL?
TRY THE UNIVERSITY. PROFESSOR TOLEDO TEACHES PHILOSOPHY, BUT HE'S A DOUBTER LIKE YOU.
YOU'VE COME ALL THE WAY FROM NEW YORK TO TALK ABOUT FOLK SUPERSTITION?
IS THAT WHAT YOU THINK CUBA IS? WE DANCE IN THE STREETS, DRINK RUM, AND PRAY TO TREE FROGS FOR RAIN?
N-NO. NOT AT ALL. I THINK CUBAN CULTURE IS FASCINATING IN ITS-- IN ITS--
I'M LYING, I DON'T REALLY KNOW MUCH ABOUT THIS PLACE.

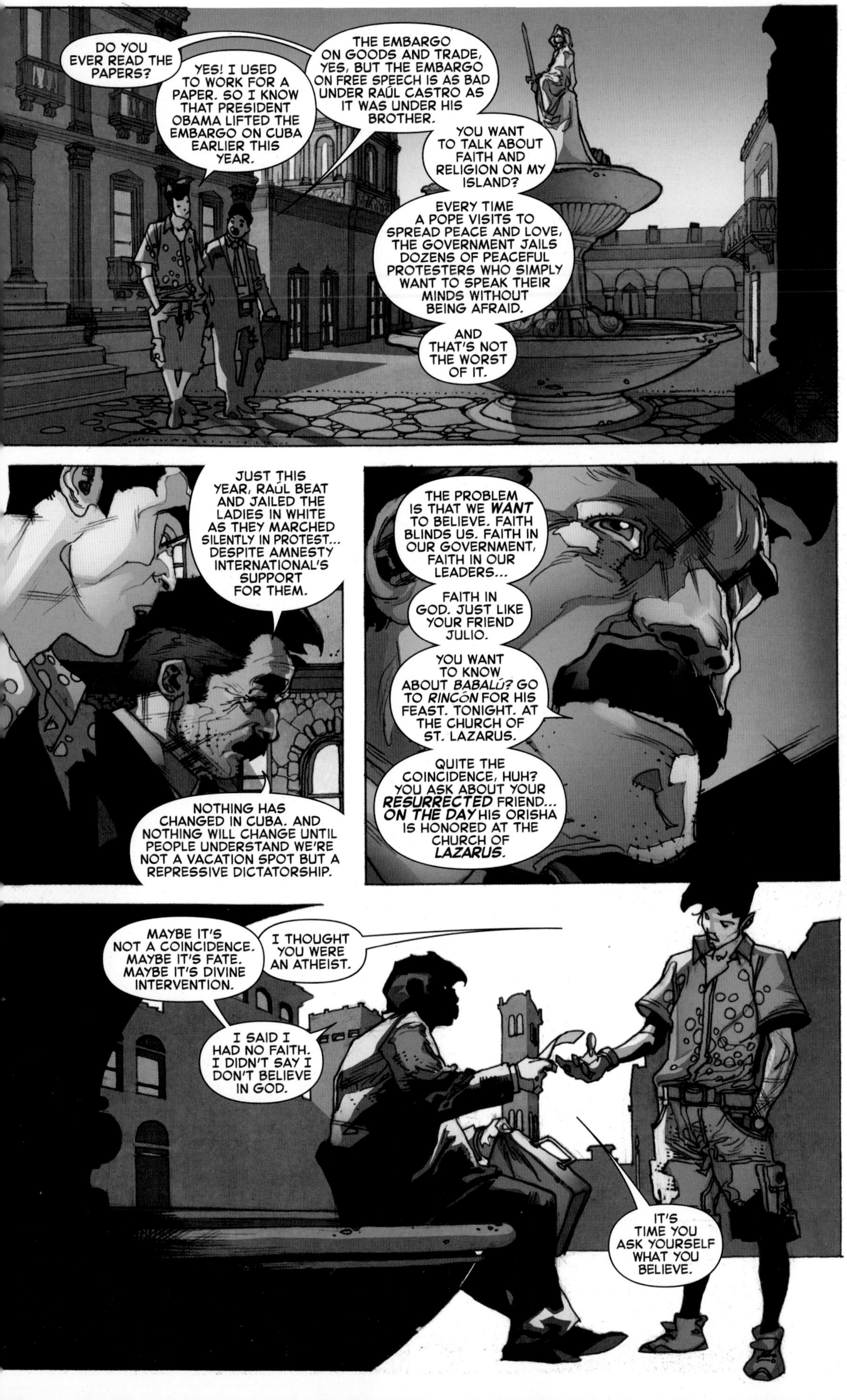
DO YOU EVER READ THE PAPERS?
YES! I USED TO WORK FOR A PAPER. SO I KNOW THAT PRESIDENT OBAMA LIFTED THE EMBARGO ON CUBA EARLIER THIS YEAR.
THE EMBARGO ON GOODS AND TRADE, YES, BUT THE EMBARGO ON FREE SPEECH IS AS BAD UNDER RAÚL CASTRO AS IT WAS UNDER HIS BROTHER.
YOU WANT TO TALK ABOUT FAITH AND RELIGION ON MY ISLAND?
EVERY TIME A POPE VISITS TO SPREAD PEACE AND LOVE, THE GOVERNMENT JAILS DOZENS OF PEACEFUL PROTESTERS WHO SIMPLY WANT TO SPEAK THEIR MINDS WITHOUT BEING AFRAID.
AND THAT'S NOT THE WORST OF IT.
JUST THIS YEAR, RAÚL BEAT AND JAILED THE LADIES IN WHITE AS THEY MARCHED SILENTLY IN PROTEST... DESPITE AMNESTY INTERNATIONAL'S SUPPORT FOR THEM.
NOTHING HAS CHANGED IN CUBA. AND NOTHING WILL CHANGE UNTIL PEOPLE UNDERSTAND WE'RE NOT A VACATION SPOT BUT A REPRESSIVE DICTATORSHIP.
THE PROBLEM IS THAT WE ***WANT*** TO BELIEVE. FAITH BLINDS US. FAITH IN OUR GOVERNMENT, FAITH IN OUR LEADERS...
FAITH IN GOD. JUST LIKE YOUR FRIEND JULIO.
YOU WANT TO KNOW ABOUT *BABALÚ?* GO TO *RINCÓN* FOR HIS FEAST. TONIGHT. AT THE CHURCH OF ST. LAZARUS.
QUITE THE COINCIDENCE, HUH? YOU ASK ABOUT YOUR ***RESURRECTED*** FRIEND... ***ON THE DAY*** HIS ORISHA IS HONORED AT THE CHURCH OF ***LAZARUS.***
MAYBE IT'S NOT A COINCIDENCE. MAYBE IT'S FATE. MAYBE IT'S DIVINE INTERVENTION.
I THOUGHT YOU WERE AN ATHEIST.
I SAID I HAD NO FAITH. I DIDN'T SAY I DON'T BELIEVE IN GOD.
IT'S TIME YOU ASK YOURSELF WHAT YOU BELIEVE.

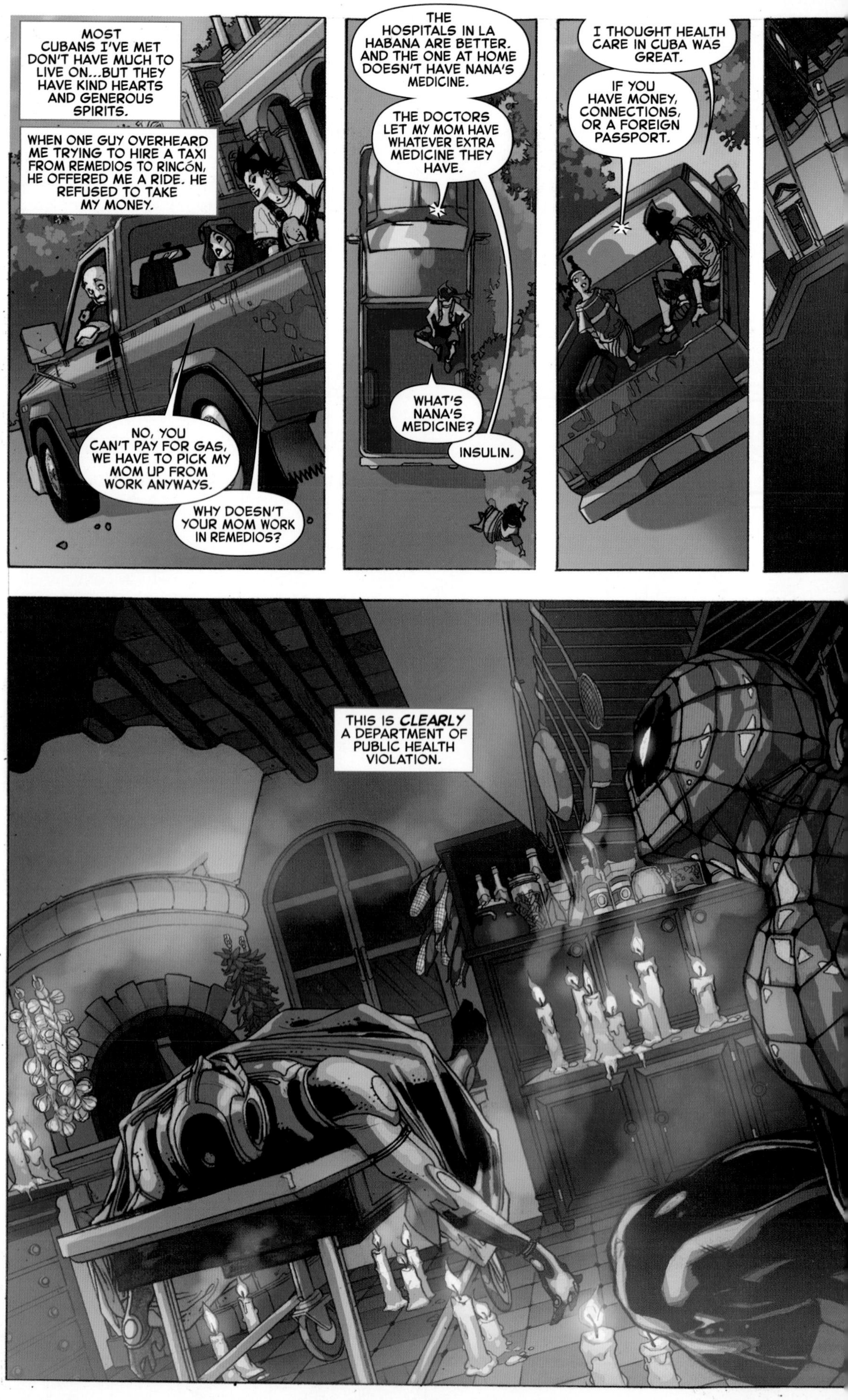
MOST CUBANS I'VE MET DON'T HAVE MUCH TO LIVE ON...BUT THEY HAVE KIND HEARTS AND GENEROUS SPIRITS.
WHEN ONE GUY OVERHEARD ME TRYING TO HIRE A TAXI FROM REMEDIOS TO RINCÓN, HE OFFERED ME A RIDE. HE REFUSED TO TAKE MY MONEY.
NO, YOU CAN'T PAY FOR GAS, WE HAVE TO PICK MY MOM UP FROM WORK ANYWAYS.
WHY DOESN'T YOUR MOM WORK IN REMEDIOS?
THE HOSPITALS IN LA HABANA ARE BETTER. AND THE ONE AT HOME DOESN'T HAVE NANA'S MEDICINE.
THE DOCTORS LET MY MOM HAVE WHATEVER EXTRA MEDICINE THEY HAVE.
WHAT'S NANA'S MEDICINE?
INSULIN.
I THOUGHT HEALTH CARE IN CUBA WAS GREAT.
IF YOU HAVE MONEY, CONNECTIONS, OR A FOREIGN PASSPORT.
THIS IS CLEARLY A DEPARTMENT OF PUBLIC HEALTH VIOLATION.

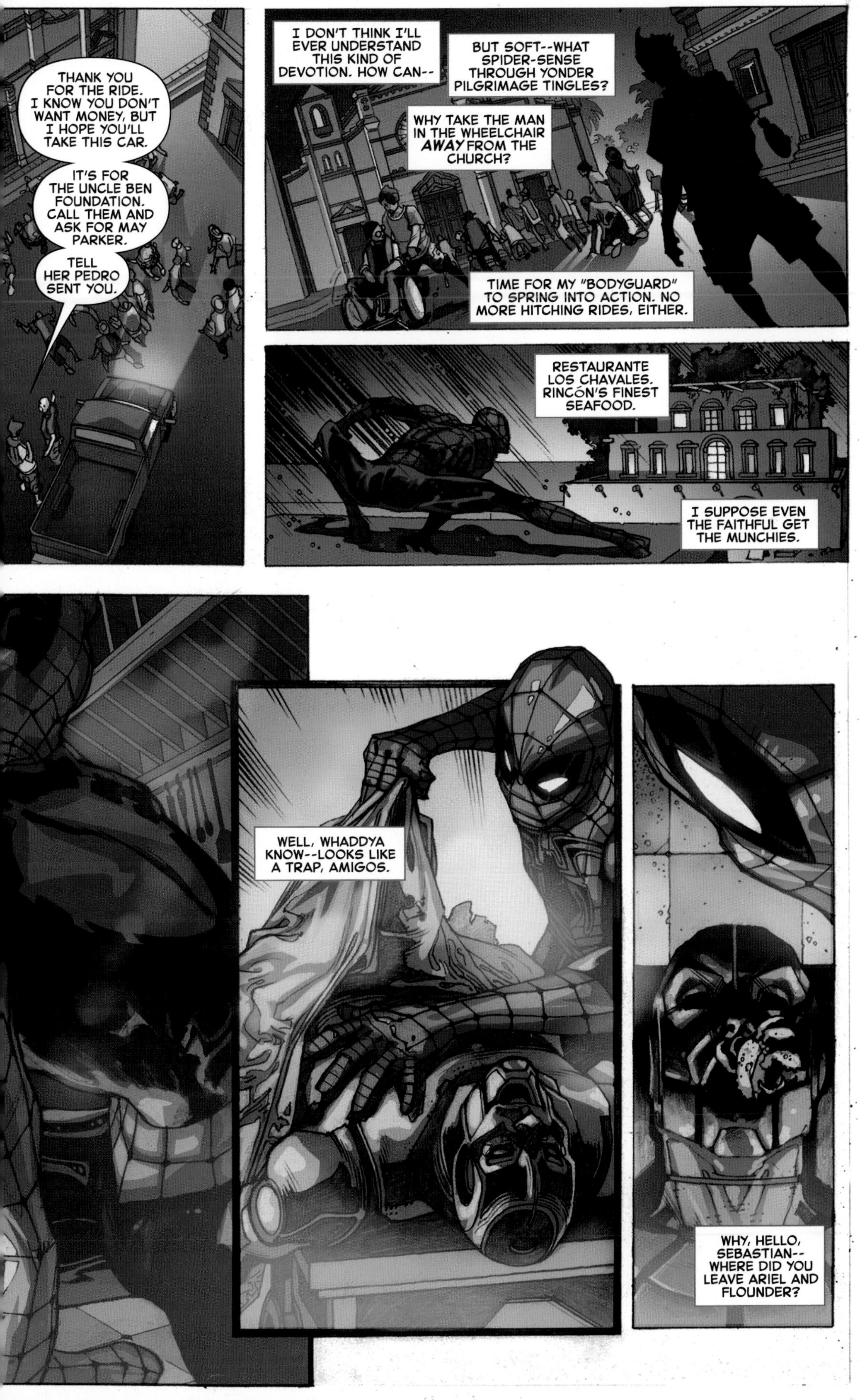
THANK YOU FOR THE RIDE. I KNOW YOU DON'T WANT MONEY, BUT I HOPE YOU'LL TAKE THIS CAR.
IT'S FOR THE UNCLE BEN FOUNDATION. CALL THEM AND ASK FOR MAY PARKER.
TELL HER PEDRO SENT YOU.
I DON'T THINK I'LL EVER UNDERSTAND THIS KIND OF DEVOTION. HOW CAN--
BUT SOFT--WHAT SPIDER-SENSE THROUGH YONDER PILGRIMAGE TINGLES?
WHY TAKE THE MAN IN THE WHEELCHAIR AWAY FROM THE CHURCH?
TIME FOR MY "BODYGUARD" TO SPRING INTO ACTION. NO MORE HITCHING RIDES, EITHER.
RESTAURANTE LOS CHAVALES. RINCÓN'S FINEST SEAFOOD.
I SUPPOSE EVEN THE FAITHFUL GET THE MUNCHIES.
WELL, WHADDYA KNOW--LOOKS LIKE A TRAP, AMIGOS.
WHY, HELLO, SEBASTIAN--WHERE DID YOU LEAVE ARIEL AND FLOUNDER?

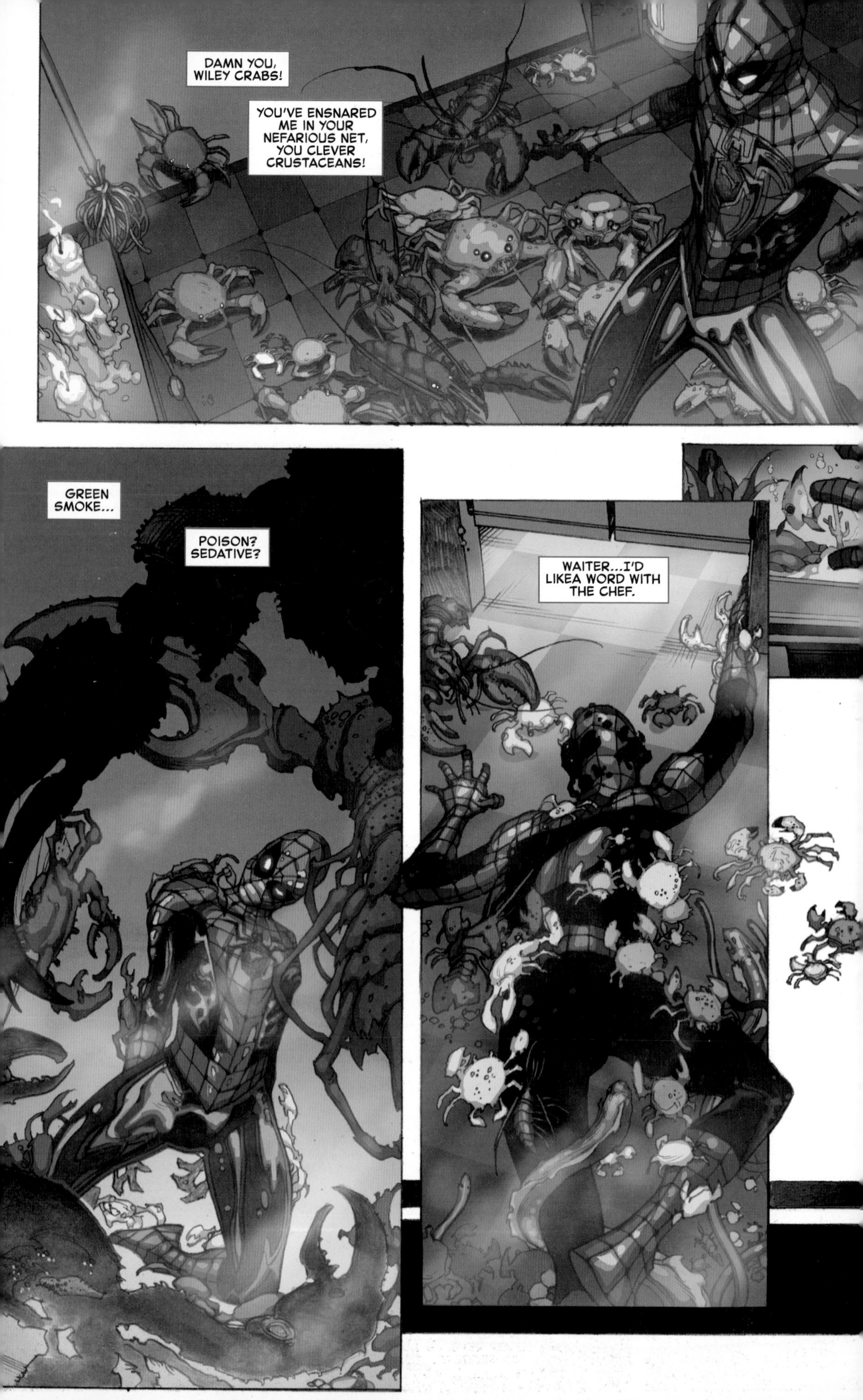
DAMN YOU, WILEY CRABS!
YOU'VE ENSNARED ME IN YOUR NEFARIOUS NET, YOU CLEVER CRUSTACEANS!
GREEN SMOKE...
POISON? SEDATIVE?
WAITER...I'D LIKEA WORD WITH THE CHEF.

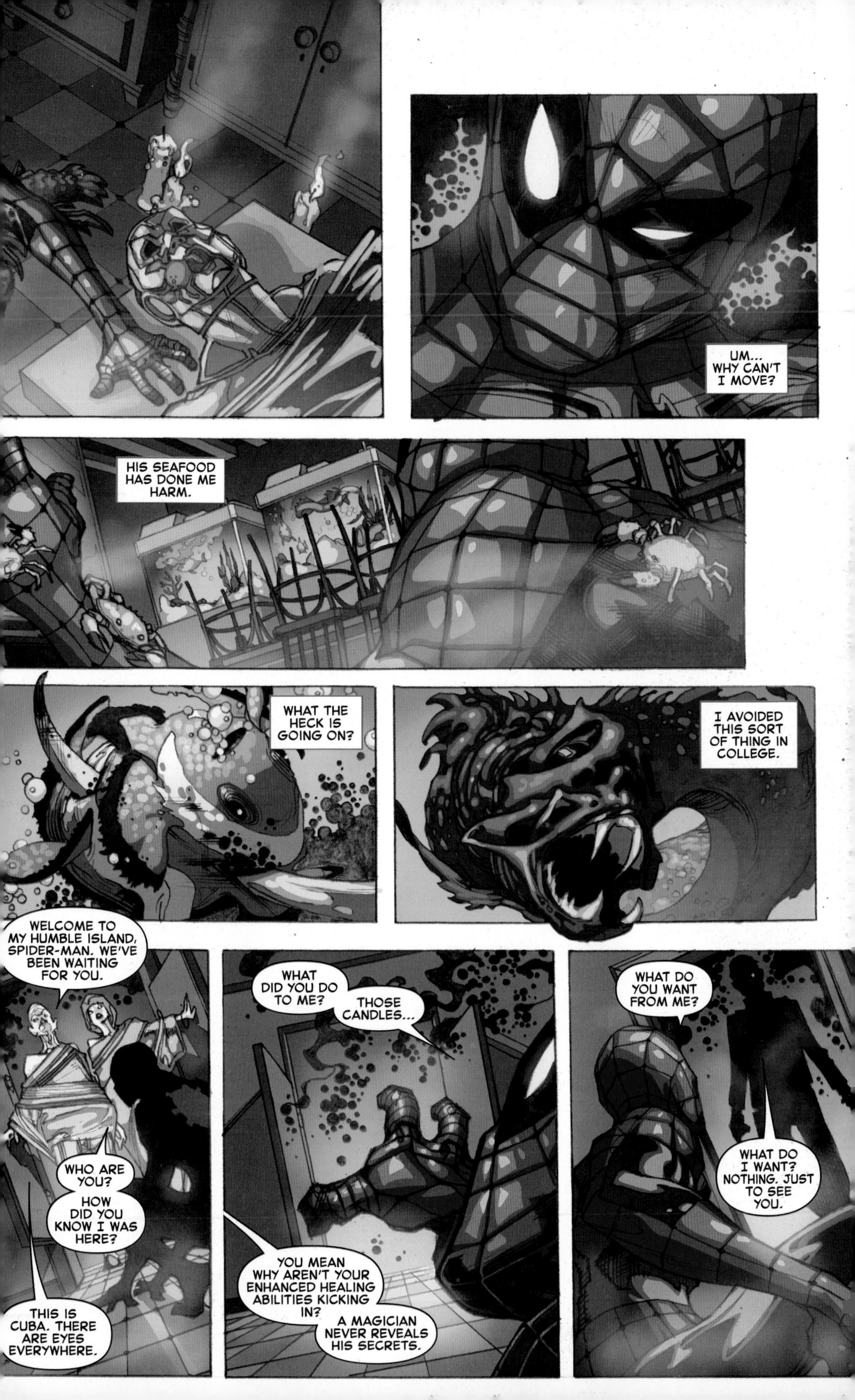
UM... WHY CAN'T I MOVE?
HIS SEAFOOD HAS DONE ME HARM.
WHAT THE HECK IS GOING ON?
I AVOIDED THIS SORT OF THING IN COLLEGE.
WELCOME TO MY HUMBLE ISLAND, SPIDER-MAN. WE'VE BEEN WAITING FOR YOU.
WHO ARE YOU?
HOW DID YOU KNOW I WAS HERE?
THIS IS CUBA. THERE ARE EYES EVERYWHERE.
WHAT DID YOU DO TO ME?
THOSE CANDLES...
YOU MEAN WHY AREN'T YOUR ENHANCED HEALING ABILITIES KICKING IN?
A MAGICIAN NEVER REVEALS HIS SECRETS.
WHAT DO YOU WANT FROM ME?
WHAT DO I WANT? NOTHING. JUST TO SEE YOU.

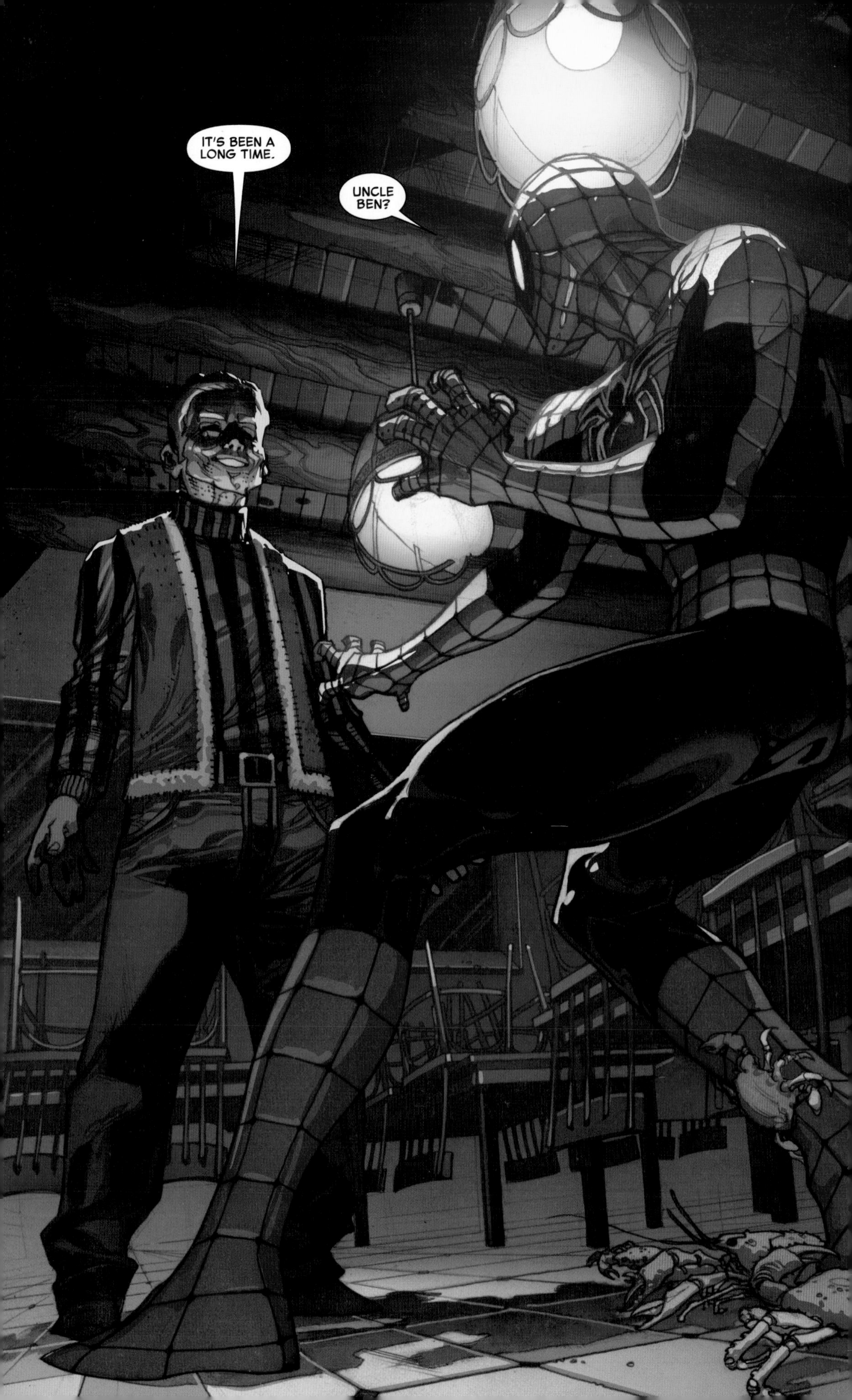
IT'S BEEN A LONG TIME.
UNCLE BEN?

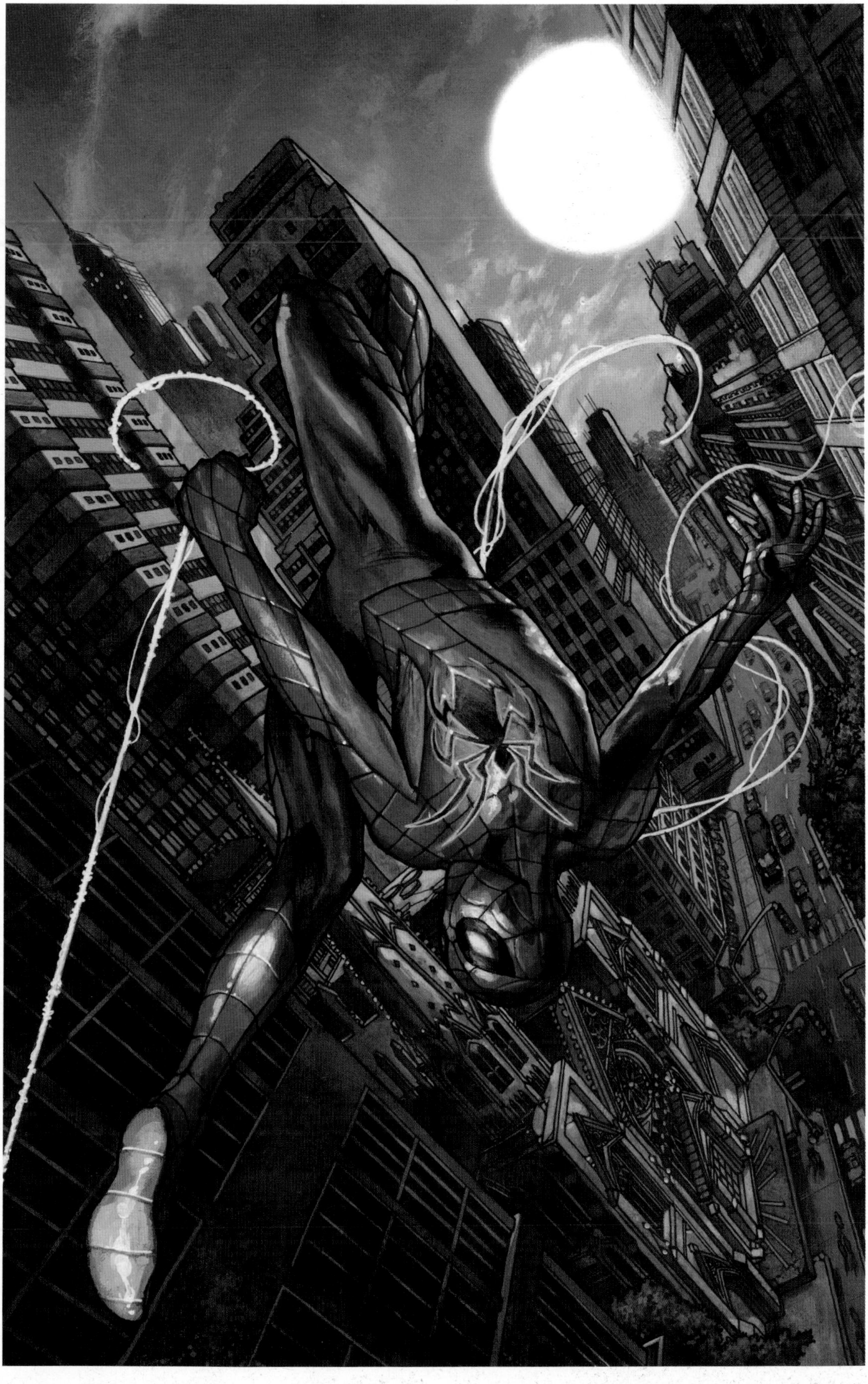

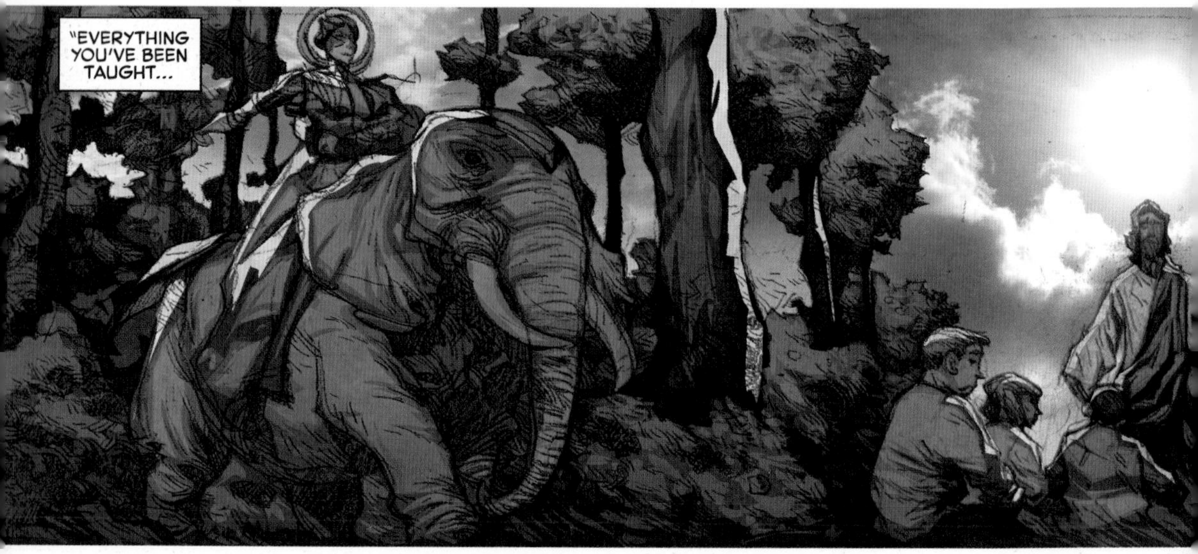
"EVERYTHING YOU'VE BEEN TAUGHT...

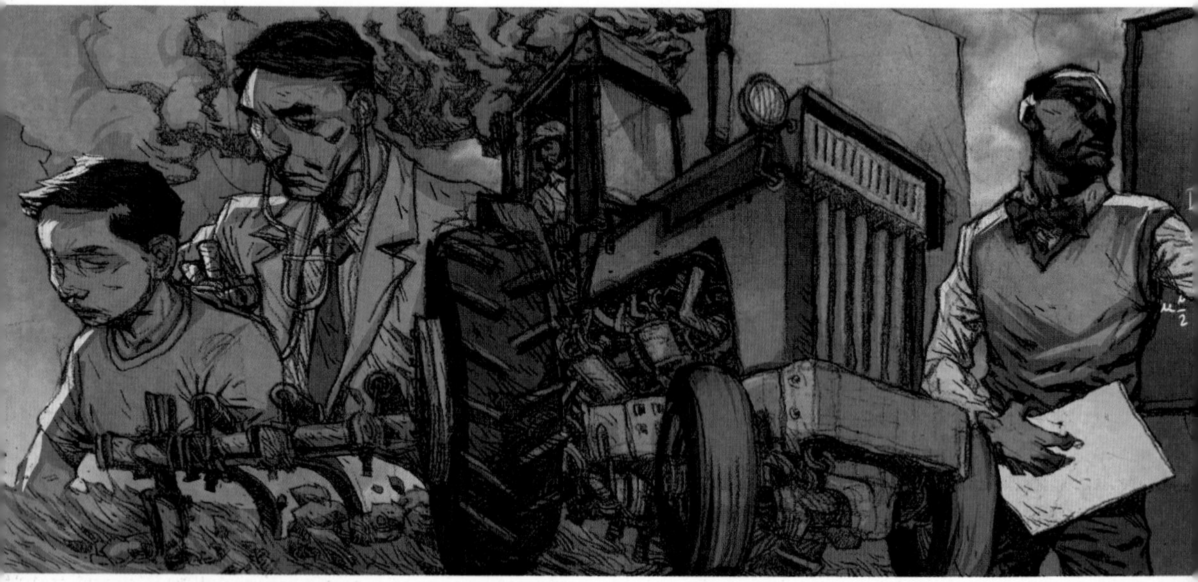

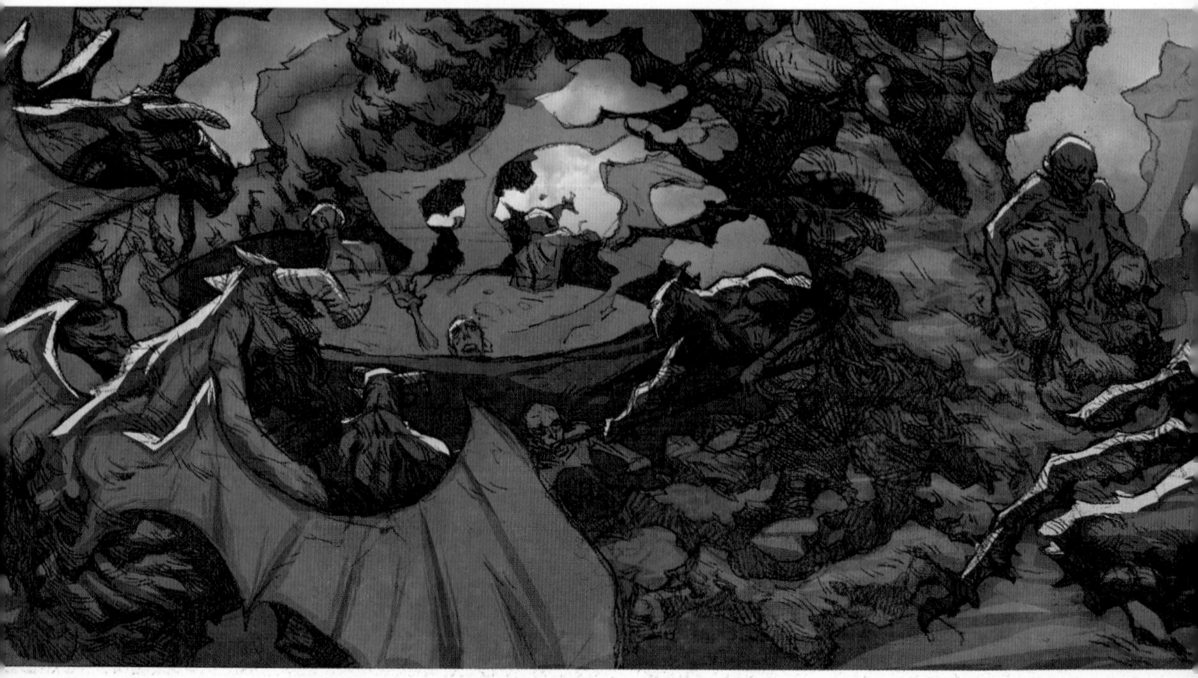

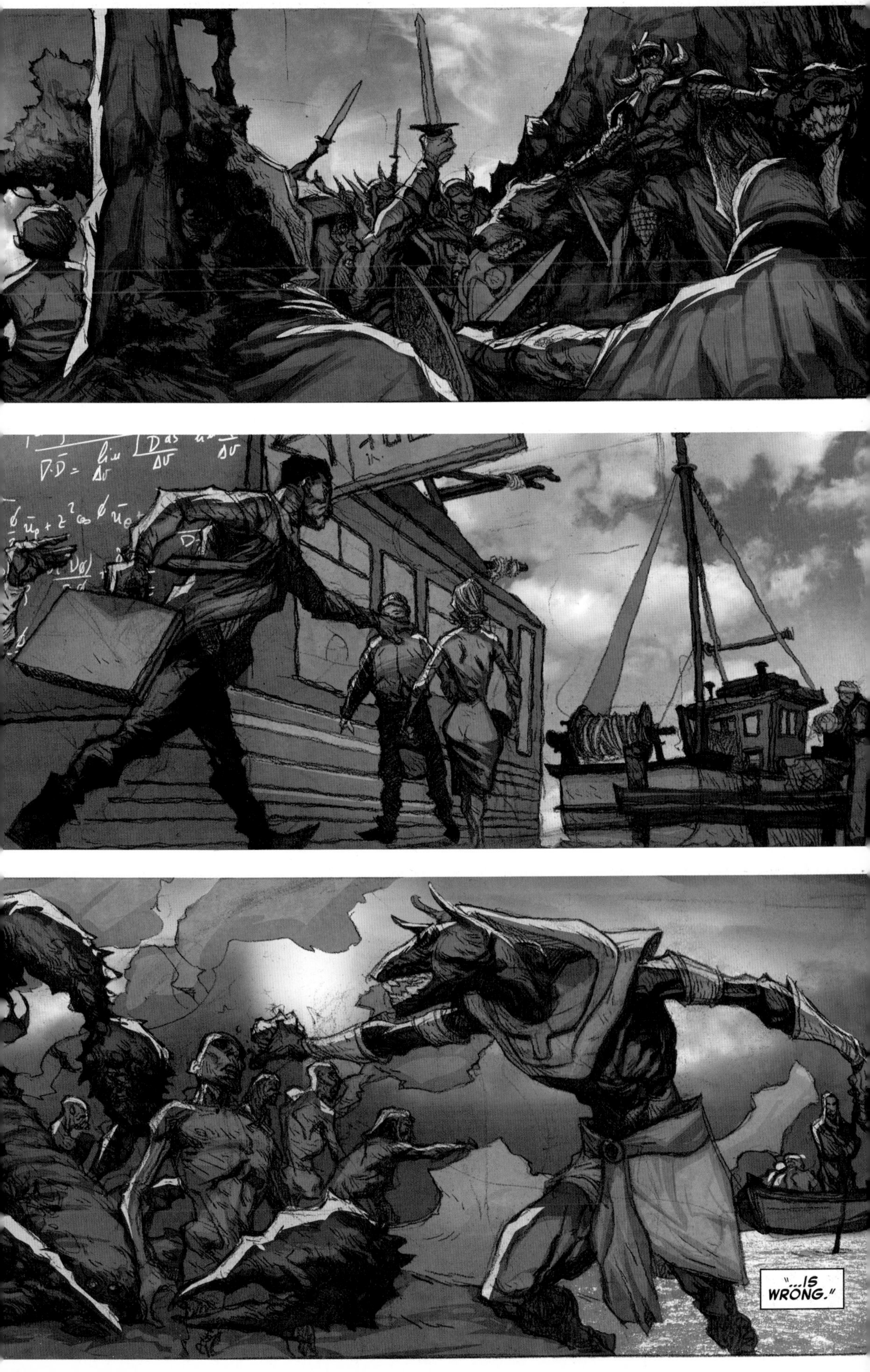
"...IS WRONG."

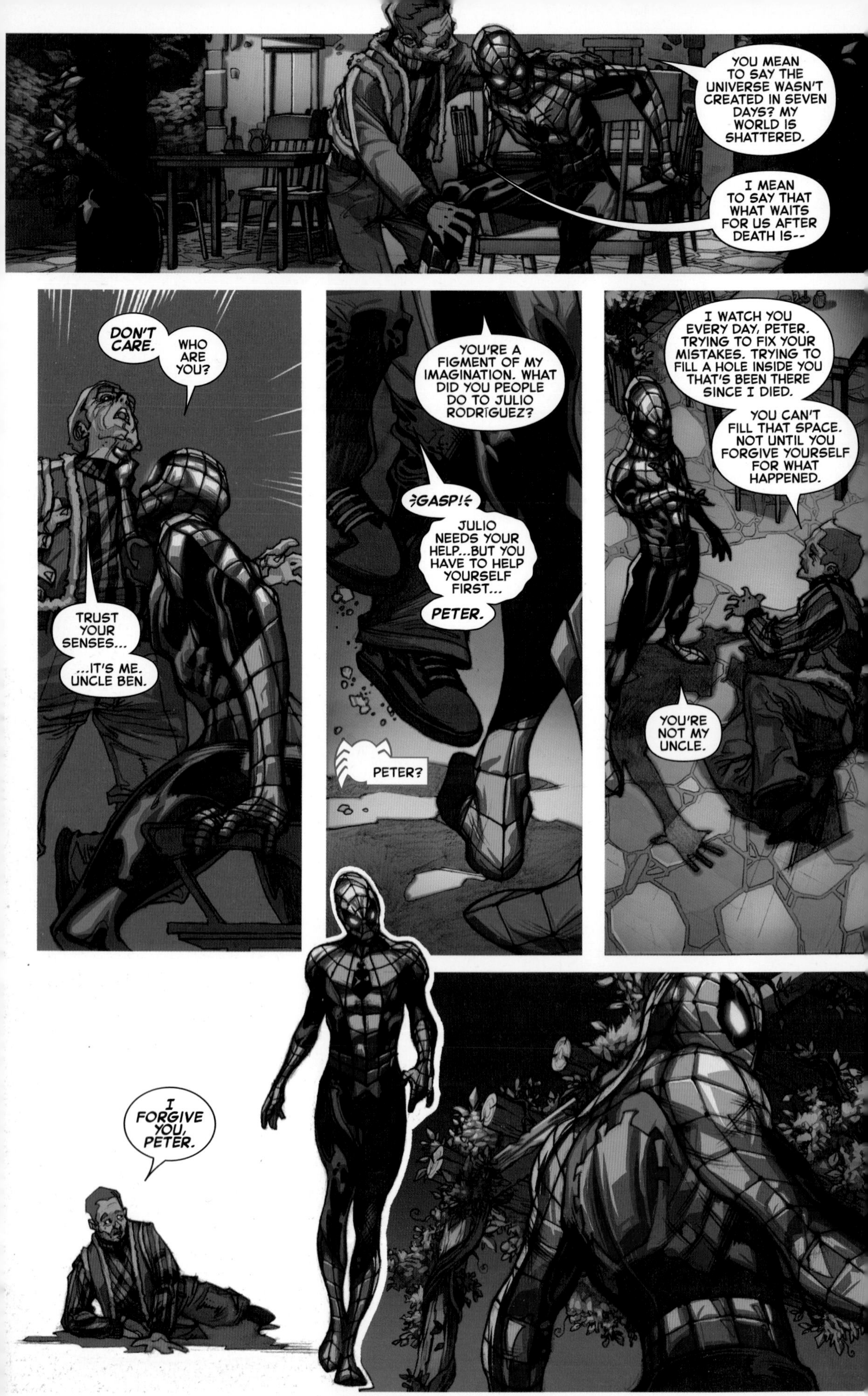
YOU MEAN TO SAY THE UNIVERSE WASN'T CREATED IN SEVEN DAYS? MY WORLD IS SHATTERED.
I MEAN TO SAY THAT WHAT WAITS FOR US AFTER DEATH IS--
DON'T CARE.
WHO ARE YOU?
TRUST YOUR SENSES...
...IT'S ME. UNCLE BEN.
YOU'RE A FIGMENT OF MY IMAGINATION. WHAT DID YOU PEOPLE DO TO JULIO RODRÍGUEZ?
GASP!
JULIO NEEDS YOUR HELP...BUT YOU HAVE TO HELP YOURSELF FIRST...
PETER.
PETER?
I WATCH YOU EVERY DAY, PETER. TRYING TO FIX YOUR MISTAKES. TRYING TO FILL A HOLE INSIDE YOU THAT'S BEEN THERE SINCE I DIED.
YOU CAN'T FILL THAT SPACE. NOT UNTIL YOU FORGIVE YOURSELF FOR WHAT HAPPENED.
YOU'RE NOT MY UNCLE.
I FORGIVE YOU, PETER.

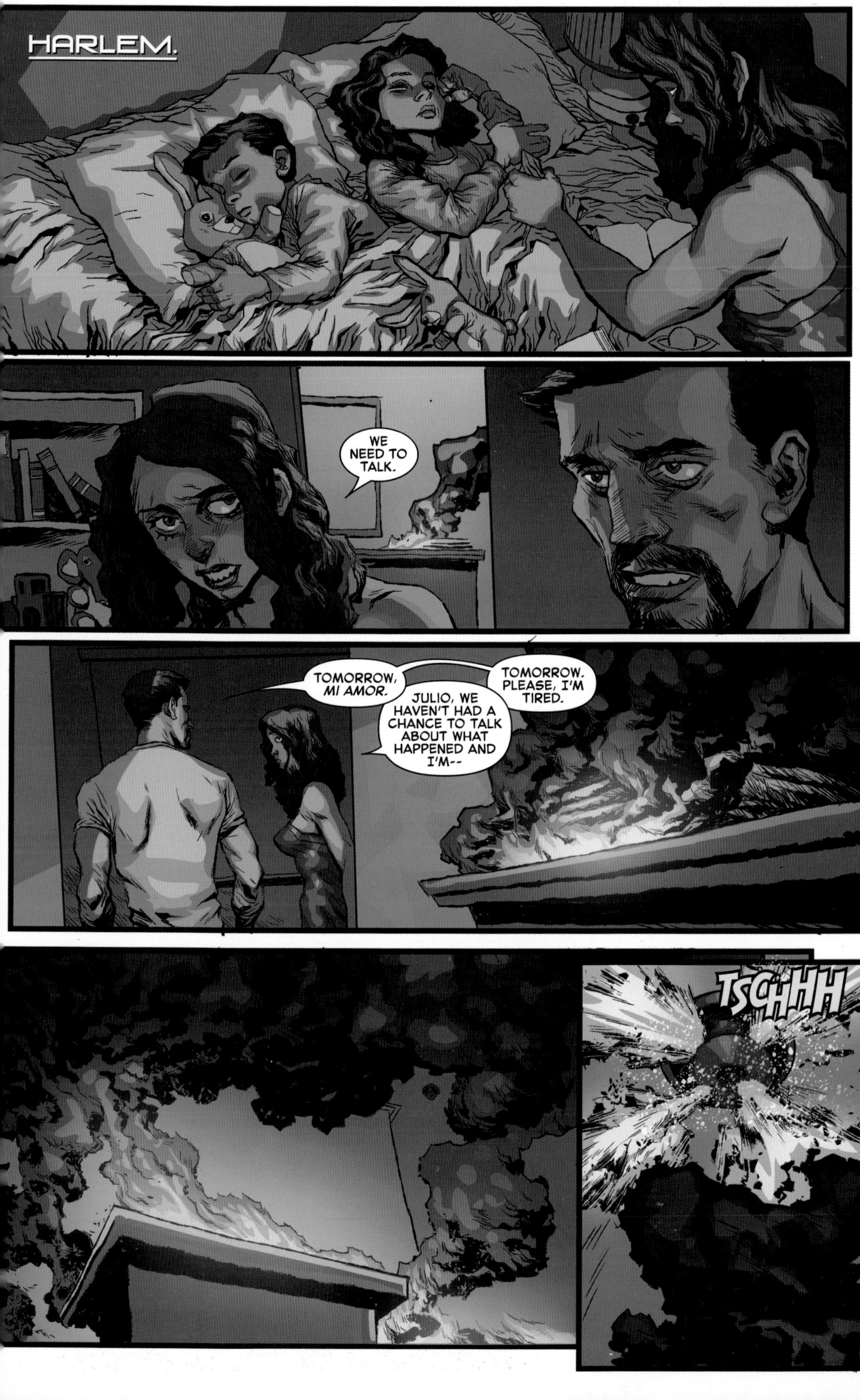
HARLEM.
WE NEED TO TALK.
TOMORROW, MI AMOR.
JULIO, WE HAVEN'T HAD A CHANCE TO TALK ABOUT WHAT HAPPENED AND I'M--
TOMORROW. PLEASE, I'M TIRED.
TSCHHH

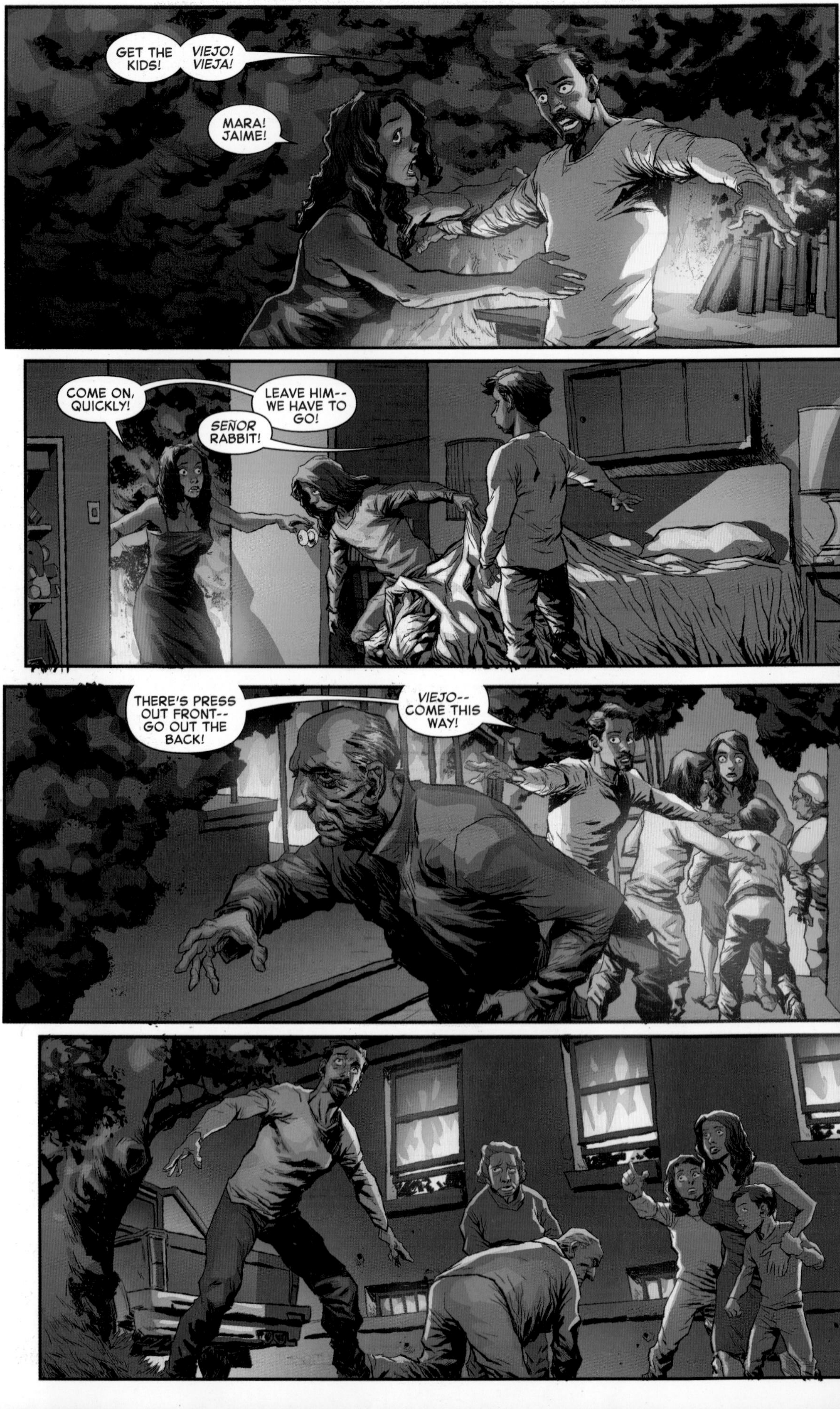
GET THE KIDS!
VIEJO! VIEJA!
MARA! JAIME!
COME ON, QUICKLY!
LEAVE HIM-- WE HAVE TO GO!
SEÑOR RABBIT!
THERE'S PRESS OUT FRONT-- GO OUT THE BACK!
VIEJO-- COME THIS WAY!

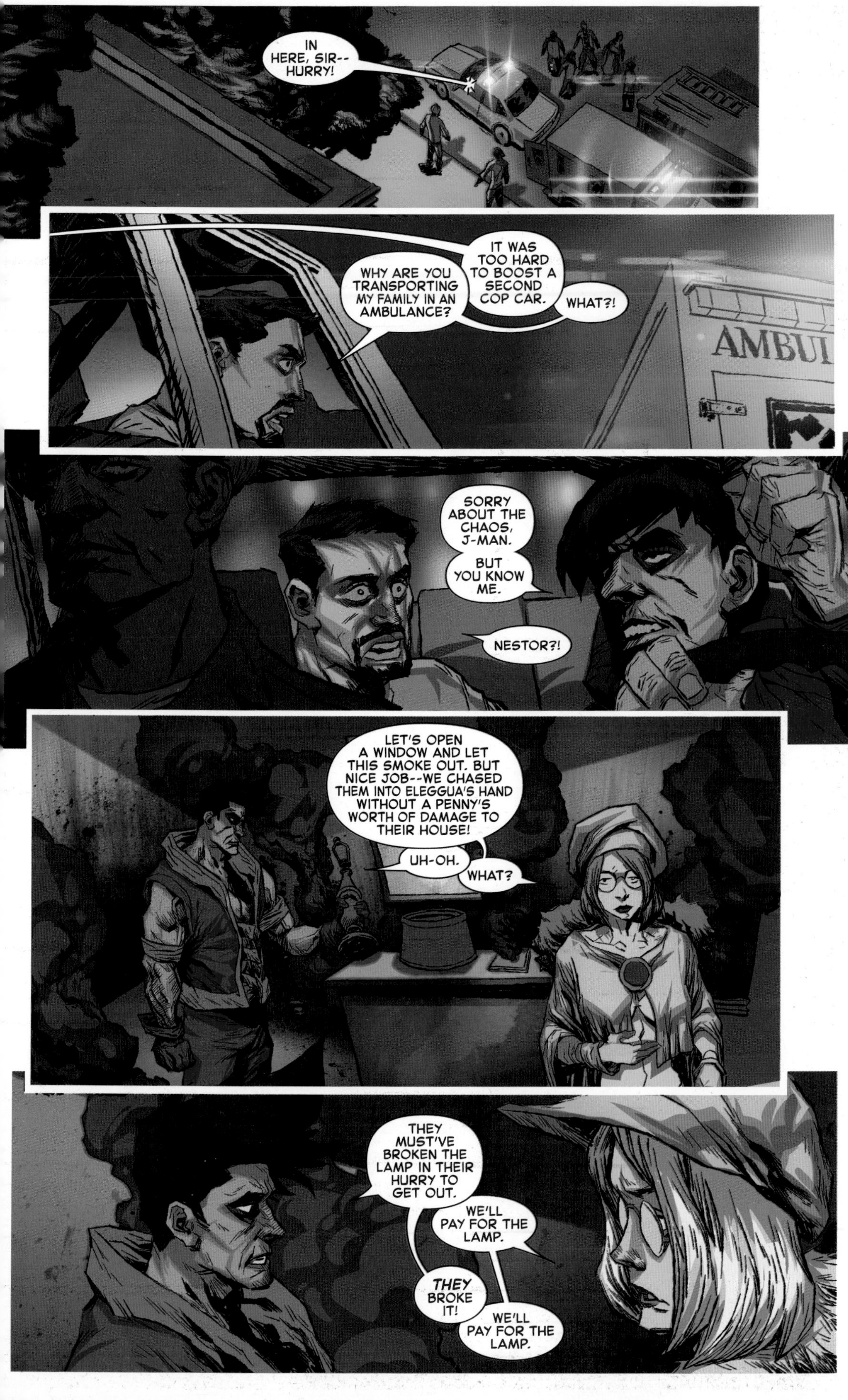
IN HERE, SIR-- HURRY!
WHY ARE YOU TRANSPORTING MY FAMILY IN AN AMBULANCE?
IT WAS TOO HARD TO BOOST A SECOND COP CAR.
WHAT?!
AMBUL
SORRY ABOUT THE CHAOS, J-MAN.
BUT YOU KNOW ME.
NESTOR?!
LET'S OPEN A WINDOW AND LET THIS SMOKE OUT. BUT NICE JOB--WE CHASED THEM INTO ELEGGUA'S HAND WITHOUT A PENNY'S WORTH OF DAMAGE TO THEIR HOUSE!
UH-OH.
WHAT?
THEY MUST'VE BROKEN THE LAMP IN THEIR HURRY TO GET OUT.
WE'LL PAY FOR THE LAMP.
THEY BROKE IT!
WE'LL PAY FOR THE LAMP.

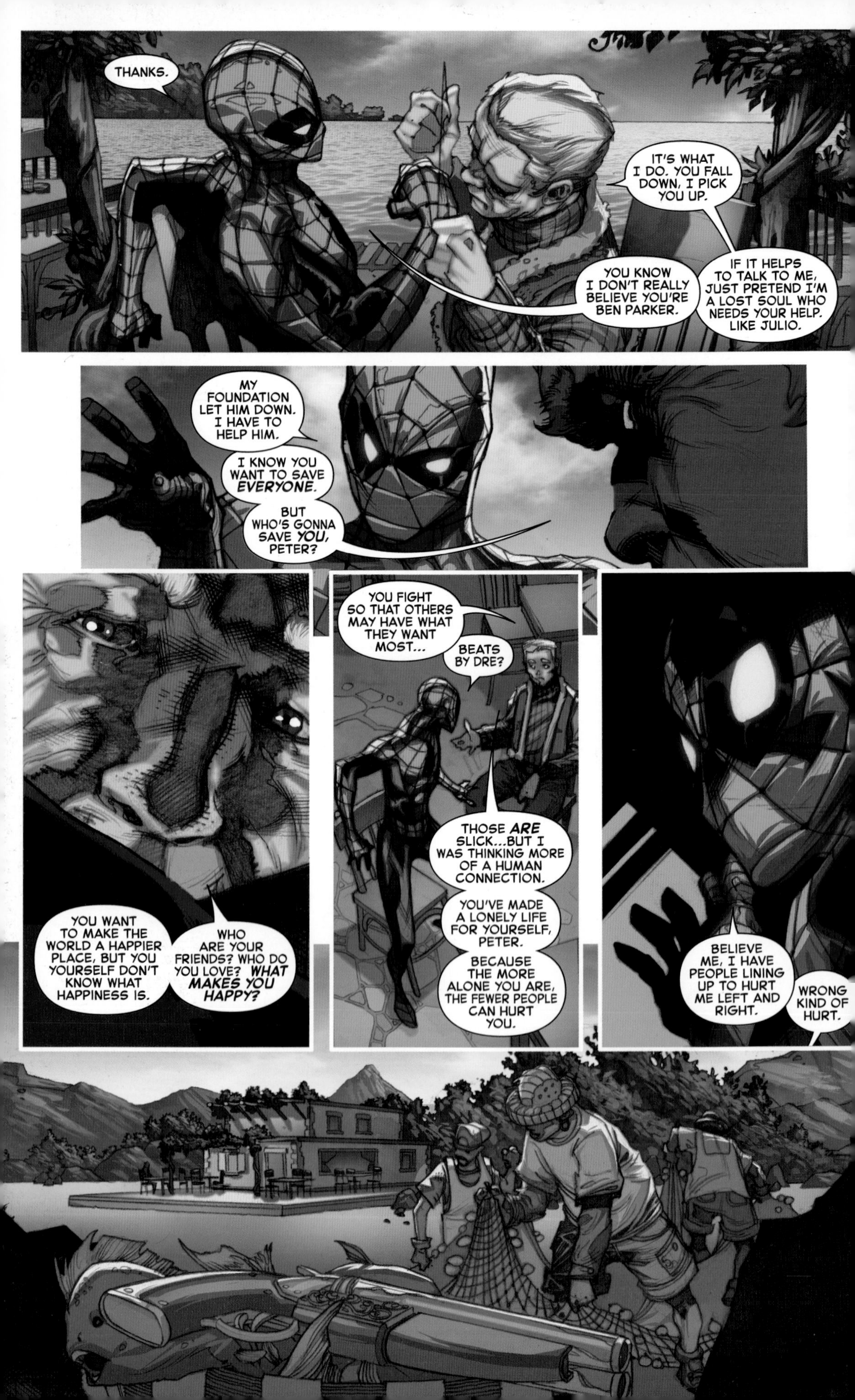
THANKS.
IT'S WHAT I DO. YOU FALL DOWN, I PICK YOU UP.
IF IT HELPS TO TALK TO ME, JUST PRETEND I'M A LOST SOUL WHO NEEDS YOUR HELP. LIKE JULIO.
YOU KNOW I DON'T REALLY BELIEVE YOU'RE BEN PARKER.
MY FOUNDATION LET HIM DOWN. I HAVE TO HELP HIM.
I KNOW YOU WANT TO SAVE EVERYONE.
BUT WHO'S GONNA SAVE YOU, PETER?
YOU WANT TO MAKE THE WORLD A HAPPIER PLACE, BUT YOU YOURSELF DON'T KNOW WHAT HAPPINESS IS.
WHO ARE YOUR FRIENDS? WHO DO YOU LOVE? WHAT MAKES YOU HAPPY?
YOU FIGHT SO THAT OTHERS MAY HAVE WHAT THEY WANT MOST...
BEATS BY DRE?
THOSE ARE SLICK...BUT I WAS THINKING MORE OF A HUMAN CONNECTION.
YOU'VE MADE A LONELY LIFE FOR YOURSELF, PETER.
BECAUSE THE MORE ALONE YOU ARE, THE FEWER PEOPLE CAN HURT YOU.
BELIEVE ME, I HAVE PEOPLE LINING UP TO HURT ME LEFT AND RIGHT.
WRONG KIND OF HURT.

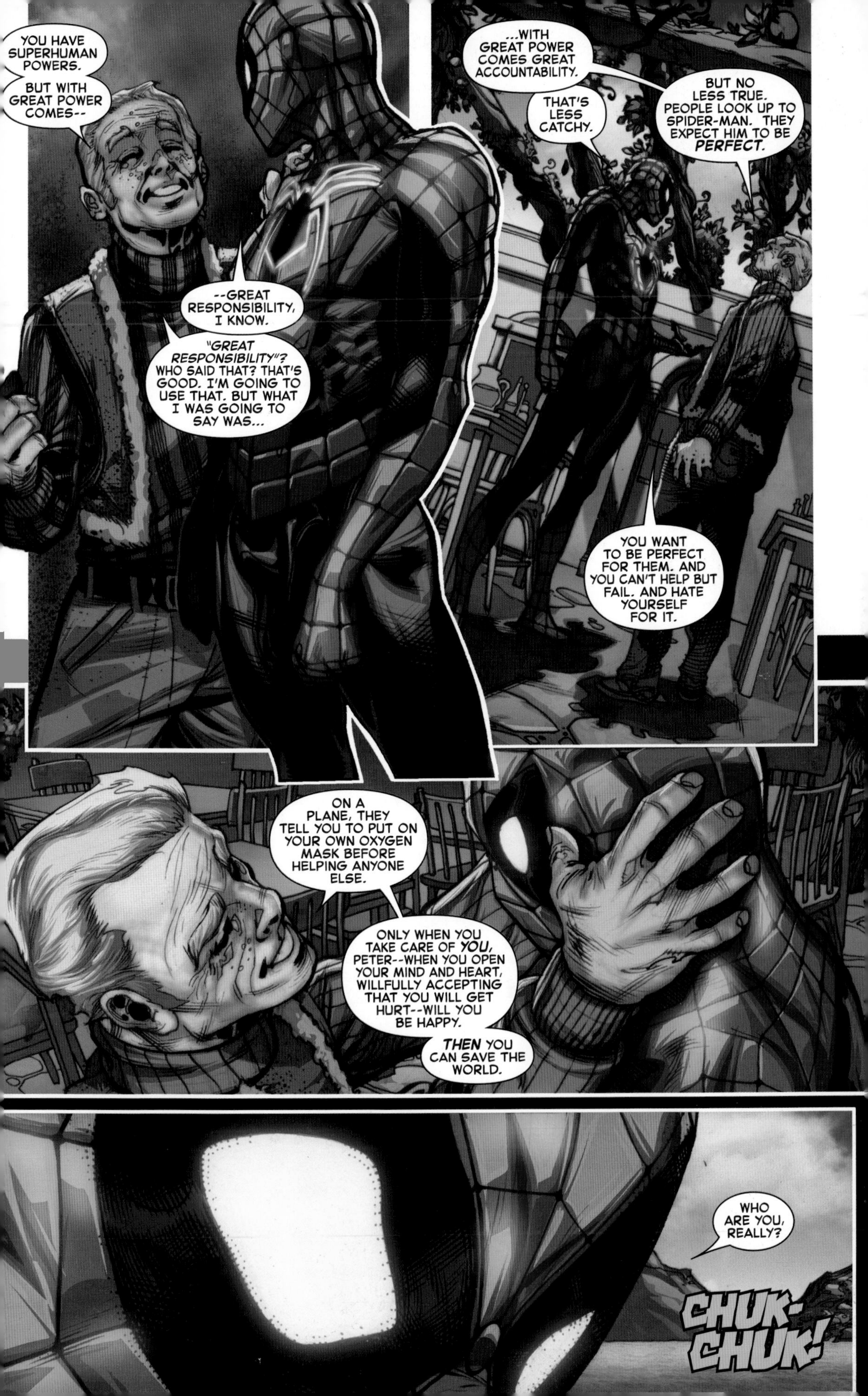
YOU HAVE SUPERHUMAN POWERS.
BUT WITH GREAT POWER COMES--
--GREAT RESPONSIBILITY, I KNOW.
"GREAT RESPONSIBILITY"? WHO SAID THAT? THAT'S GOOD. I'M GOING TO USE THAT. BUT WHAT I WAS GOING TO SAY WAS...
...WITH GREAT POWER COMES GREAT ACCOUNTABILITY.
THAT'S LESS CATCHY.
BUT NO LESS TRUE. PEOPLE LOOK UP TO SPIDER-MAN. THEY EXPECT HIM TO BE PERFECT.
YOU WANT TO BE PERFECT FOR THEM. AND YOU CAN'T HELP BUT FAIL. AND HATE YOURSELF FOR IT.
ON A PLANE, THEY TELL YOU TO PUT ON YOUR OWN OXYGEN MASK BEFORE HELPING ANYONE ELSE.
ONLY WHEN YOU TAKE CARE OF YOU, PETER--WHEN YOU OPEN YOUR MIND AND HEART, WILLFULLY ACCEPTING THAT YOU WILL GET HURT--WILL YOU BE HAPPY.
THEN YOU CAN SAVE THE WORLD.
WHO ARE YOU, REALLY?
CHUK-CHUK!

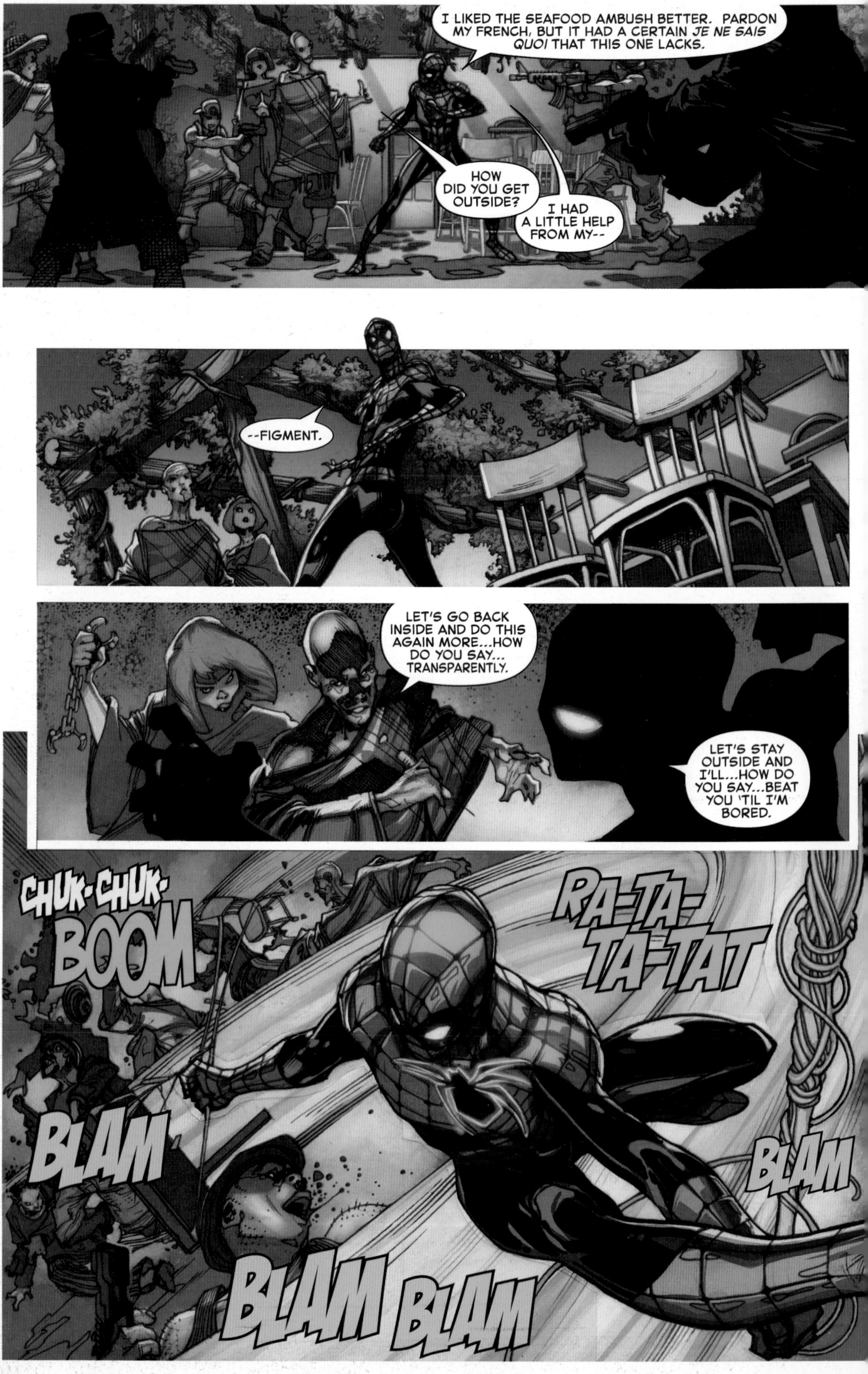
I LIKED THE SEAFOOD AMBUSH BETTER. PARDON MY FRENCH, BUT IT HAD A CERTAIN *JE NE SAIS QUOI* THAT THIS ONE LACKS.
HOW DID YOU GET OUTSIDE?
I HAD A LITTLE HELP FROM MY--
--FIGMENT.
LET'S GO BACK INSIDE AND DO THIS AGAIN MORE...HOW DO YOU SAY... TRANSPARENTLY.
LET'S STAY OUTSIDE AND I'LL...HOW DO YOU SAY...BEAT YOU 'TIL I'M BORED.
CHUK-CHUK-BOOM
RA-TA-TA-TAT
BLAM
BLAM
BLAM BLAM

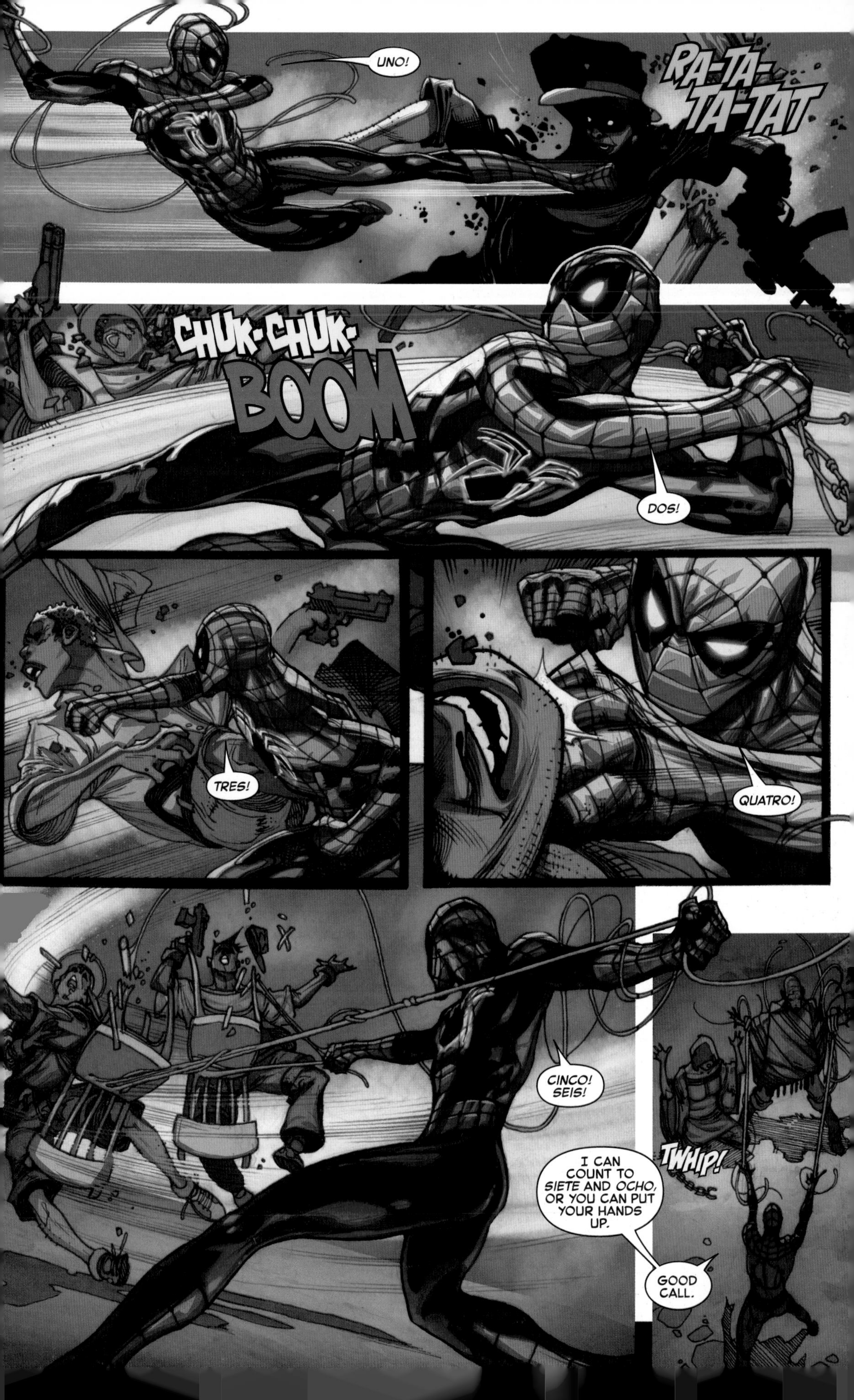
UNO!
RA-TA-TA-TAT
CHUK-CHUK-BOOM
DOS!
TRES!
QUATRO!
CINCO! SEIS!
TWHIP!
I CAN COUNT TO SIETE AND OCHO, OR YOU CAN PUT YOUR HANDS UP.
GOOD CALL.

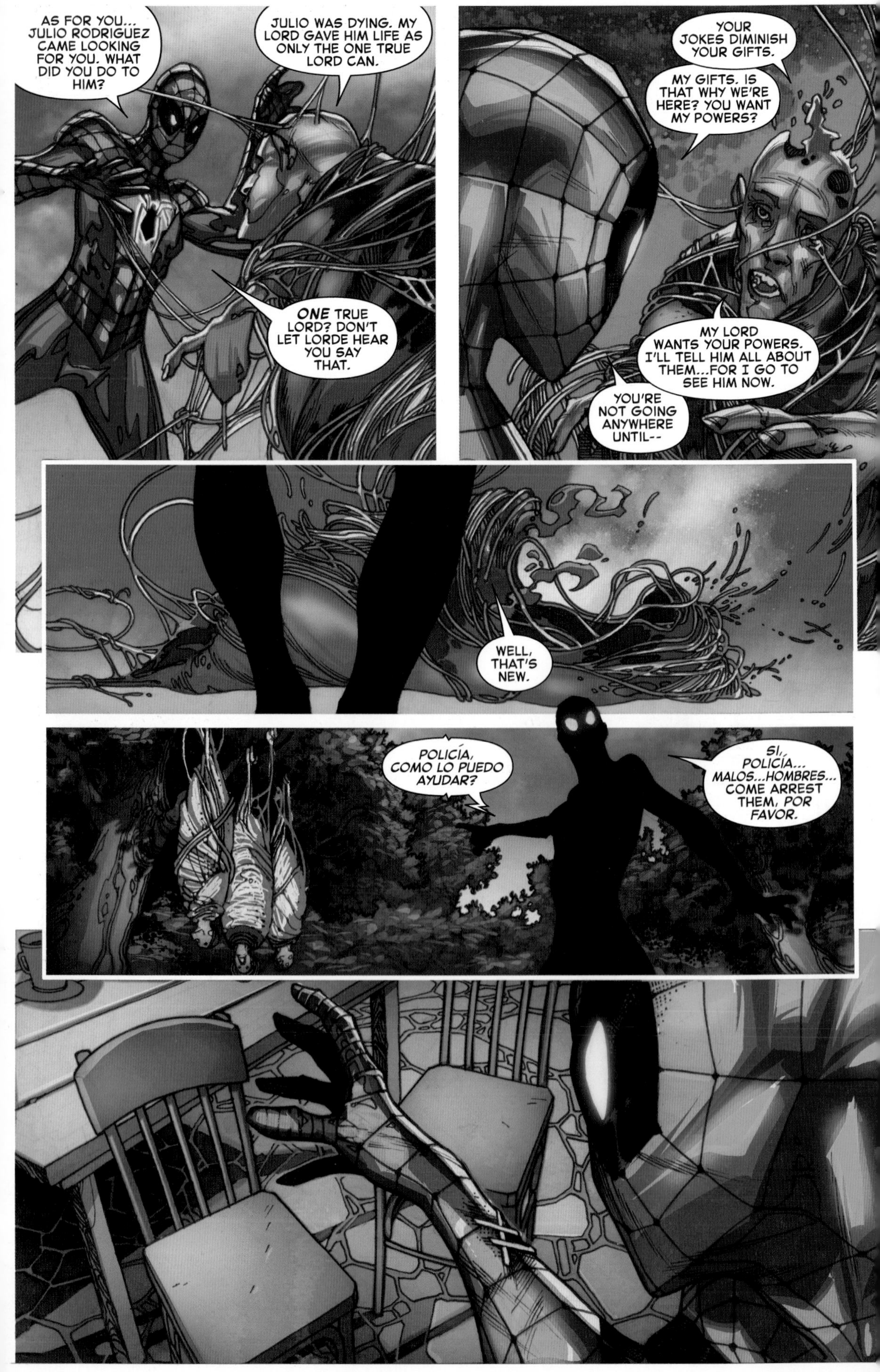
AS FOR YOU... JULIO RODRIGUEZ CAME LOOKING FOR YOU. WHAT DID YOU DO TO HIM?
JULIO WAS DYING. MY LORD GAVE HIM LIFE AS ONLY THE ONE TRUE LORD CAN.
ONE TRUE LORD? DON'T LET LORDE HEAR YOU SAY THAT.
YOUR JOKES DIMINISH YOUR GIFTS.
MY GIFTS. IS THAT WHY WE'RE HERE? YOU WANT MY POWERS?
MY LORD WANTS YOUR POWERS. I'LL TELL HIM ALL ABOUT THEM...FOR I GO TO SEE HIM NOW.
YOU'RE NOT GOING ANYWHERE UNTIL--
WELL, THAT'S NEW.
POLICÍA, COMO LO PUEDO AYUDAR?
SI, POLICÍA... MALOS...HOMBRES... COME ARREST THEM, *POR FAVOR.*

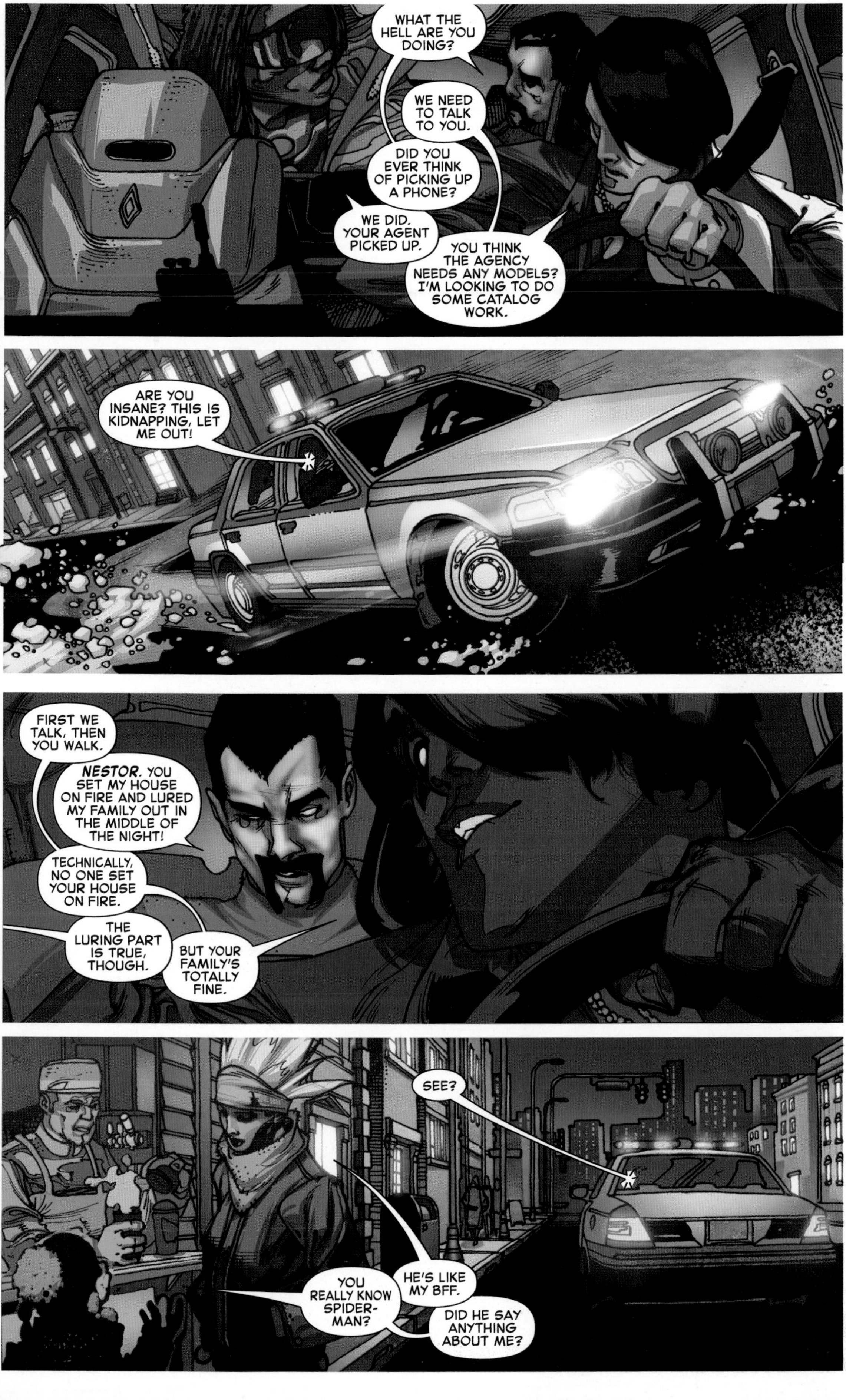
WHAT THE HELL ARE YOU DOING?
WE NEED TO TALK TO YOU.
DID YOU EVER THINK OF PICKING UP A PHONE?
WE DID. YOUR AGENT PICKED UP.
YOU THINK THE AGENCY NEEDS ANY MODELS? I'M LOOKING TO DO SOME CATALOG WORK.
ARE YOU INSANE? THIS IS KIDNAPPING, LET ME OUT!
FIRST WE TALK, THEN YOU WALK.
NESTOR. YOU SET MY HOUSE ON FIRE AND LURED MY FAMILY OUT IN THE MIDDLE OF THE NIGHT!
TECHNICALLY, NO ONE SET YOUR HOUSE ON FIRE.
THE LURING PART IS TRUE, THOUGH.
BUT YOUR FAMILY'S TOTALLY FINE.
SEE?
YOU REALLY KNOW SPIDER-MAN?
HE'S LIKE MY BFF.
DID HE SAY ANYTHING ABOUT ME?

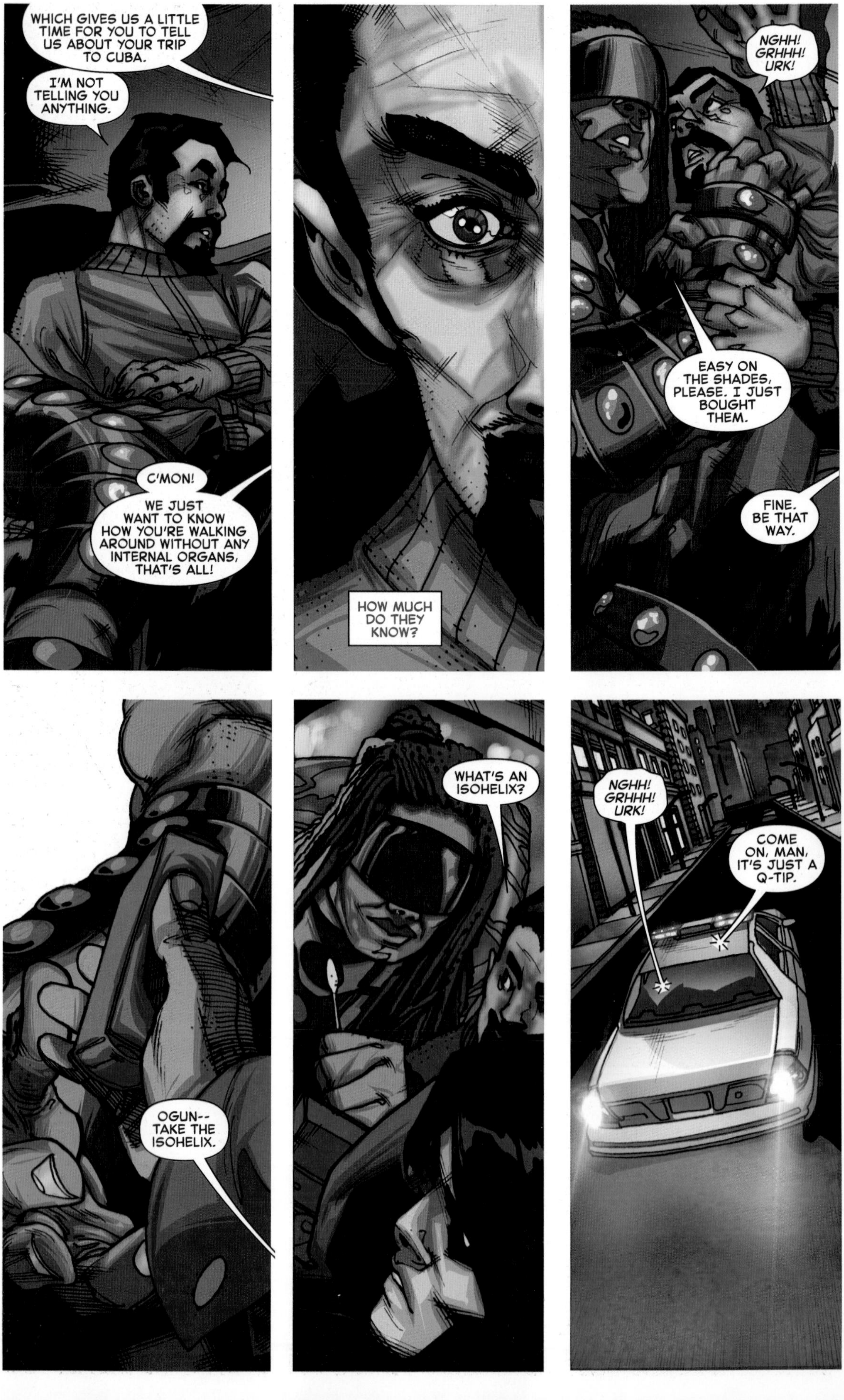
WHICH GIVES US A LITTLE TIME FOR YOU TO TELL US ABOUT YOUR TRIP TO CUBA.
I'M NOT TELLING YOU ANYTHING.
C'MON!
WE JUST WANT TO KNOW HOW YOU'RE WALKING AROUND WITHOUT ANY INTERNAL ORGANS, THAT'S ALL!
HOW MUCH DO THEY KNOW?
NGHH! GRHHH! URK!
EASY ON THE SHADES, PLEASE. I JUST BOUGHT THEM.
FINE. BE THAT WAY.
OGUN-- TAKE THE ISOHELIX.
WHAT'S AN ISOHELIX?
NGHH! GRHHH! URK!
COME ON, MAN, IT'S JUST A Q-TIP.

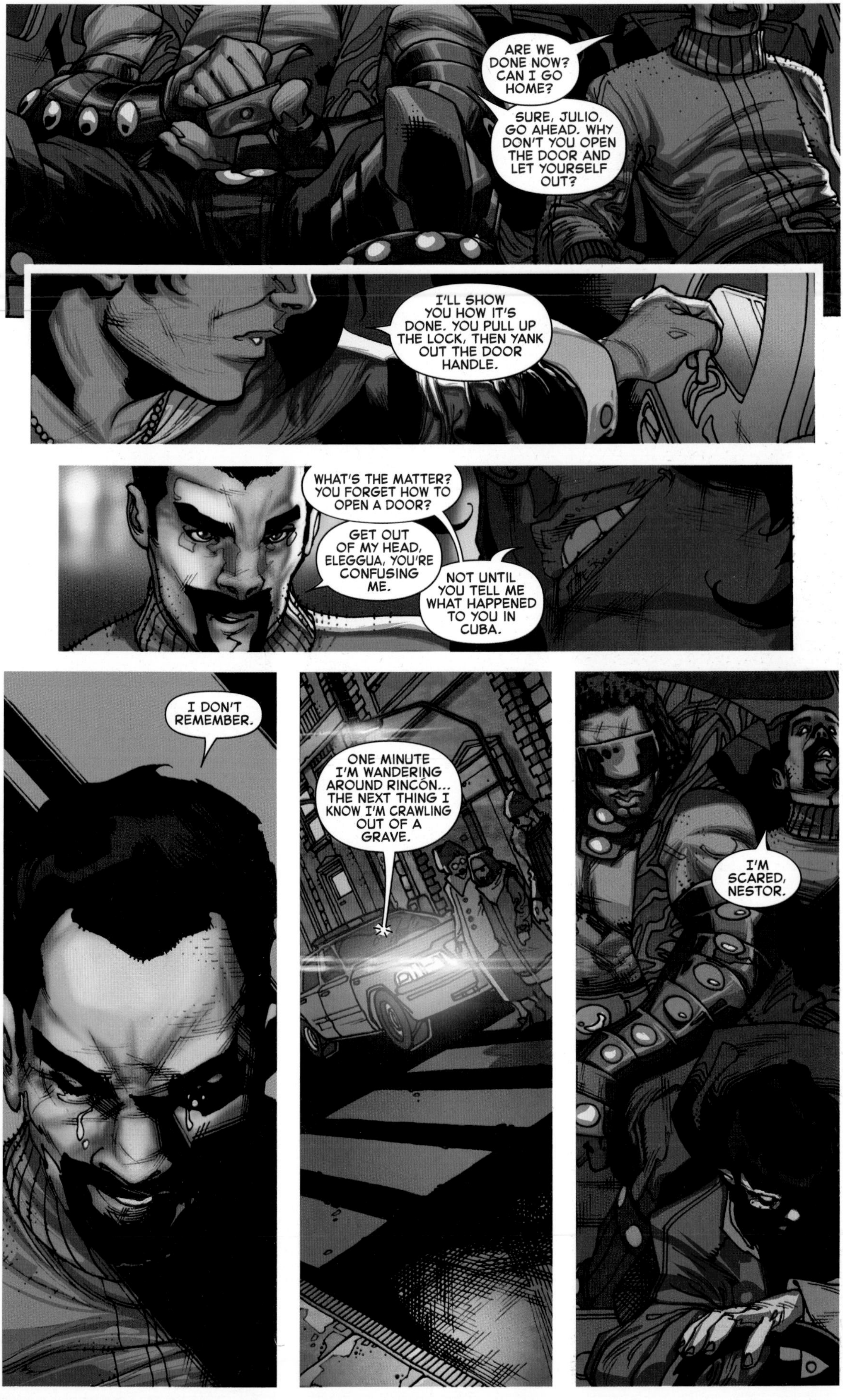
ARE WE DONE NOW? CAN I GO HOME?
SURE, JULIO, GO AHEAD. WHY DON'T YOU OPEN THE DOOR AND LET YOURSELF OUT?
I'LL SHOW YOU HOW IT'S DONE. YOU PULL UP THE LOCK, THEN YANK OUT THE DOOR HANDLE.
WHAT'S THE MATTER? YOU FORGET HOW TO OPEN A DOOR?
GET OUT OF MY HEAD, ELEGGUA, YOU'RE CONFUSING ME.
NOT UNTIL YOU TELL ME WHAT HAPPENED TO YOU IN CUBA.
I DON'T REMEMBER.
ONE MINUTE I'M WANDERING AROUND RINCÓN... THE NEXT THING I KNOW I'M CRAWLING OUT OF A GRAVE.
I'M SCARED, NESTOR.

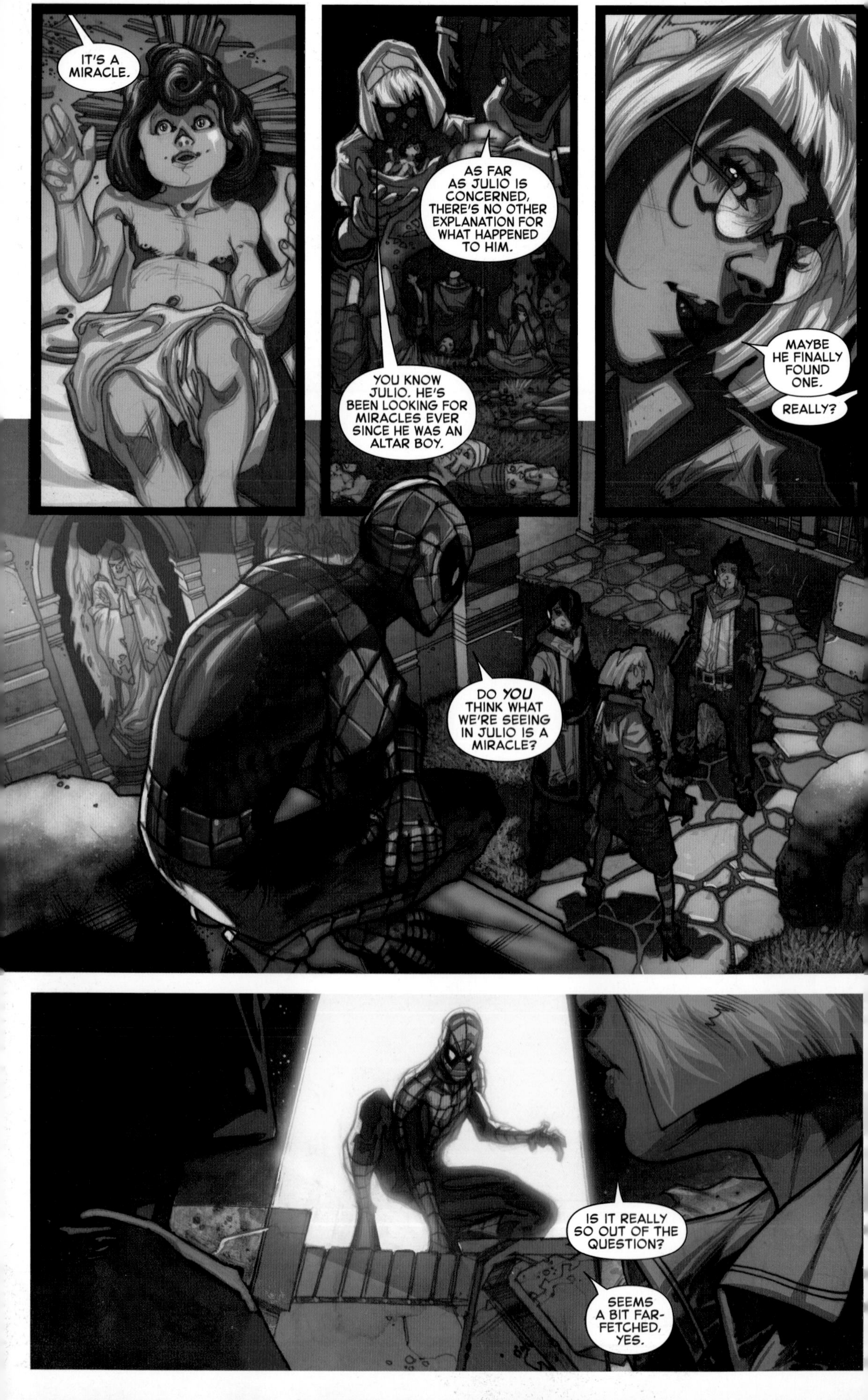
IT'S A MIRACLE.
AS FAR AS JULIO IS CONCERNED, THERE'S NO OTHER EXPLANATION FOR WHAT HAPPENED TO HIM.
YOU KNOW JULIO. HE'S BEEN LOOKING FOR MIRACLES EVER SINCE HE WAS AN ALTAR BOY.
MAYBE HE FINALLY FOUND ONE.
REALLY?
DO *YOU* THINK WHAT WE'RE SEEING IN JULIO IS A MIRACLE?
IS IT REALLY SO OUT OF THE QUESTION?
SEEMS A BIT FAR-FETCHED, YES.

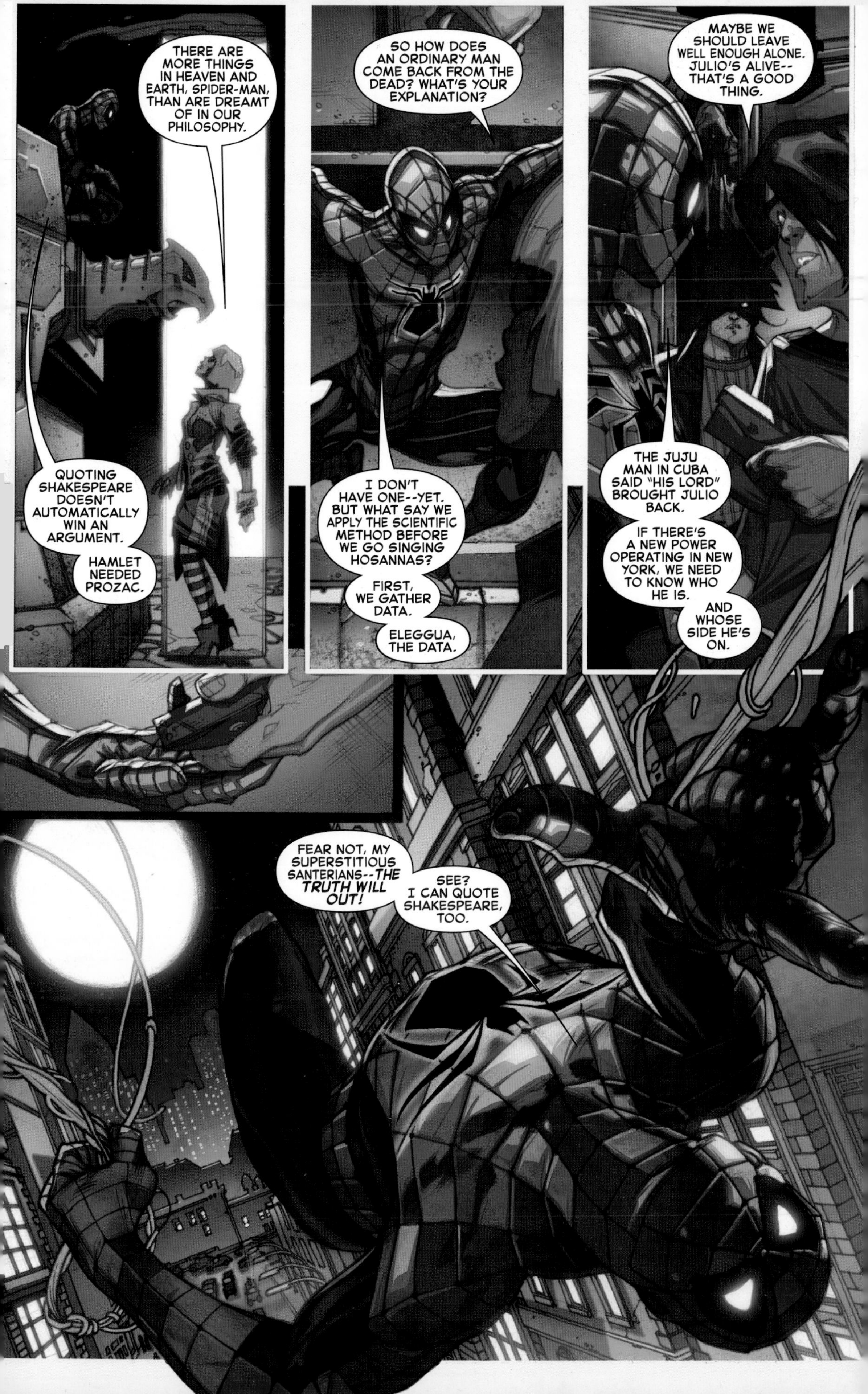
THERE ARE MORE THINGS IN HEAVEN AND EARTH, SPIDER-MAN, THAN ARE DREAMT OF IN OUR PHILOSOPHY.
QUOTING SHAKESPEARE DOESN'T AUTOMATICALLY WIN AN ARGUMENT.
HAMLET NEEDED PROZAC.
SO HOW DOES AN ORDINARY MAN COME BACK FROM THE DEAD? WHAT'S YOUR EXPLANATION?
I DON'T HAVE ONE--YET. BUT WHAT SAY WE APPLY THE SCIENTIFIC METHOD BEFORE WE GO SINGING HOSANNAS?
FIRST, WE GATHER DATA.
ELEGGUA, THE DATA.
MAYBE WE SHOULD LEAVE WELL ENOUGH ALONE. JULIO'S ALIVE-- THAT'S A GOOD THING.
THE JUJU MAN IN CUBA SAID "HIS LORD" BROUGHT JULIO BACK.
IF THERE'S A NEW POWER OPERATING IN NEW YORK, WE NEED TO KNOW WHO HE IS.
AND WHOSE SIDE HE'S ON.
FEAR NOT, MY SUPERSTITIOUS SANTERIANS--THE TRUTH WILL OUT!
SEE? I CAN QUOTE SHAKESPEARE, TOO.

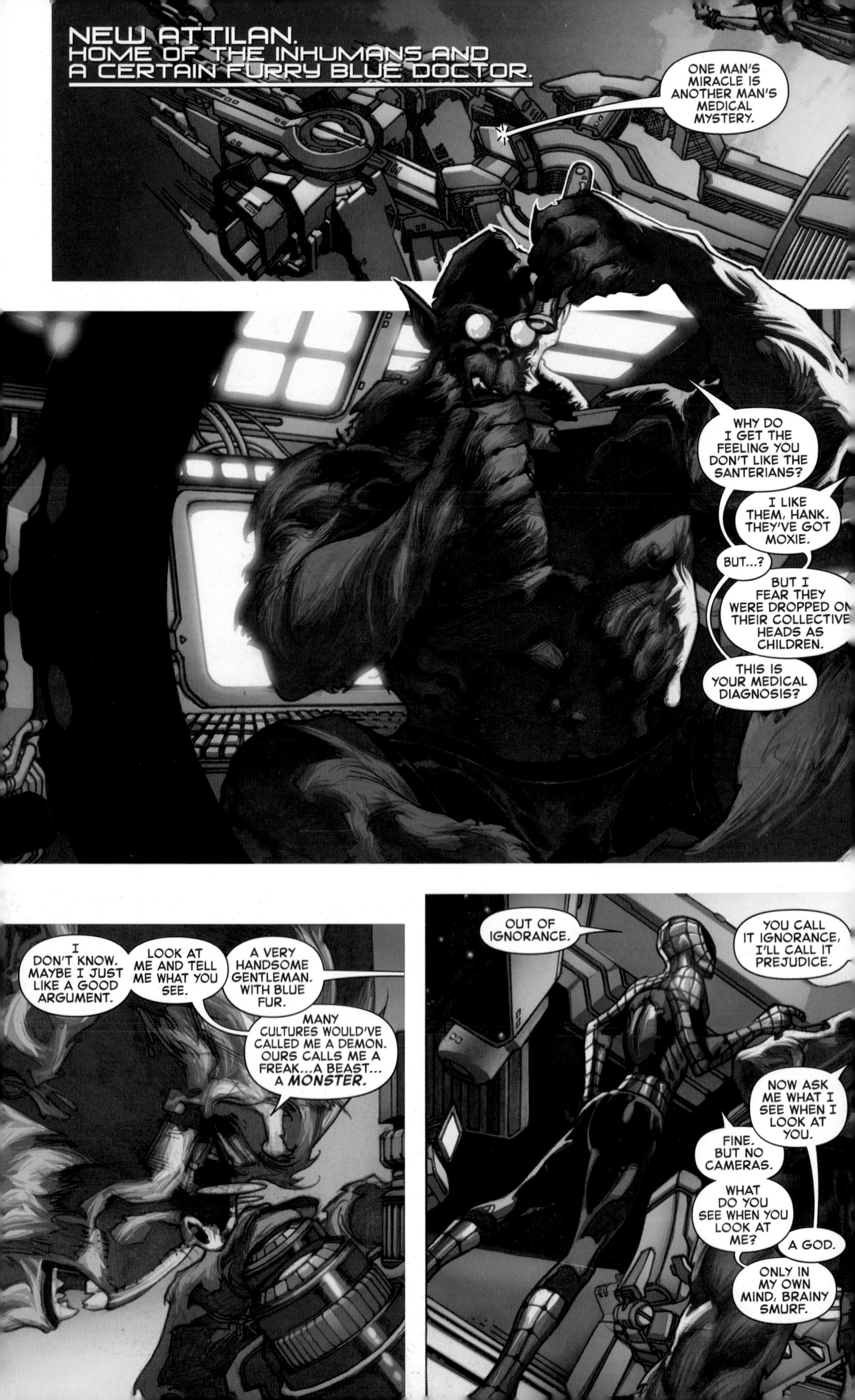

NEW ATTILAN.
HOME OF THE INHUMANS AND A CERTAIN FURRY BLUE DOCTOR.
ONE MAN'S MIRACLE IS ANOTHER MAN'S MEDICAL MYSTERY.
WHY DO I GET THE FEELING YOU DON'T LIKE THE SANTERIANS?
I LIKE THEM, HANK. THEY'VE GOT MOXIE.
BUT...?
BUT I FEAR THEY WERE DROPPED ON THEIR COLLECTIVE HEADS AS CHILDREN.
THIS IS YOUR MEDICAL DIAGNOSIS?
I DON'T KNOW. MAYBE I JUST LIKE A GOOD ARGUMENT.
LOOK AT ME AND TELL ME WHAT YOU SEE.
A VERY HANDSOME GENTLEMAN. WITH BLUE FUR.
MANY CULTURES WOULD'VE CALLED ME A DEMON. OURS CALLS ME A FREAK...A BEAST... A *MONSTER.*
OUT OF IGNORANCE.
YOU CALL IT IGNORANCE, I'LL CALL IT PREJUDICE.
NOW ASK ME WHAT I SEE WHEN I LOOK AT YOU.
FINE. BUT NO CAMERAS.
WHAT DO YOU SEE WHEN YOU LOOK AT ME?
A GOD.
ONLY IN MY OWN MIND, BRAINY SMURF.

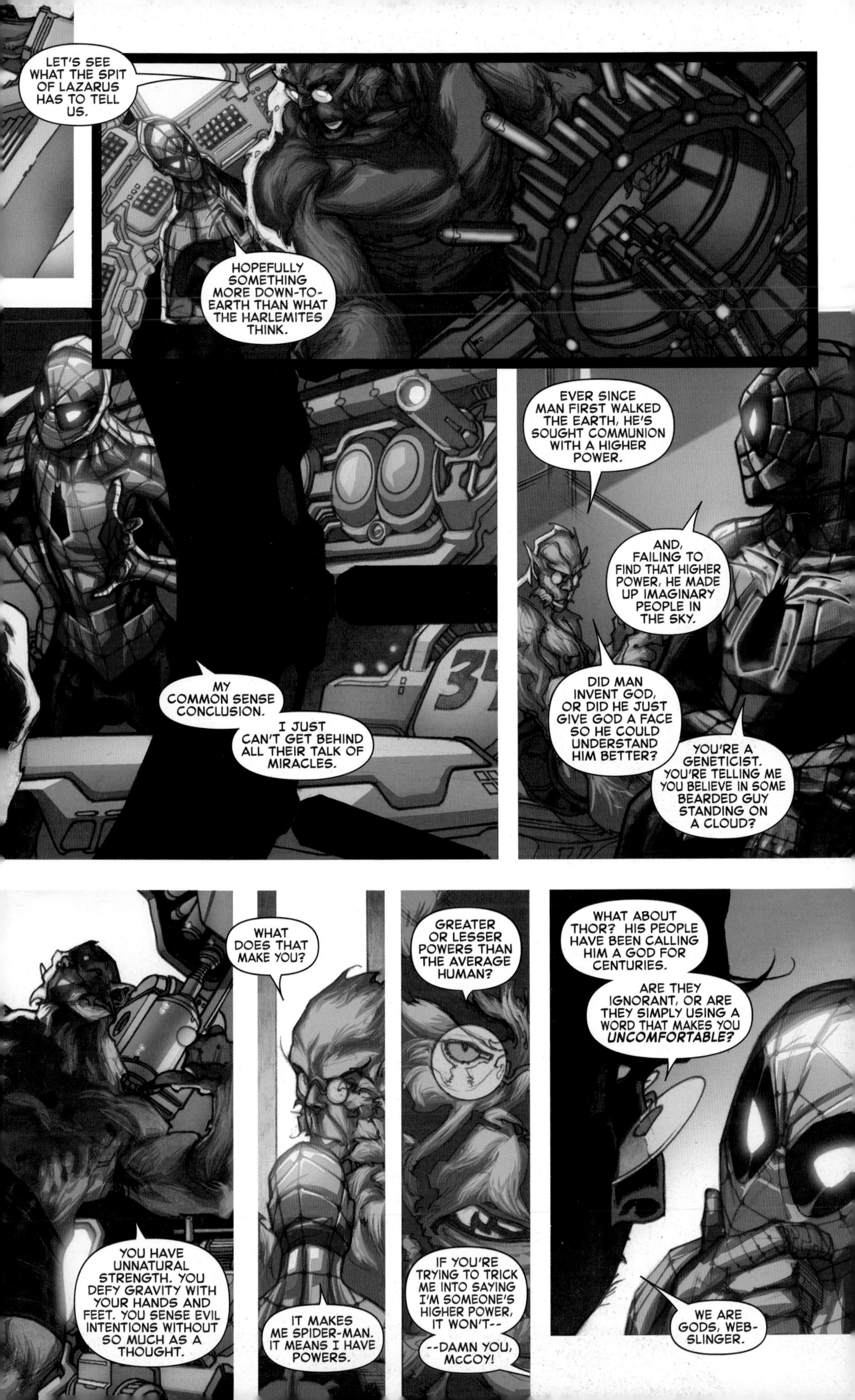

LET'S SEE WHAT THE SPIT OF LAZARUS HAS TO TELL US.
HOPEFULLY SOMETHING MORE DOWN-TO-EARTH THAN WHAT THE HARLEMITES THINK.
MY COMMON SENSE CONCLUSION.
I JUST CAN'T GET BEHIND ALL THEIR TALK OF MIRACLES.
EVER SINCE MAN FIRST WALKED THE EARTH, HE'S SOUGHT COMMUNION WITH A HIGHER POWER.
AND, FAILING TO FIND THAT HIGHER POWER, HE MADE UP IMAGINARY PEOPLE IN THE SKY.
DID MAN INVENT GOD, OR DID HE JUST GIVE GOD A FACE SO HE COULD UNDERSTAND HIM BETTER?
YOU'RE A GENETICIST. YOU'RE TELLING ME YOU BELIEVE IN SOME BEARDED GUY STANDING ON A CLOUD?
YOU HAVE UNNATURAL STRENGTH. YOU DEFY GRAVITY WITH YOUR HANDS AND FEET. YOU SENSE EVIL INTENTIONS WITHOUT SO MUCH AS A THOUGHT.
WHAT DOES THAT MAKE YOU?
IT MAKES ME SPIDER-MAN. IT MEANS I HAVE POWERS.
GREATER OR LESSER POWERS THAN THE AVERAGE HUMAN?
IF YOU'RE TRYING TO TRICK ME INTO SAYING I'M SOMEONE'S HIGHER POWER, IT WON'T--
--DAMN YOU, McCOY!
WHAT ABOUT THOR? HIS PEOPLE HAVE BEEN CALLING HIM A GOD FOR CENTURIES.
ARE THEY IGNORANT, OR ARE THEY SIMPLY USING A WORD THAT MAKES YOU *UNCOMFORTABLE?*
WE ARE GODS, WEB-SLINGER.

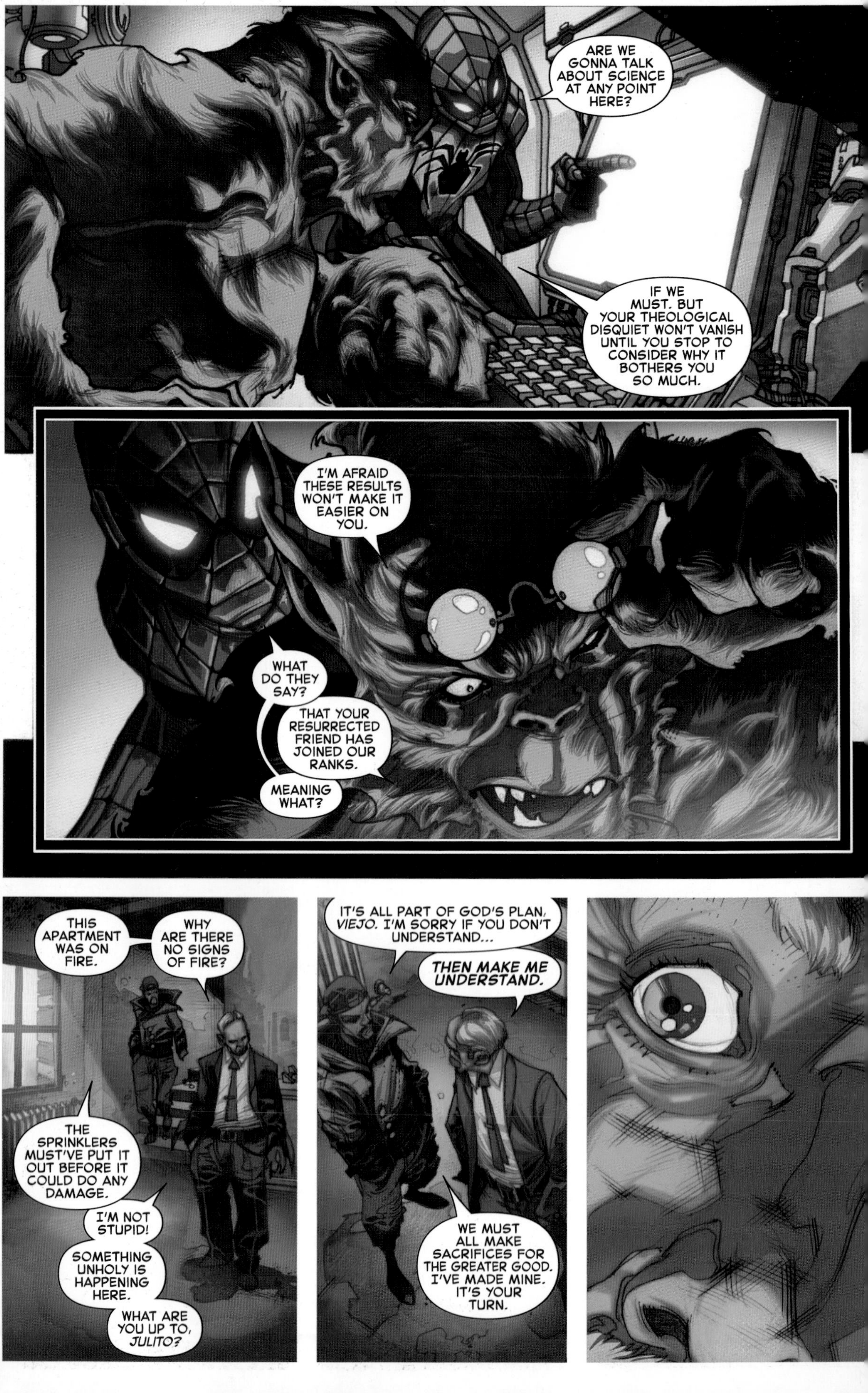

ARE WE GONNA TALK ABOUT SCIENCE AT ANY POINT HERE?
IF WE MUST. BUT YOUR THEOLOGICAL DISQUIET WON'T VANISH UNTIL YOU STOP TO CONSIDER WHY IT BOTHERS YOU SO MUCH.
I'M AFRAID THESE RESULTS WON'T MAKE IT EASIER ON YOU.
WHAT DO THEY SAY?
THAT YOUR RESURRECTED FRIEND HAS JOINED OUR RANKS.
MEANING WHAT?
THIS APARTMENT WAS ON FIRE.
WHY ARE THERE NO SIGNS OF FIRE?
THE SPRINKLERS MUST'VE PUT IT OUT BEFORE IT COULD DO ANY DAMAGE.
I'M NOT STUPID!
SOMETHING UNHOLY IS HAPPENING HERE.
WHAT ARE YOU UP TO, *JULITO?*
IT'S ALL PART OF GOD'S PLAN, *VIEJO.* I'M SORRY IF YOU DON'T UNDERSTAND...
THEN MAKE ME UNDERSTAND.
WE MUST ALL MAKE SACRIFICES FOR THE GREATER GOOD. I'VE MADE MINE. IT'S YOUR TURN.

I'M NOT SAYING HE'S A GOD...

BUT HE'S NO LONGER HUMAN.

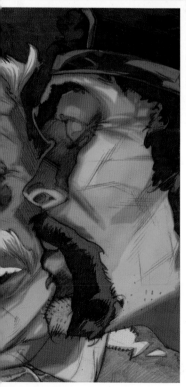

I LOVE YOU, VIEJO.

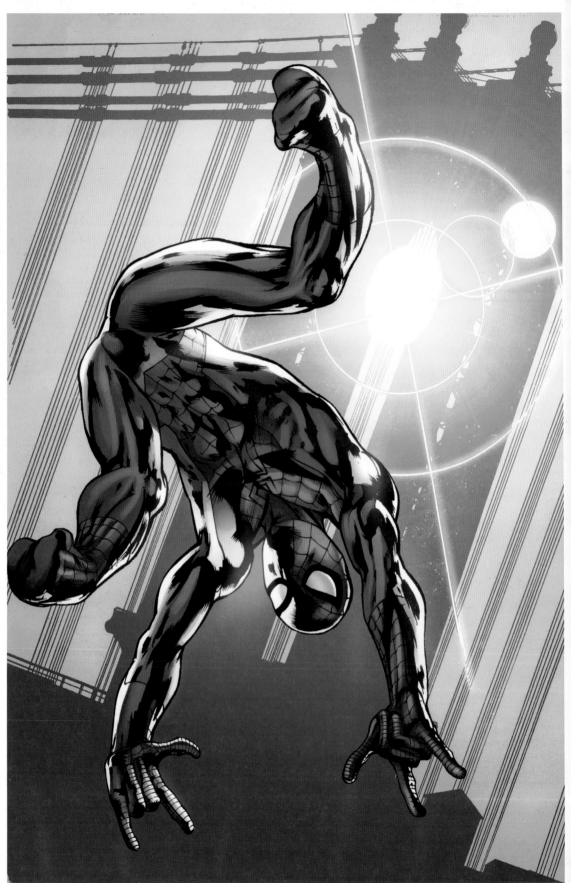

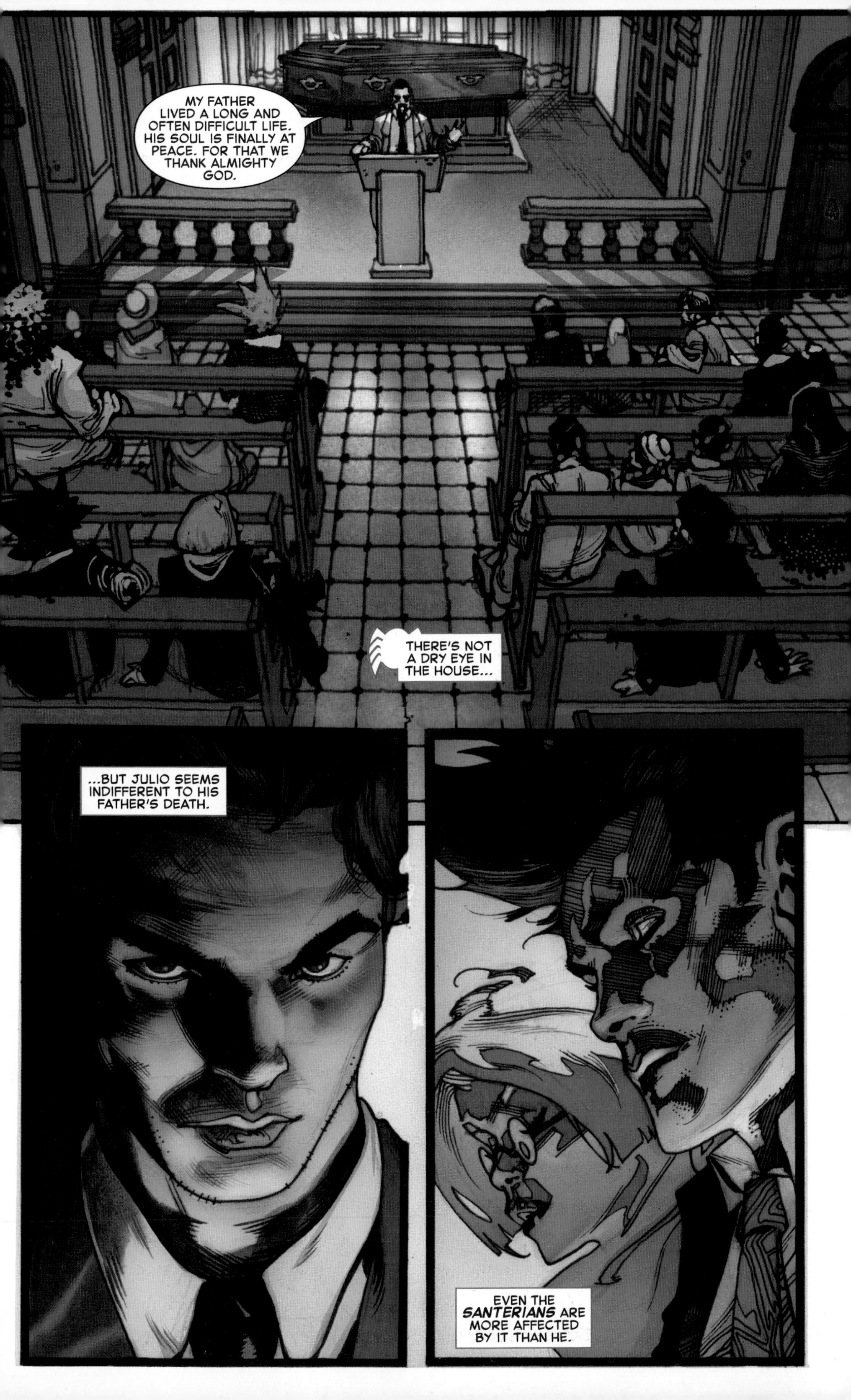
MY FATHER LIVED A LONG AND OFTEN DIFFICULT LIFE. HIS SOUL IS FINALLY AT PEACE. FOR THAT WE THANK ALMIGHTY GOD.
THERE'S NOT A DRY EYE IN THE HOUSE...
...BUT JULIO SEEMS INDIFFERENT TO HIS FATHER'S DEATH.
EVEN THE *SANTERIANS* ARE MORE AFFECTED BY IT THAN HE.

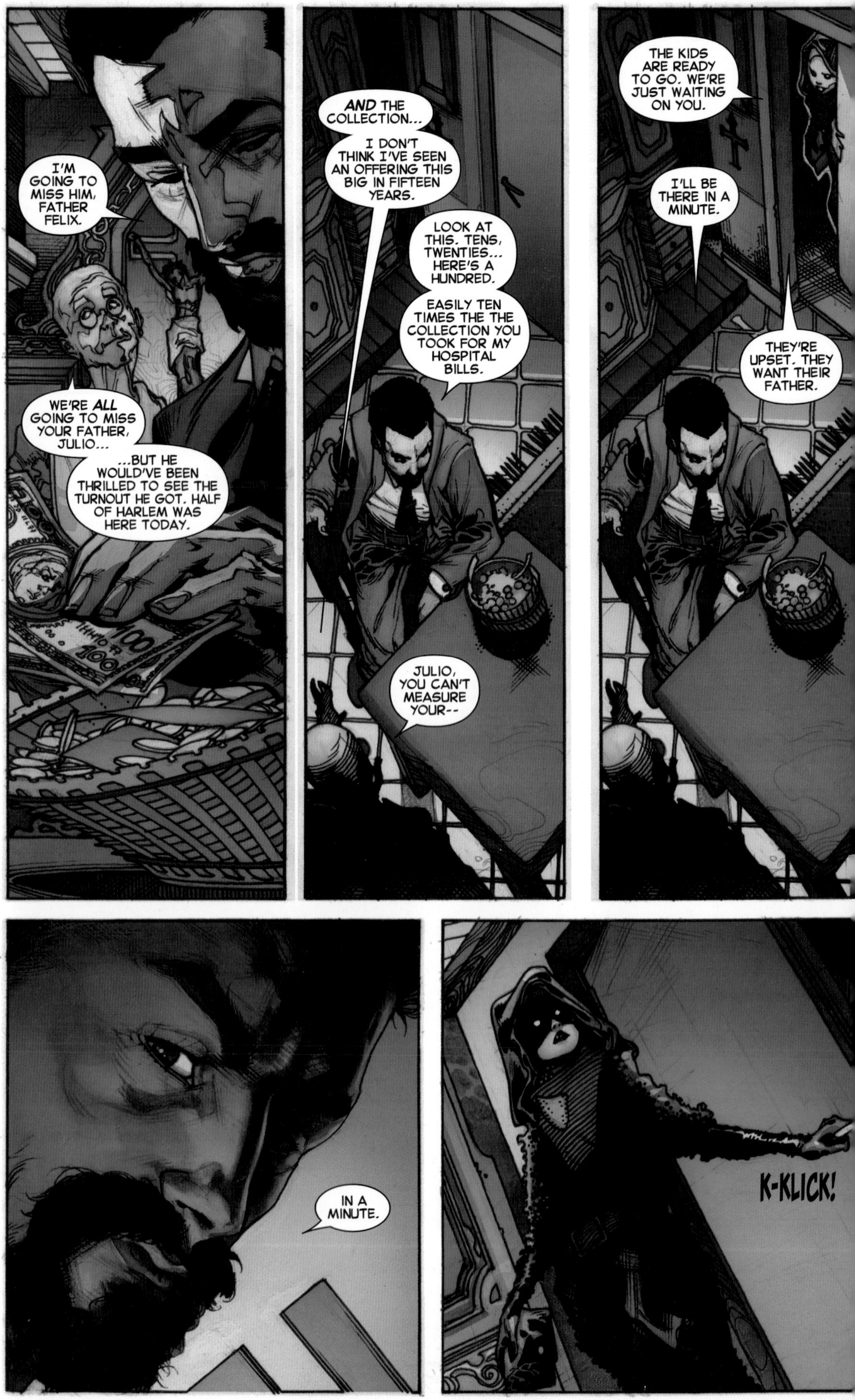
I'M GOING TO MISS HIM, FATHER FELIX.
WE'RE ALL GOING TO MISS YOUR FATHER, JULIO...
...BUT HE WOULD'VE BEEN THRILLED TO SEE THE TURNOUT HE GOT. HALF OF HARLEM WAS HERE TODAY.
AND THE COLLECTION...
I DON'T THINK I'VE SEEN AN OFFERING THIS BIG IN FIFTEEN YEARS.
LOOK AT THIS. TENS, TWENTIES... HERE'S A HUNDRED.
EASILY TEN TIMES THE THE COLLECTION YOU TOOK FOR MY HOSPITAL BILLS.
JULIO, YOU CAN'T MEASURE YOUR--
THE KIDS ARE READY TO GO. WE'RE JUST WAITING ON YOU.
I'LL BE THERE IN A MINUTE.
THEY'RE UPSET. THEY WANT THEIR FATHER.
IN A MINUTE.
K-KLICK!

YOU CAN'T MEASURE YOUR COLLECTION AGAINST YOUR FATHER'S.

YOUR FATHER TOUCHED THOUSANDS OF LIVES, OF COURSE THEY WANTED TO PAY THEIR RESPECTS.

THEY DIDN'T COME FOR MY FATHER.

THEY CAME FOR ME.

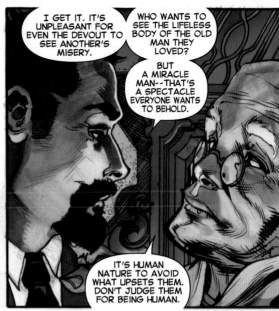

I GET IT. IT'S UNPLEASANT FOR EVEN THE DEVOUT TO SEE ANOTHER'S MISERY.

WHO WANTS TO SEE THE LIFELESS BODY OF THE OLD MAN THEY LOVED?

BUT A MIRACLE MAN--THAT'S A SPECTACLE EVERYONE WANTS TO BEHOLD.

IT'S HUMAN NATURE TO AVOID WHAT UPSETS THEM. DON'T JUDGE THEM FOR BEING HUMAN.

I DON'T. NOTHING COULD MAKE ME HAPPIER THAN SEEING SO MANY OLD FACES BACK IN CHURCH.

YOUR FLOCK STRAYED, FATHER. IF MY ORDEAL RENEWS THEIR FAITH, THEN ALL MY SUFFERING WAS WORTH IT.

THE QUESTION IS: HOW DO WE KEEP THEM FROM WANDERING AGAIN?

YOUR PRESENCE IS ENOUGH. EVEN SAINT THOMAS HAD TO SEE THE MIRACLE OF CHRIST'S RESURRECTION BEFORE HE BELIEVED.

SOME WILL ALWAYS TAKE MORE CONVINCING THAN OTHERS.

IF THEY NEED TO SEE TO BELIEVE...

...I'LL SHOW THEM.

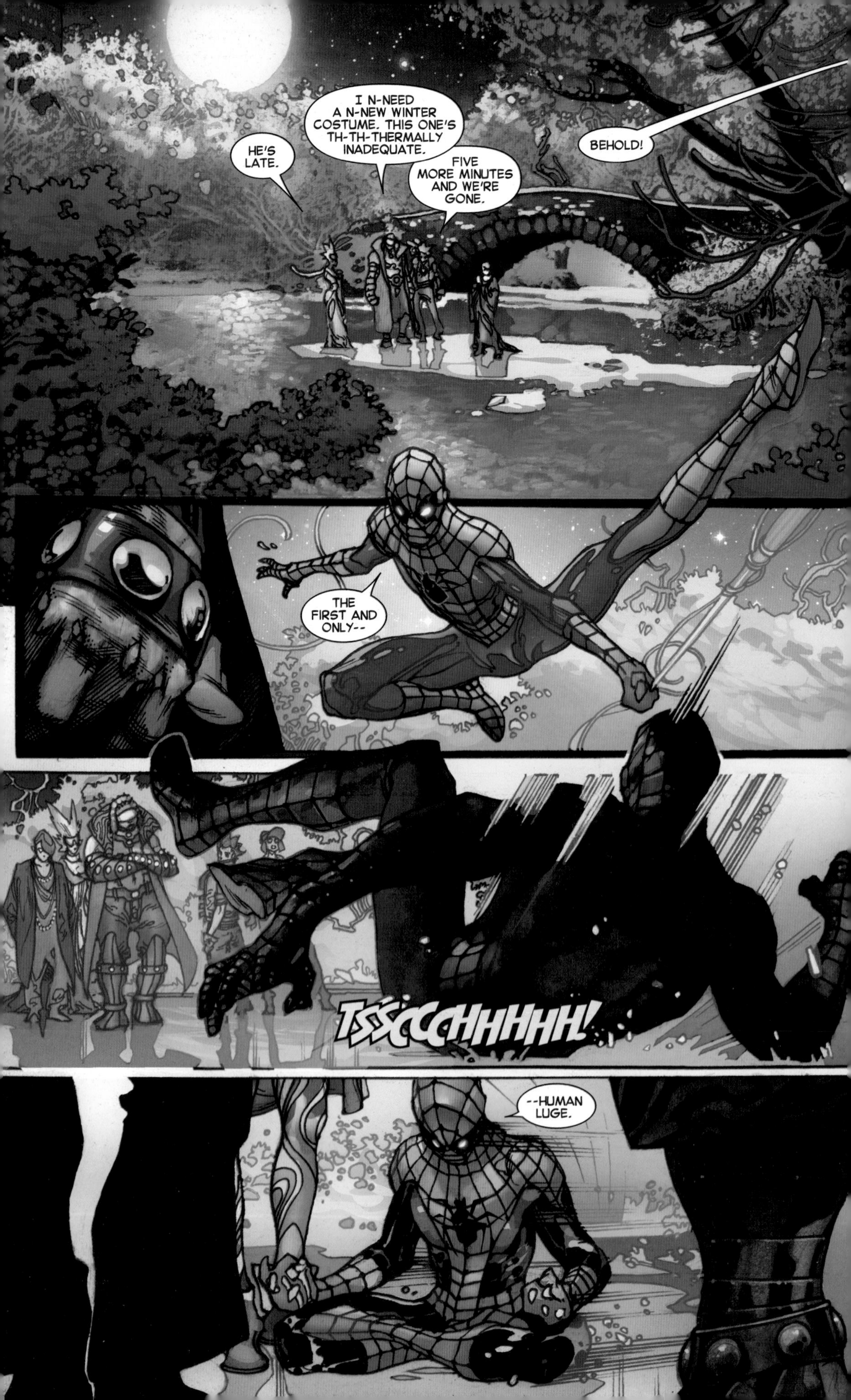
HE'S LATE.
I N-NEED A N-NEW WINTER COSTUME. THIS ONE'S TH-TH-THERMALLY INADEQUATE.
FIVE MORE MINUTES AND WE'RE GONE.
BEHOLD!
THE FIRST AND ONLY--
TSSCCHHHHH!
--HUMAN LUGE.

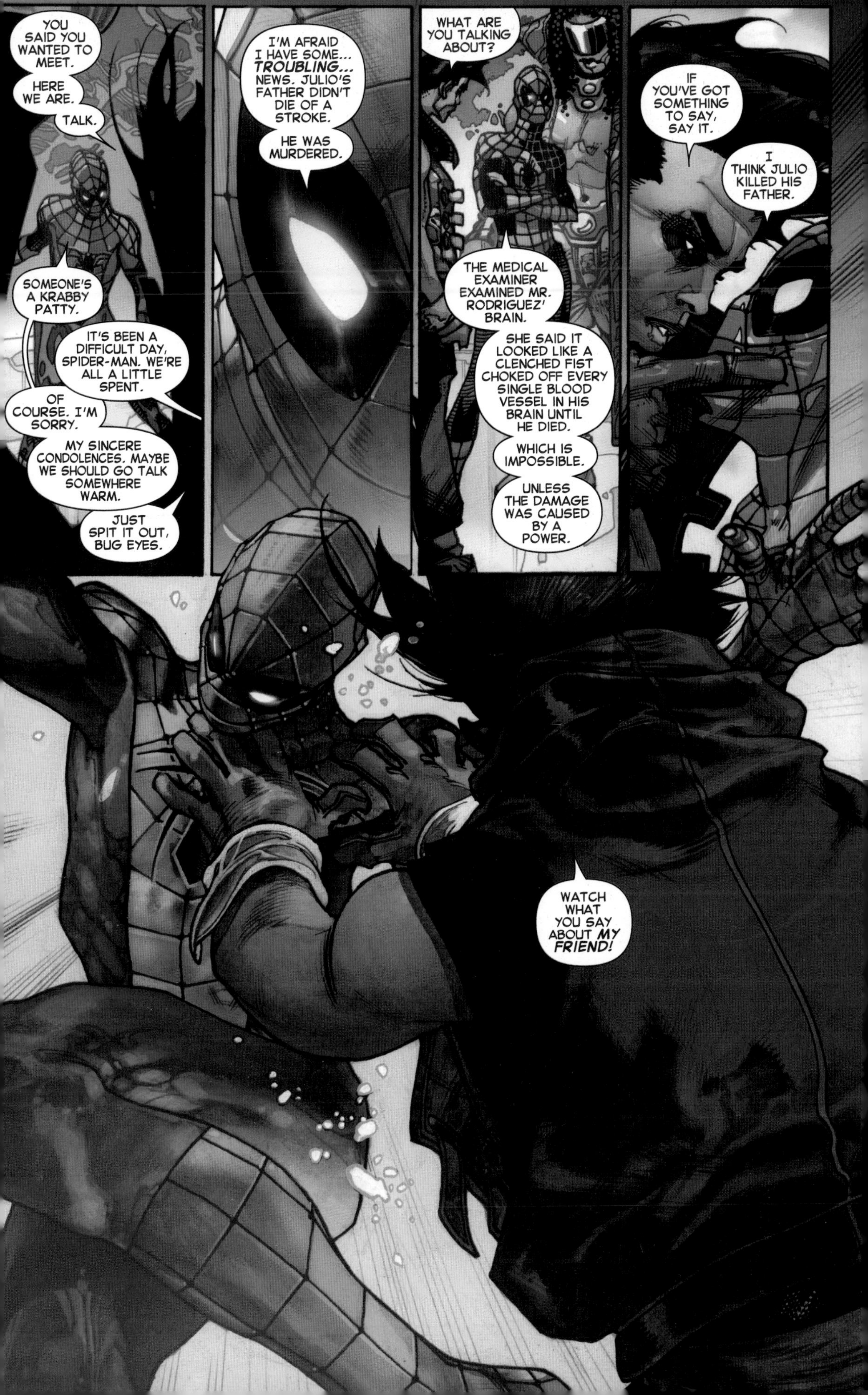
YOU SAID YOU WANTED TO MEET.
HERE WE ARE.
TALK.
SOMEONE'S A KRABBY PATTY.
IT'S BEEN A DIFFICULT DAY, SPIDER-MAN. WE'RE ALL A LITTLE SPENT.
OF COURSE. I'M SORRY.
MY SINCERE CONDOLENCES. MAYBE WE SHOULD GO TALK SOMEWHERE WARM.
JUST SPIT IT OUT, BUG EYES.
I'M AFRAID I HAVE SOME... TROUBLING... NEWS. JULIO'S FATHER DIDN'T DIE OF A STROKE.
HE WAS MURDERED.
WHAT ARE YOU TALKING ABOUT?
THE MEDICAL EXAMINER EXAMINED MR. RODRIGUEZ' BRAIN.
SHE SAID IT LOOKED LIKE A CLENCHED FIST CHOKED OFF EVERY SINGLE BLOOD VESSEL IN HIS BRAIN UNTIL HE DIED.
WHICH IS IMPOSSIBLE.
UNLESS THE DAMAGE WAS CAUSED BY A POWER.
IF YOU'VE GOT SOMETHING TO SAY, SAY IT.
I THINK JULIO KILLED HIS FATHER.
WATCH WHAT YOU SAY ABOUT MY FRIEND!

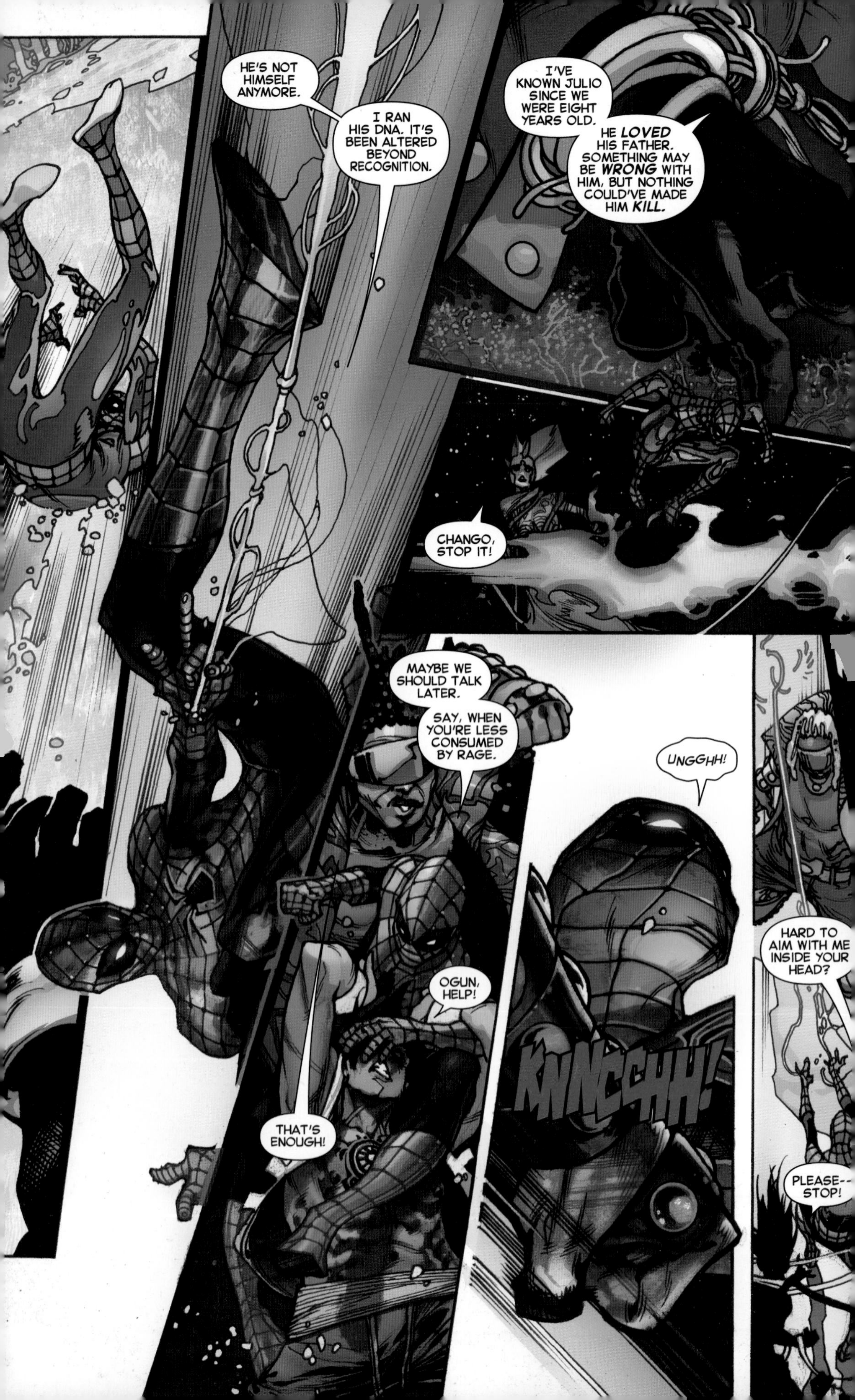
HE'S NOT HIMSELF ANYMORE.
I RAN HIS DNA. IT'S BEEN ALTERED BEYOND RECOGNITION.
I'VE KNOWN JULIO SINCE WE WERE EIGHT YEARS OLD.
HE LOVED HIS FATHER. SOMETHING MAY BE WRONG WITH HIM, BUT NOTHING COULD'VE MADE HIM KILL.
CHANGO, STOP IT!
MAYBE WE SHOULD TALK LATER.
SAY, WHEN YOU'RE LESS CONSUMED BY RAGE.
OGUN, HELP!
THAT'S ENOUGH!
UNGGHH!
KNNCGHH!
HARD TO AIM WITH ME INSIDE YOUR HEAD?
PLEASE-- STOP!

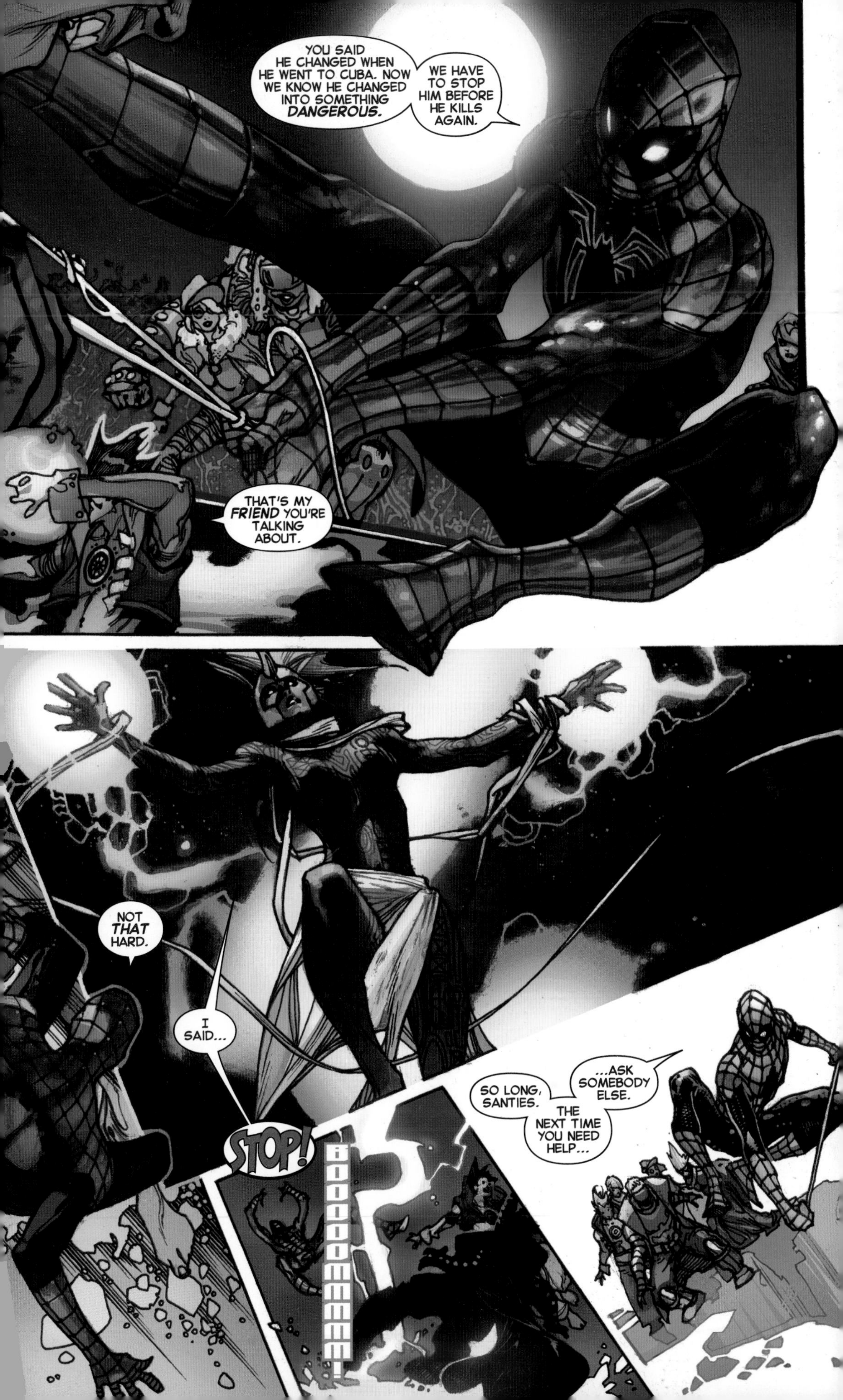
YOU SAID HE CHANGED WHEN HE WENT TO CUBA. NOW WE KNOW HE CHANGED INTO SOMETHING DANGEROUS.
WE HAVE TO STOP HIM BEFORE HE KILLS AGAIN.
THAT'S MY FRIEND YOU'RE TALKING ABOUT.
NOT THAT HARD.
I SAID...
STOP!
BOOOOOMMMMM!
THE NEXT TIME YOU NEED HELP...
...ASK SOMEBODY ELSE.
SO LONG, SANTIES.

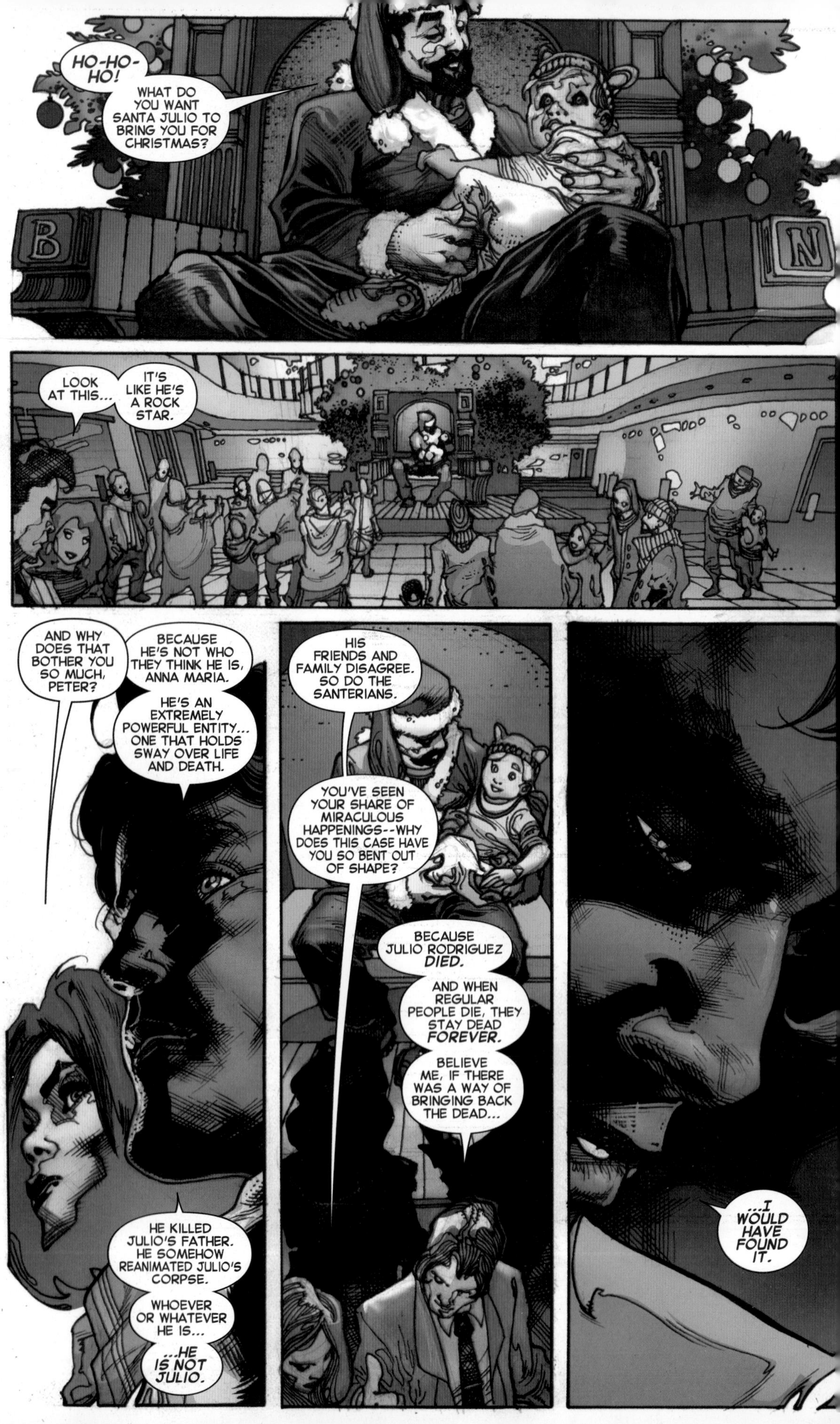

HO-HO-HO!
WHAT DO YOU WANT SANTA JULIO TO BRING YOU FOR CHRISTMAS?
LOOK AT THIS...
IT'S LIKE HE'S A ROCK STAR.
AND WHY DOES THAT BOTHER YOU SO MUCH, PETER?
BECAUSE HE'S NOT WHO THEY THINK HE IS, ANNA MARIA.
HE'S AN EXTREMELY POWERFUL ENTITY... ONE THAT HOLDS SWAY OVER LIFE AND DEATH.
HE KILLED JULIO'S FATHER. HE SOMEHOW REANIMATED JULIO'S CORPSE.
WHOEVER OR WHATEVER HE IS...
...HE IS NOT JULIO.
HIS FRIENDS AND FAMILY DISAGREE. SO DO THE SANTERIANS.
YOU'VE SEEN YOUR SHARE OF MIRACULOUS HAPPENINGS--WHY DOES THIS CASE HAVE YOU SO BENT OUT OF SHAPE?
BECAUSE JULIO RODRIGUEZ DIED.
AND WHEN REGULAR PEOPLE DIE, THEY STAY DEAD FOREVER.
BELIEVE ME, IF THERE WAS A WAY OF BRINGING BACK THE DEAD...
...I WOULD HAVE FOUND IT.

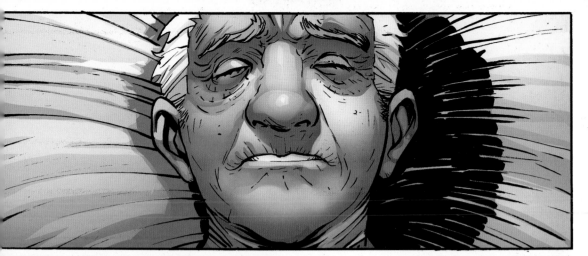

PARKER, BENJAMIN. TIME OF DEATH, 12:04 AM.

YOU HAVE ALL THE POWER. EVERYTHING IS POSSIBLE TO YOU.

YOU LET HIM DIE.

YOU ARE A LIE.

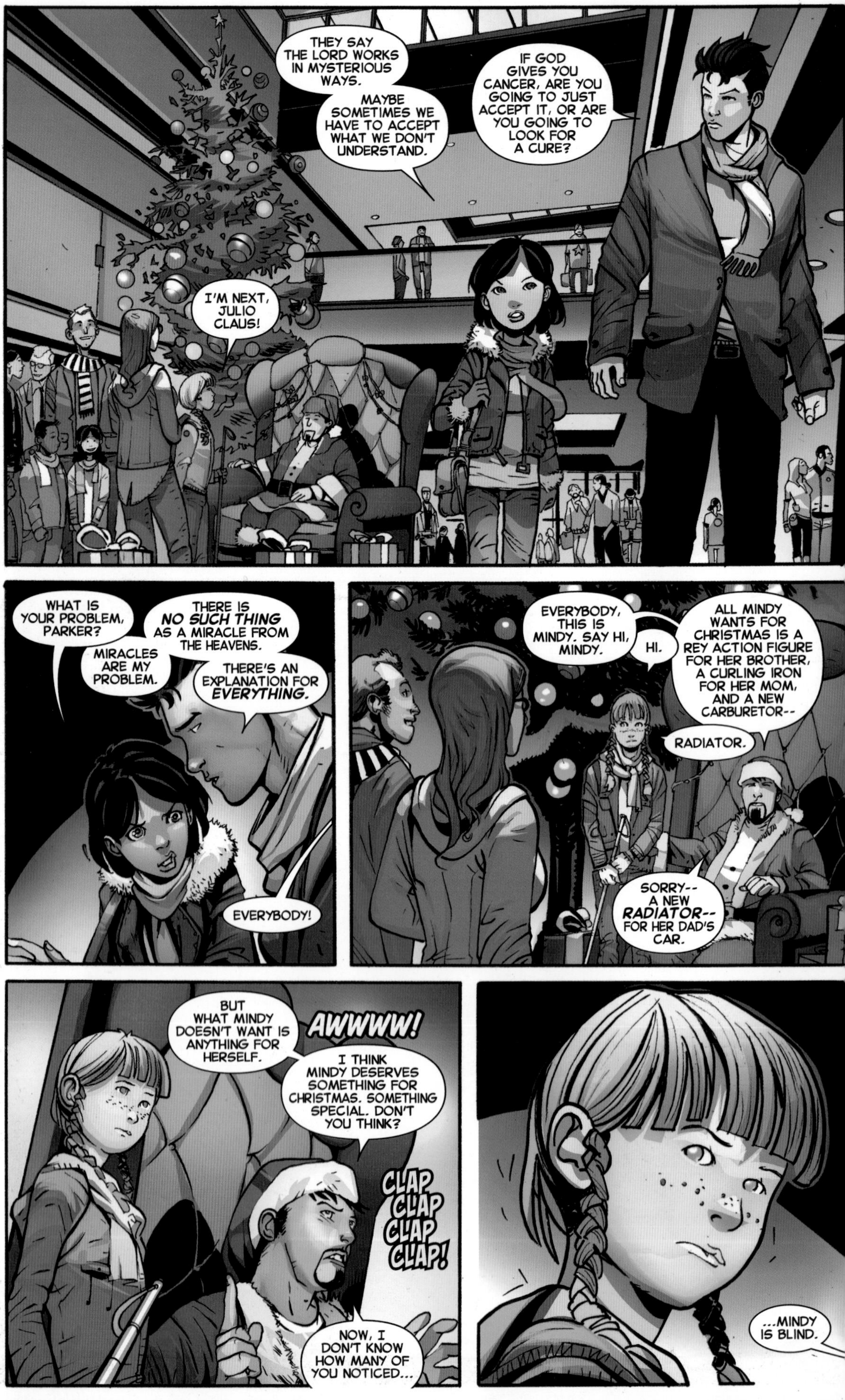
THEY SAY THE LORD WORKS IN MYSTERIOUS WAYS.
MAYBE SOMETIMES WE HAVE TO ACCEPT WHAT WE DON'T UNDERSTAND.
IF GOD GIVES YOU CANCER, ARE YOU GOING TO JUST ACCEPT IT, OR ARE YOU GOING TO LOOK FOR A CURE?
I'M NEXT, JULIO CLAUS!
WHAT IS YOUR PROBLEM, PARKER?
MIRACLES ARE MY PROBLEM.
THERE IS *NO SUCH THING* AS A MIRACLE FROM THE HEAVENS.
THERE'S AN EXPLANATION FOR *EVERYTHING.*
EVERYBODY!
EVERYBODY, THIS IS MINDY. SAY HI, MINDY.
HI.
ALL MINDY WANTS FOR CHRISTMAS IS A REY ACTION FIGURE FOR HER BROTHER, A CURLING IRON FOR HER MOM, AND A NEW CARBURETOR--
RADIATOR.
SORRY-- A NEW *RADIATOR--* FOR HER DAD'S CAR.
BUT WHAT MINDY DOESN'T WANT IS ANYTHING FOR HERSELF.
AWWWW!
I THINK MINDY DESERVES SOMETHING FOR CHRISTMAS. SOMETHING SPECIAL. DON'T YOU THINK?
CLAP CLAP CLAP CLAP!
NOW, I DON'T KNOW HOW MANY OF YOU NOTICED...
...MINDY IS BLIND.

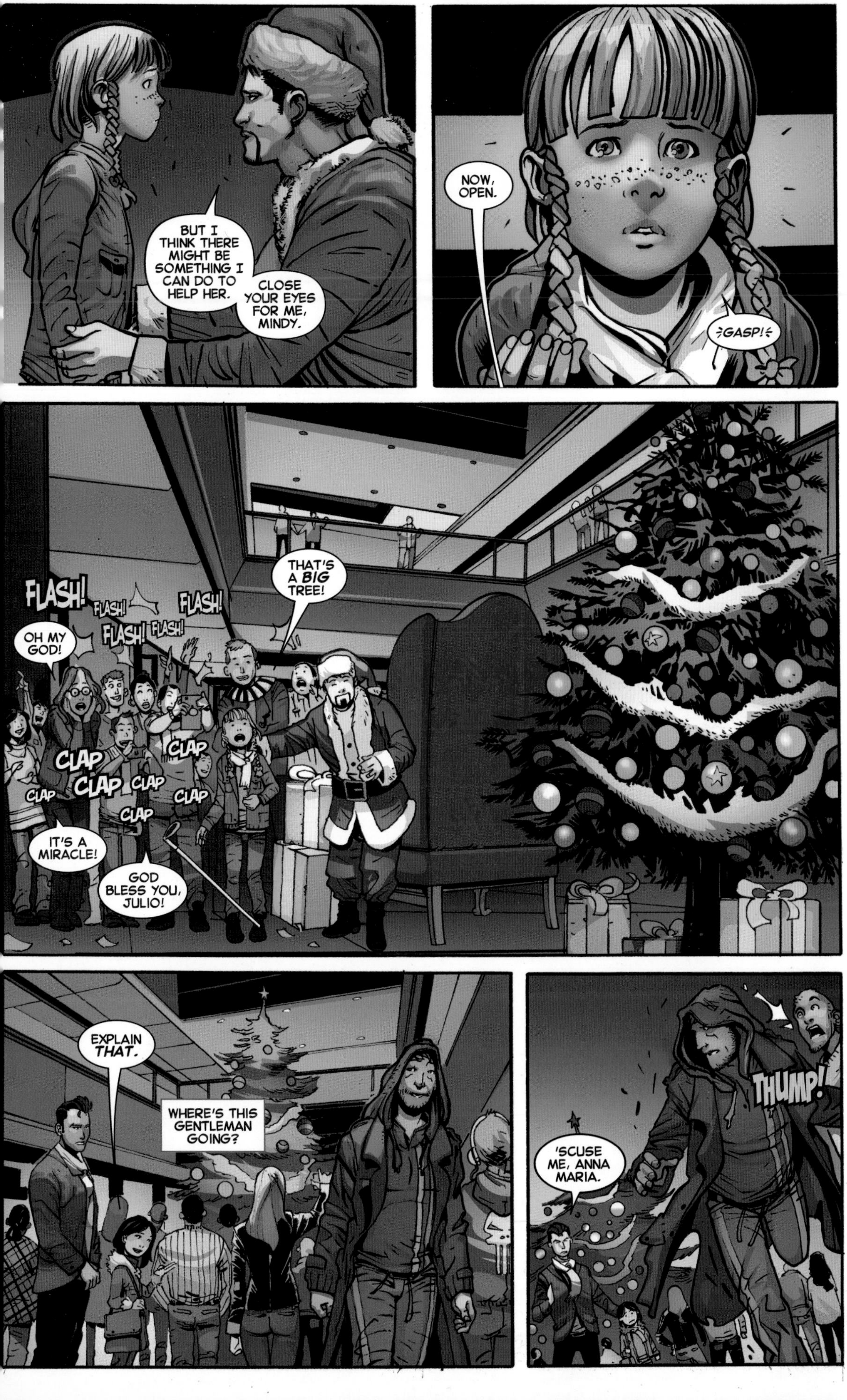
BUT I THINK THERE MIGHT BE SOMETHING I CAN DO TO HELP HER.
CLOSE YOUR EYES FOR ME, MINDY.
NOW, OPEN.
GASP!
FLASH!
FLASH!
FLASH!
FLASH!
FLASH!
THAT'S A BIG TREE!
OH MY GOD!
CLAP
CLAP
CLAP
CLAP
CLAP
CLAP
CLAP
IT'S A MIRACLE!
GOD BLESS YOU, JULIO!
EXPLAIN THAT.
WHERE'S THIS GENTLEMAN GOING?
THUMP!
'SCUSE ME, ANNA MARIA.

THIS IS MY HAPPY FACE.

WHAT'S THAT? HOW'D WE GET HERE?

I RAN THIS GUY DOWN AND SLUNG HIM UP HERE.

IT WAS BORING, YOU DON'T NEED TO SEE WHAT HAPPENED.

HE WET HIS PANTS, OKAY? ARE YOU HAPPY?

YOU KNOW ME, RIGHT? HAPPY-GO-LUCKY CRIME-FIGHTER, JOKE-CRACKING WEB-SLINGER, AND ALL-AROUND GOOD GUY.

EXCEPT WHEN I'M ANGRY.

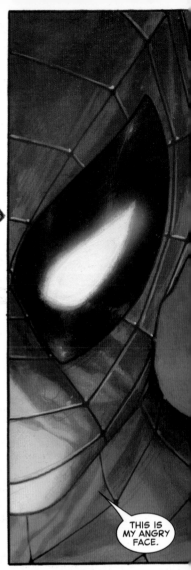

THIS IS MY ANGRY FACE.

MAN, THIS SCAFFOLD IS KINDA SHAKY. I'LL JUST BE UP HERE--WHERE WAS I?

OH, YEAH. WHEN YOU SAW JULIO RODRIGUEZ, YOU LOOKED LIKE YOU'D SEEN A GHOST. WHY?

B-BECAUSE HE IS A GHOST.

I K-KKK-K-- I KK-K-KK--

YOU C-C-CAJOLED HIM? YOU CANOODLED HIM? YOU CREME DE CACAO'D HIM? GOTTA SAY, I'M HAVING A HARD TIME FOLLOWING YOU.

I KILLED HIM!

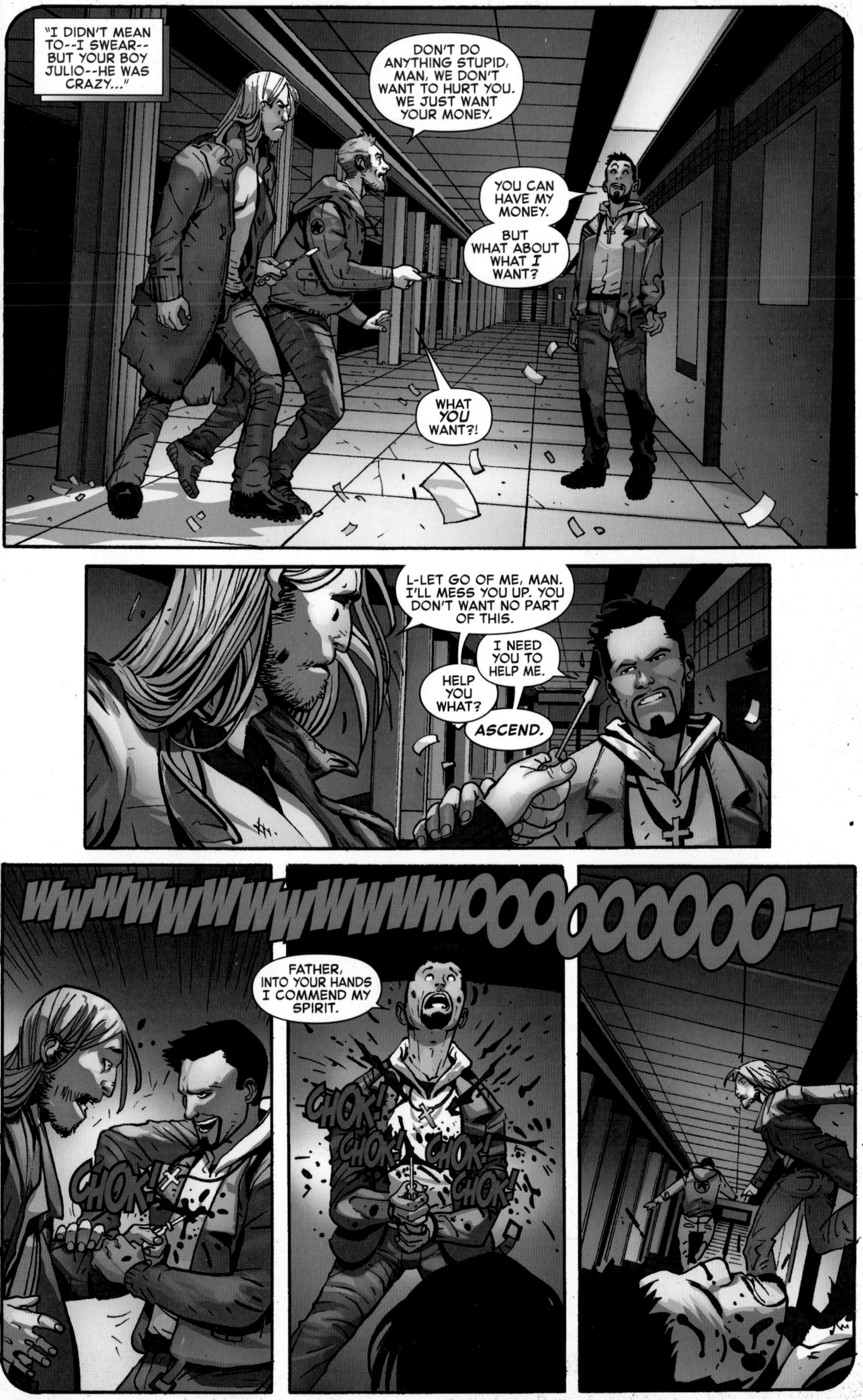
"I DIDN'T MEAN TO--I SWEAR--BUT YOUR BOY JULIO--HE WAS CRAZY..."
DON'T DO ANYTHING STUPID, MAN, WE DON'T WANT TO HURT YOU. WE JUST WANT YOUR MONEY.
YOU CAN HAVE MY MONEY.
BUT WHAT ABOUT WHAT *I* WANT?
WHAT *YOU* WANT?!
L-LET GO OF ME, MAN. I'LL MESS YOU UP. YOU DON'T WANT NO PART OF THIS.
I NEED YOU TO HELP ME.
HELP YOU WHAT?
ASCEND.
WWWWWWWWWWWWOOOOOOOOOO--
CHOK!
FATHER, INTO YOUR HANDS I COMMEND MY SPIRIT.
CHOK! CHOK! CHOK! CHOK!

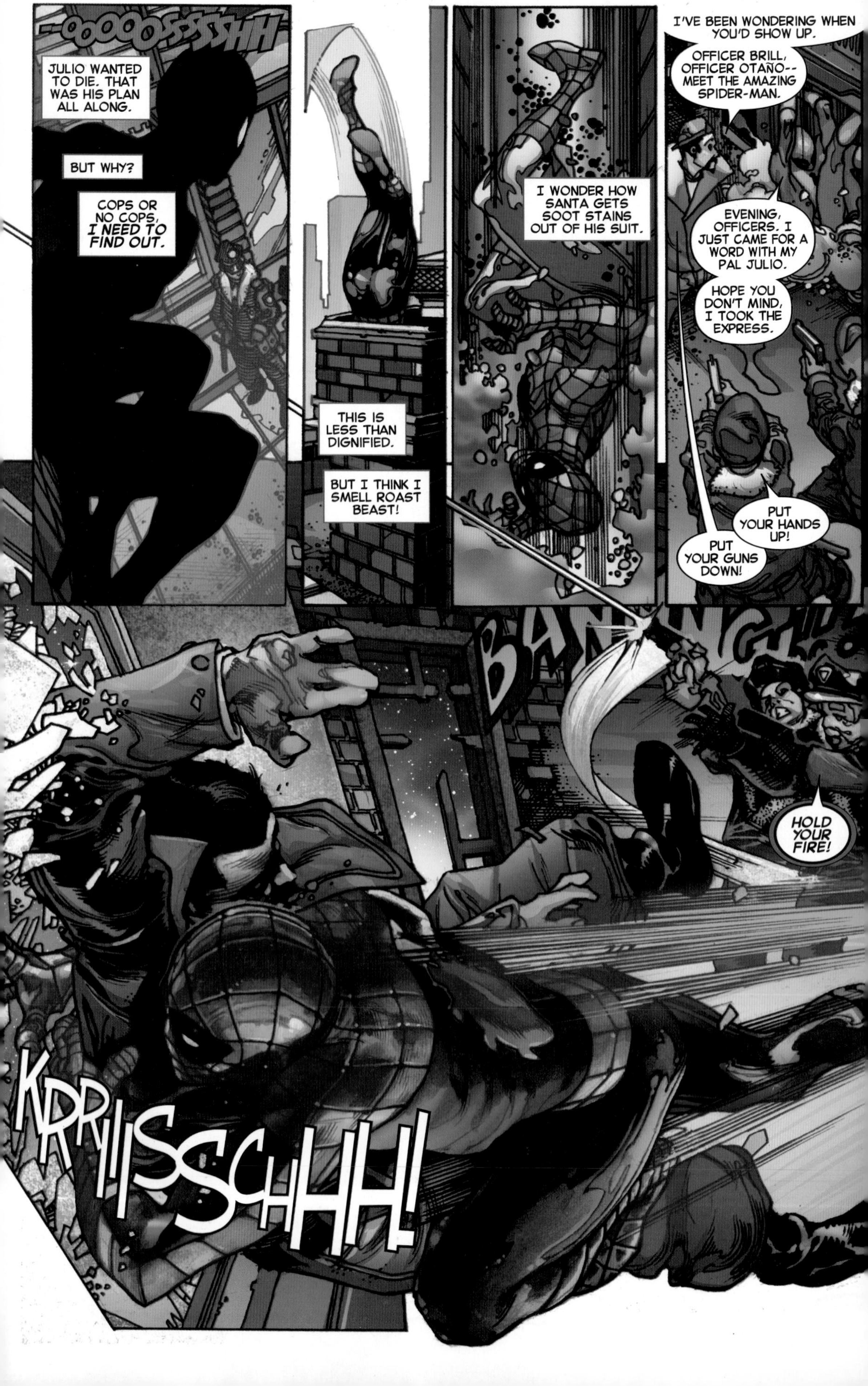
-OOOOOSSSSSHH
JULIO WANTED TO DIE. THAT WAS HIS PLAN ALL ALONG.
BUT WHY?
COPS OR NO COPS, *I NEED TO FIND OUT.*
THIS IS LESS THAN DIGNIFIED.
BUT I THINK I SMELL ROAST BEAST!
I WONDER HOW SANTA GETS SOOT STAINS OUT OF HIS SUIT.
I'VE BEEN WONDERING WHEN YOU'D SHOW UP.
OFFICER BRILL, OFFICER OTAÑO-- MEET THE AMAZING SPIDER-MAN.
EVENING, OFFICERS. I JUST CAME FOR A WORD WITH MY PAL JULIO.
HOPE YOU DON'T MIND, I TOOK THE EXPRESS.
PUT YOUR HANDS UP!
PUT YOUR GUNS DOWN!
HOLD YOUR FIRE!
KRRIIISSCHHH!

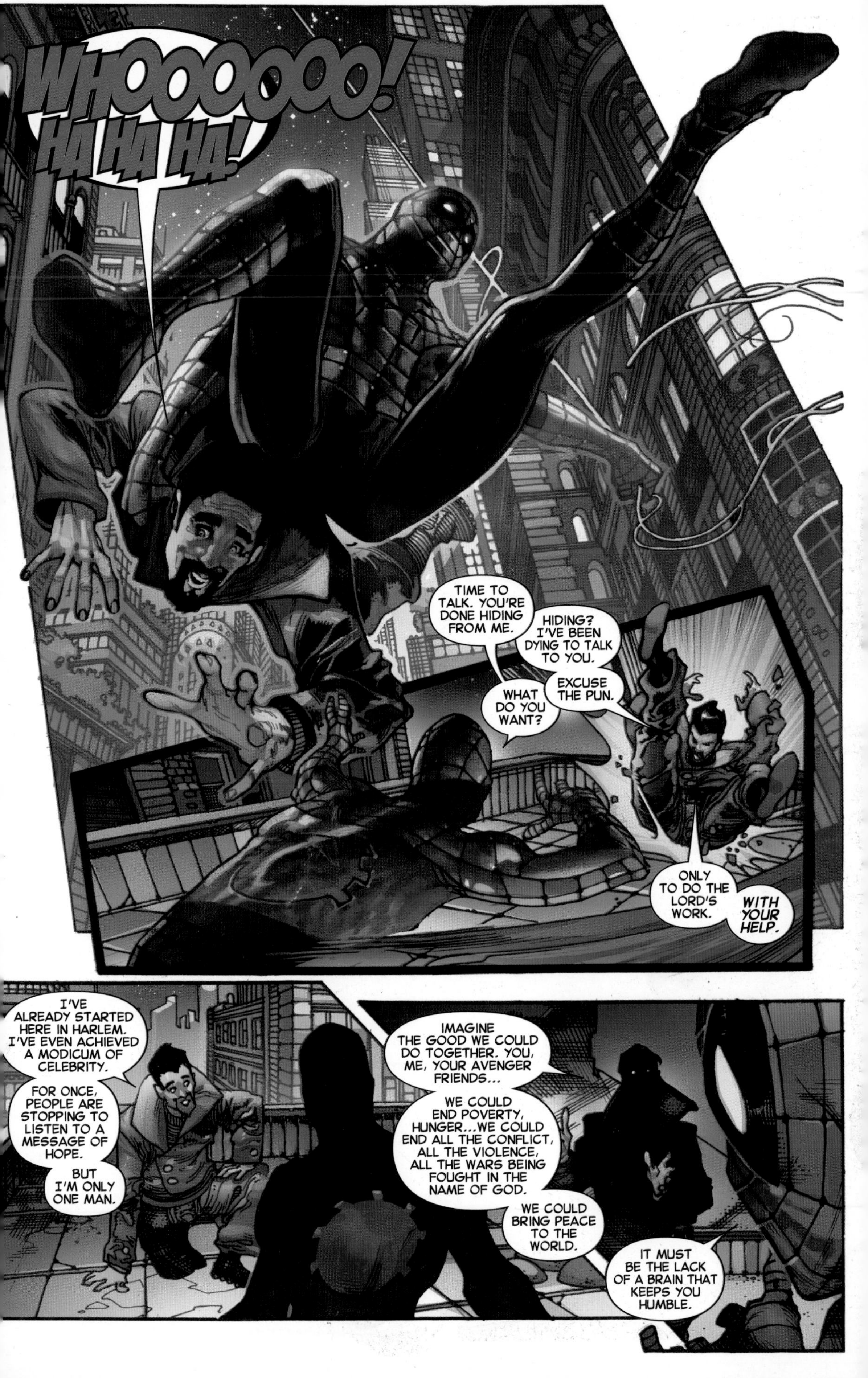
WHOOOOOO! HA HA HA!
TIME TO TALK. YOU'RE DONE HIDING FROM ME.
HIDING? I'VE BEEN DYING TO TALK TO YOU.
EXCUSE THE PUN.
WHAT DO YOU WANT?
ONLY TO DO THE LORD'S WORK.
WITH YOUR HELP.
I'VE ALREADY STARTED HERE IN HARLEM. I'VE EVEN ACHIEVED A MODICUM OF CELEBRITY.
FOR ONCE, PEOPLE ARE STOPPING TO LISTEN TO A MESSAGE OF HOPE.
BUT I'M ONLY ONE MAN.
IMAGINE THE GOOD WE COULD DO TOGETHER. YOU, ME, YOUR AVENGER FRIENDS...
WE COULD END POVERTY, HUNGER...WE COULD END ALL THE CONFLICT, ALL THE VIOLENCE, ALL THE WARS BEING FOUGHT IN THE NAME OF GOD.
WE COULD BRING PEACE TO THE WORLD.
IT MUST BE THE LACK OF A BRAIN THAT KEEPS YOU HUMBLE.

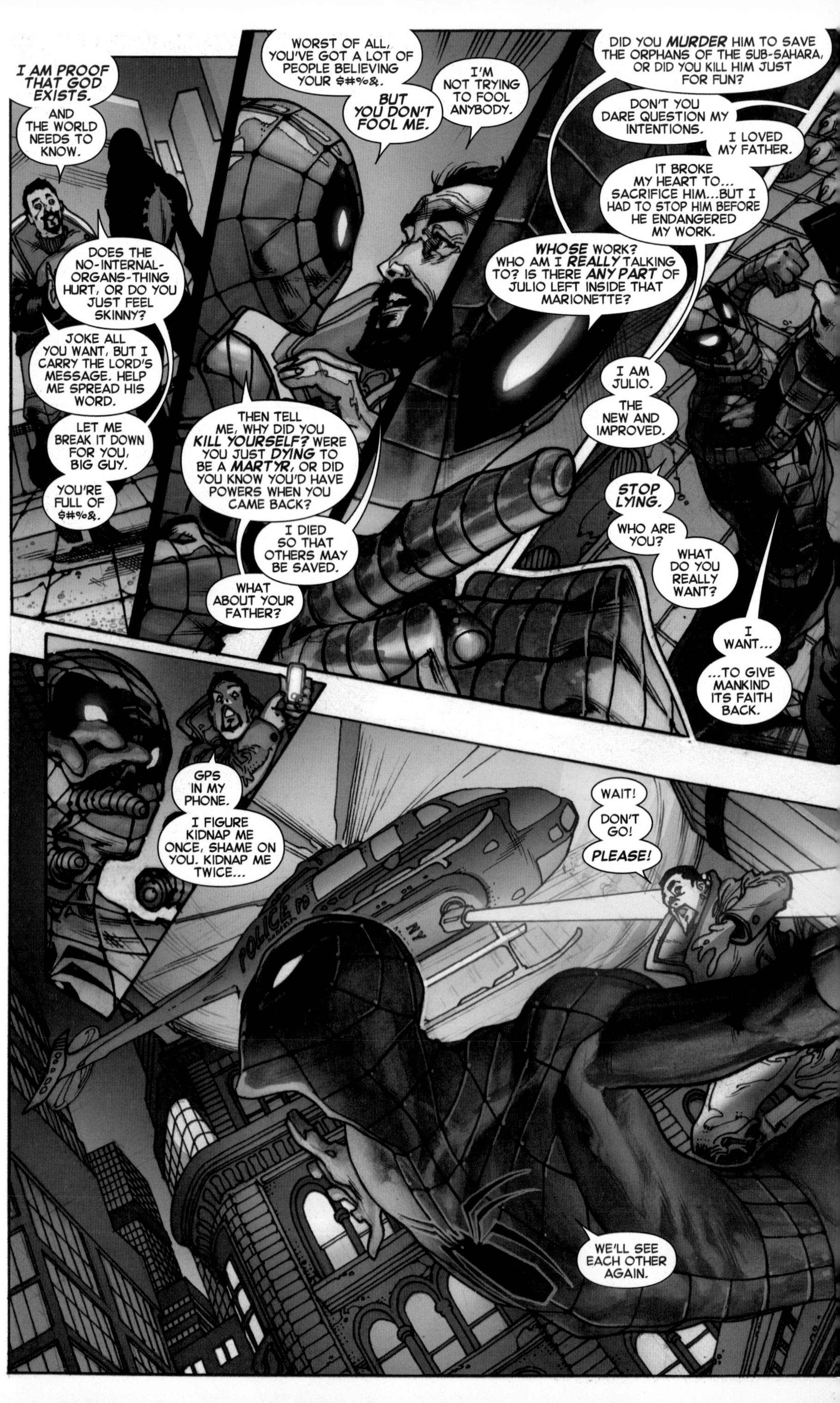
I AM PROOF THAT GOD EXISTS.
AND THE WORLD NEEDS TO KNOW.
DOES THE NO-INTERNAL-ORGANS-THING HURT, OR DO YOU JUST FEEL SKINNY?
JOKE ALL YOU WANT, BUT I CARRY THE LORD'S MESSAGE. HELP ME SPREAD HIS WORD.
LET ME BREAK IT DOWN FOR YOU, BIG GUY.
YOU'RE FULL OF $#%&.
WORST OF ALL, YOU'VE GOT A LOT OF PEOPLE BELIEVING YOUR $#%&.
BUT YOU DON'T FOOL ME.
I'M NOT TRYING TO FOOL ANYBODY.
THEN TELL ME, WHY DID YOU KILL YOURSELF? WERE YOU JUST DYING TO BE A MARTYR, OR DID YOU KNOW YOU'D HAVE POWERS WHEN YOU CAME BACK?
I DIED SO THAT OTHERS MAY BE SAVED.
WHAT ABOUT YOUR FATHER?
DID YOU MURDER HIM TO SAVE THE ORPHANS OF THE SUB-SAHARA, OR DID YOU KILL HIM JUST FOR FUN?
DON'T YOU DARE QUESTION MY INTENTIONS.
I LOVED MY FATHER.
IT BROKE MY HEART TO... SACRIFICE HIM...BUT I HAD TO STOP HIM BEFORE HE ENDANGERED MY WORK.
WHOSE WORK? WHO AM I REALLY TALKING TO? IS THERE ANY PART OF JULIO LEFT INSIDE THAT MARIONETTE?
I AM JULIO.
THE NEW AND IMPROVED.
STOP LYING.
WHO ARE YOU?
WHAT DO YOU REALLY WANT?
I WANT...
...TO GIVE MANKIND ITS FAITH BACK.
GPS IN MY PHONE.
I FIGURE KIDNAP ME ONCE, SHAME ON YOU. KIDNAP ME TWICE...
WAIT!
DON'T GO!
PLEASE!
POLICE
NY
WE'LL SEE EACH OTHER AGAIN.

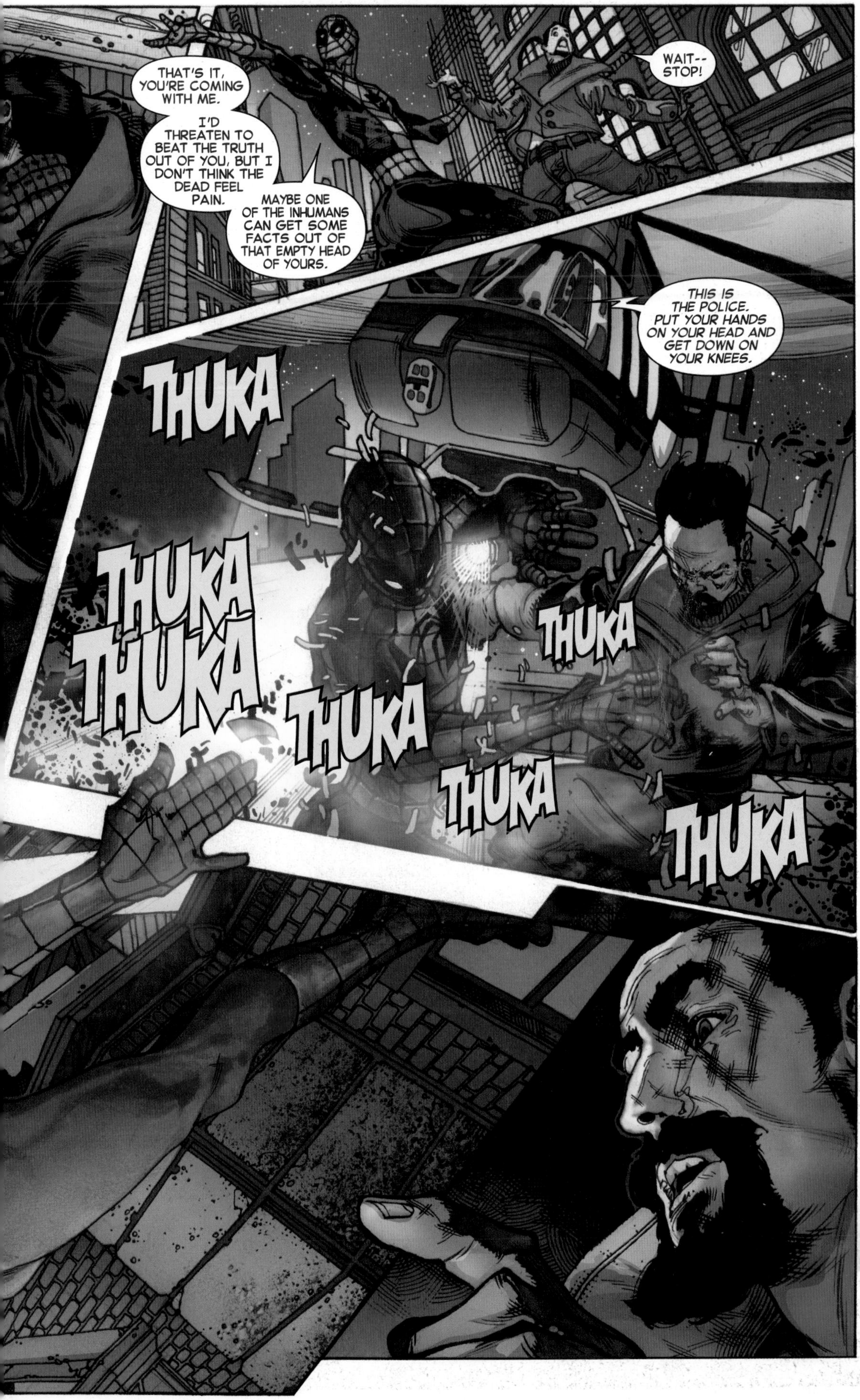
THAT'S IT, YOU'RE COMING WITH ME.
I'D THREATEN TO BEAT THE TRUTH OUT OF YOU, BUT I DON'T THINK THE DEAD FEEL PAIN.
WAIT-- STOP!
MAYBE ONE OF THE INHUMANS CAN GET SOME FACTS OUT OF THAT EMPTY HEAD OF YOURS.
THIS IS THE POLICE. PUT YOUR HANDS ON YOUR HEAD AND GET DOWN ON YOUR KNEES.
THUKA
THUKA
THUKA
THUKA
THUKA
THUKA
THUKA

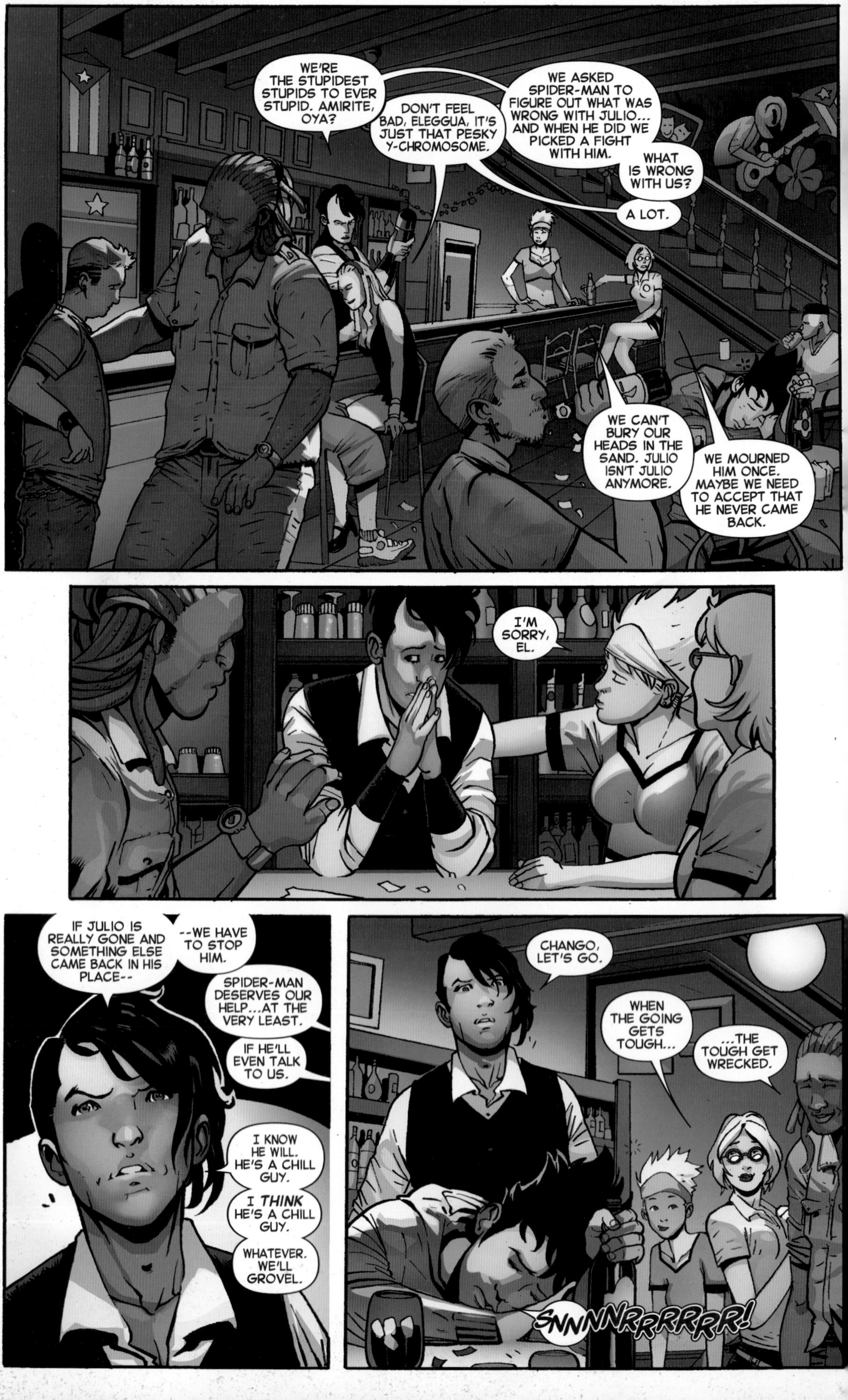

WE'RE THE STUPIDEST STUPIDS TO EVER STUPID. AMIRITE, OYA?
DON'T FEEL BAD, ELEGGUA, IT'S JUST THAT PESKY Y-CHROMOSOME.
WE ASKED SPIDER-MAN TO FIGURE OUT WHAT WAS WRONG WITH JULIO... AND WHEN HE DID WE PICKED A FIGHT WITH HIM.
WHAT IS WRONG WITH US?
A LOT.
WE CAN'T BURY OUR HEADS IN THE SAND. JULIO ISN'T JULIO ANYMORE.
WE MOURNED HIM ONCE. MAYBE WE NEED TO ACCEPT THAT HE NEVER CAME BACK.
I'M SORRY, EL.
IF JULIO IS REALLY GONE AND SOMETHING ELSE CAME BACK IN HIS PLACE--
--WE HAVE TO STOP HIM.
SPIDER-MAN DESERVES OUR HELP...AT THE VERY LEAST.
IF HE'LL EVEN TALK TO US.
I KNOW HE WILL. HE'S A CHILL GUY.
I *THINK* HE'S A CHILL GUY.
WHATEVER. WE'LL GROVEL.
CHANGO, LET'S GO.
WHEN THE GOING GETS TOUGH...
...THE TOUGH GET WRECKED.
SNNNNRRRRRR!

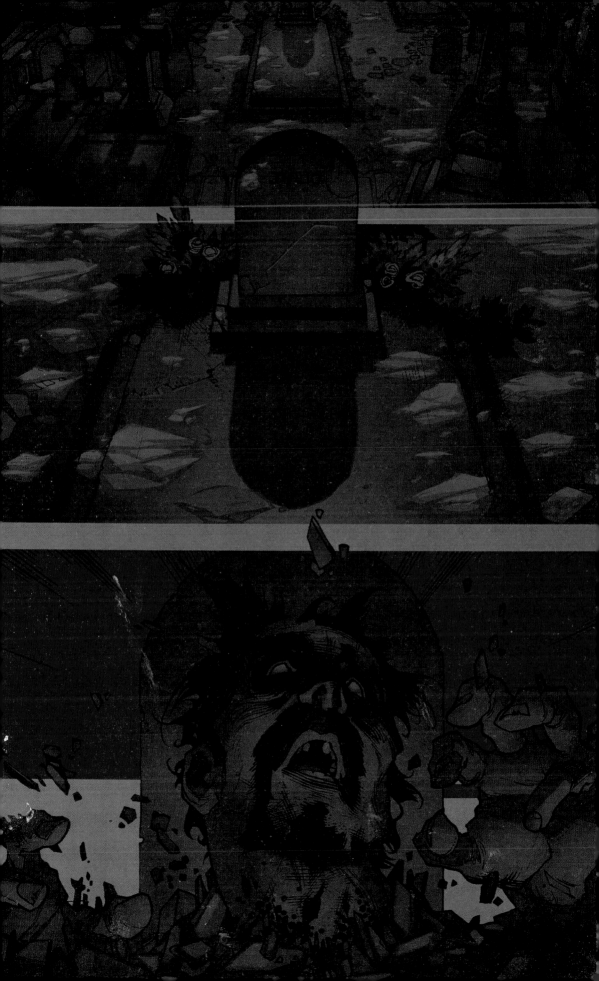

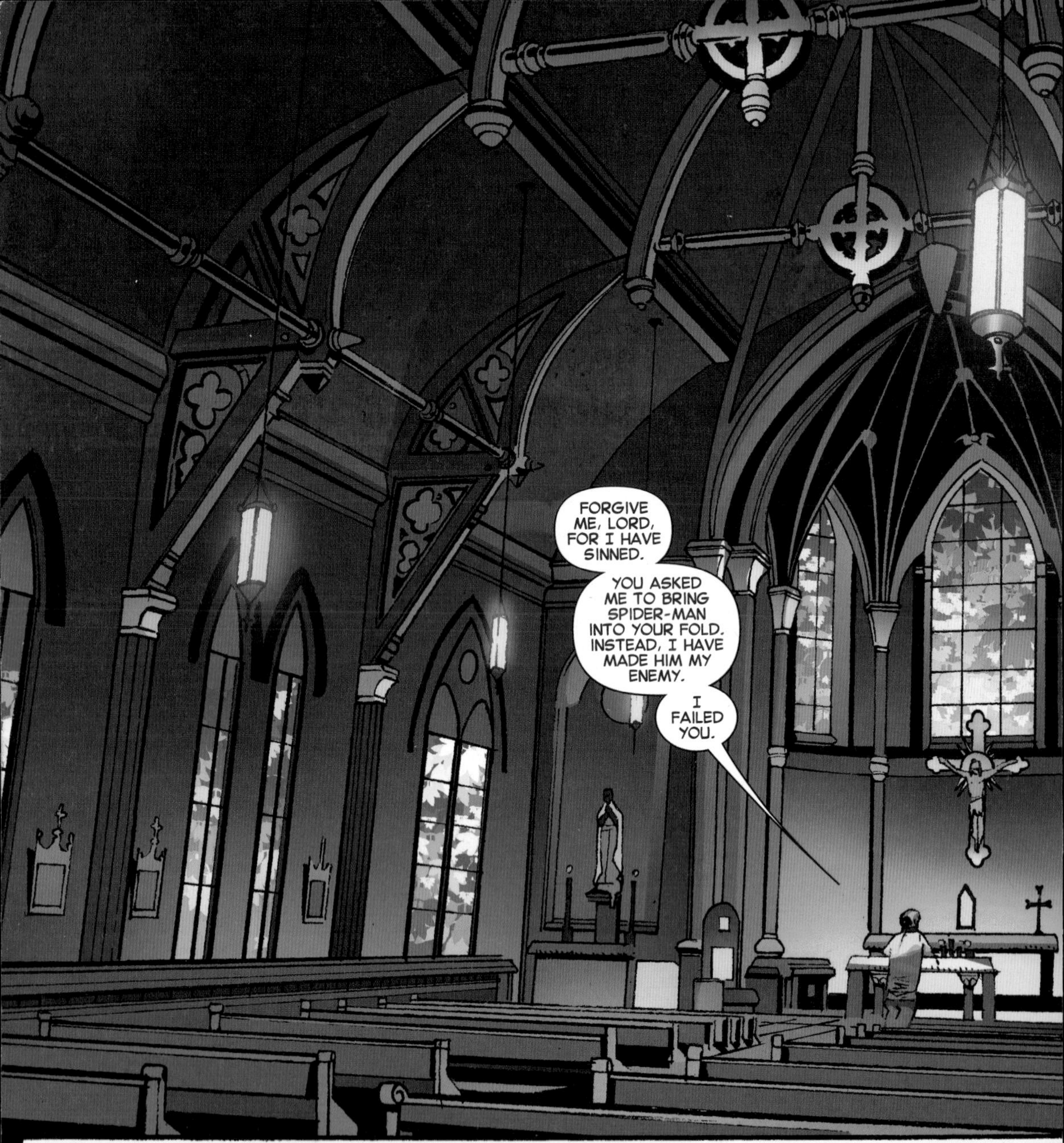
FORGIVE ME, LORD, FOR I HAVE SINNED.
YOU ASKED ME TO BRING SPIDER-MAN INTO YOUR FOLD. INSTEAD, I HAVE MADE HIM MY ENEMY.
I FAILED YOU.

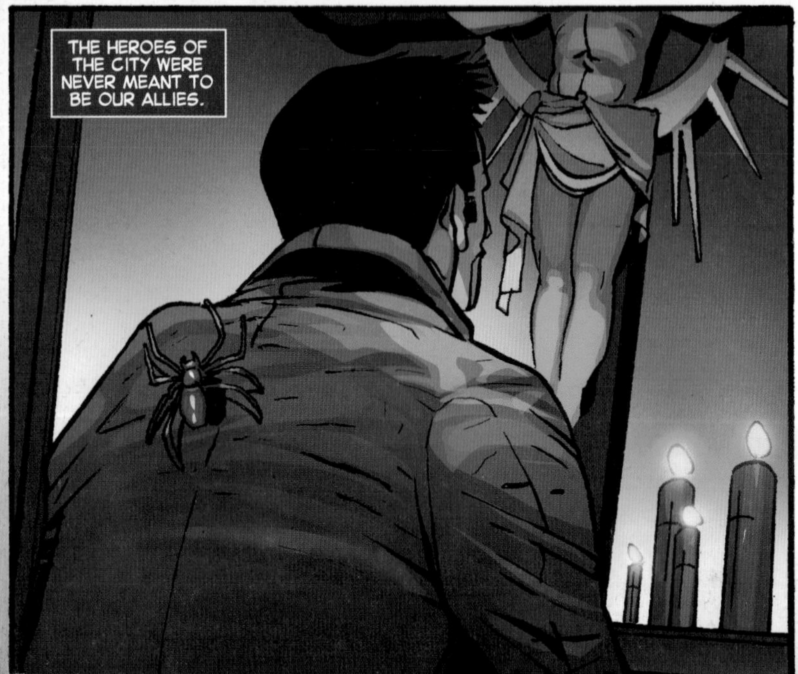
THE HEROES OF THE CITY WERE NEVER MEANT TO BE OUR ALLIES.

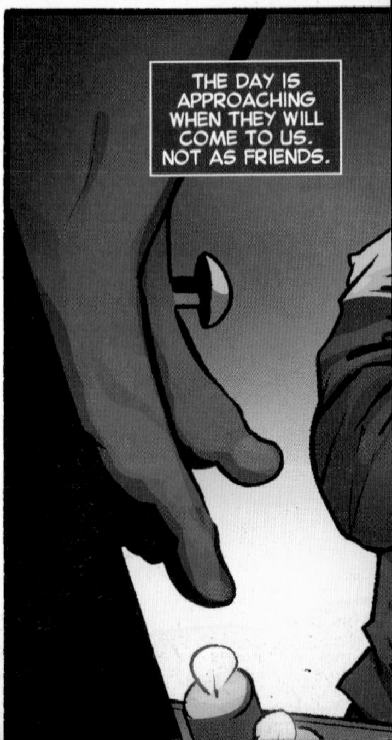
THE DAY IS APPROACHING WHEN THEY WILL COME TO US. NOT AS FRIENDS.

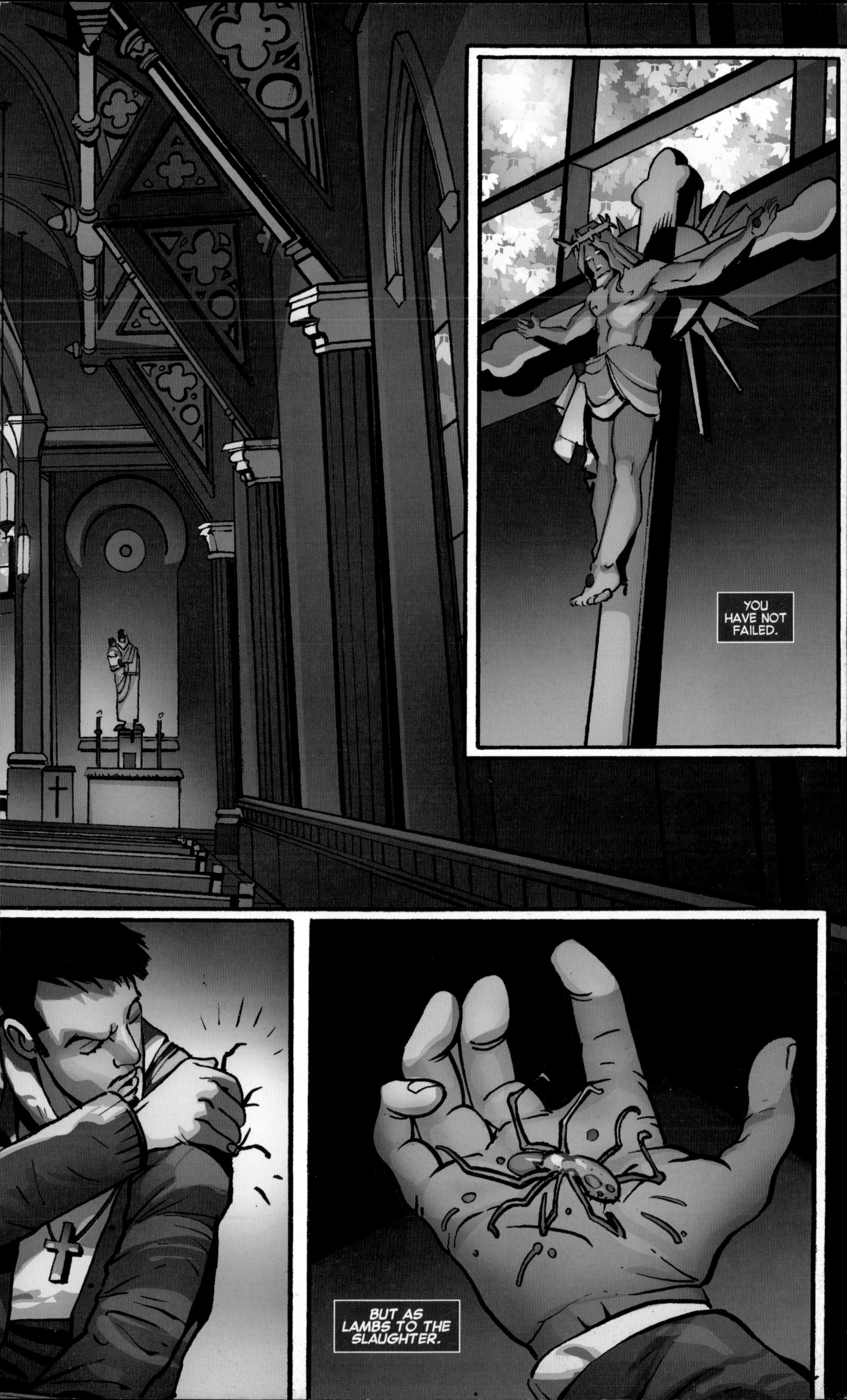
YOU HAVE NOT FAILED.
BUT AS LAMBS TO THE SLAUGHTER.

The AMAZING SPIDER-MAN Variant Covers

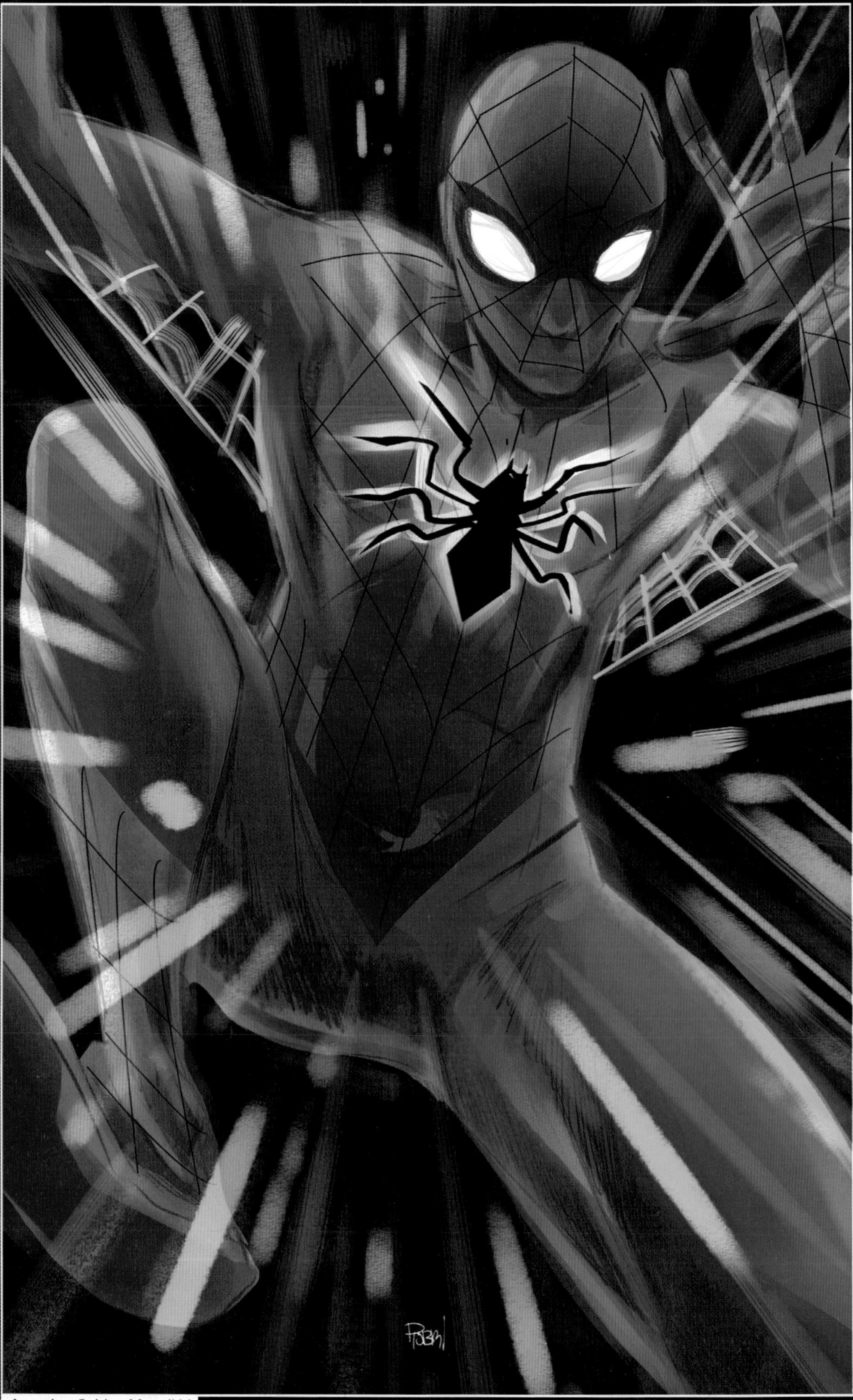

Amazing Spider-Man #1.1
by Robbi Rodriguez

MARVEL GRAPHIC NOVEL AMAZING SPIDER-MAN VOL 5 #1.5

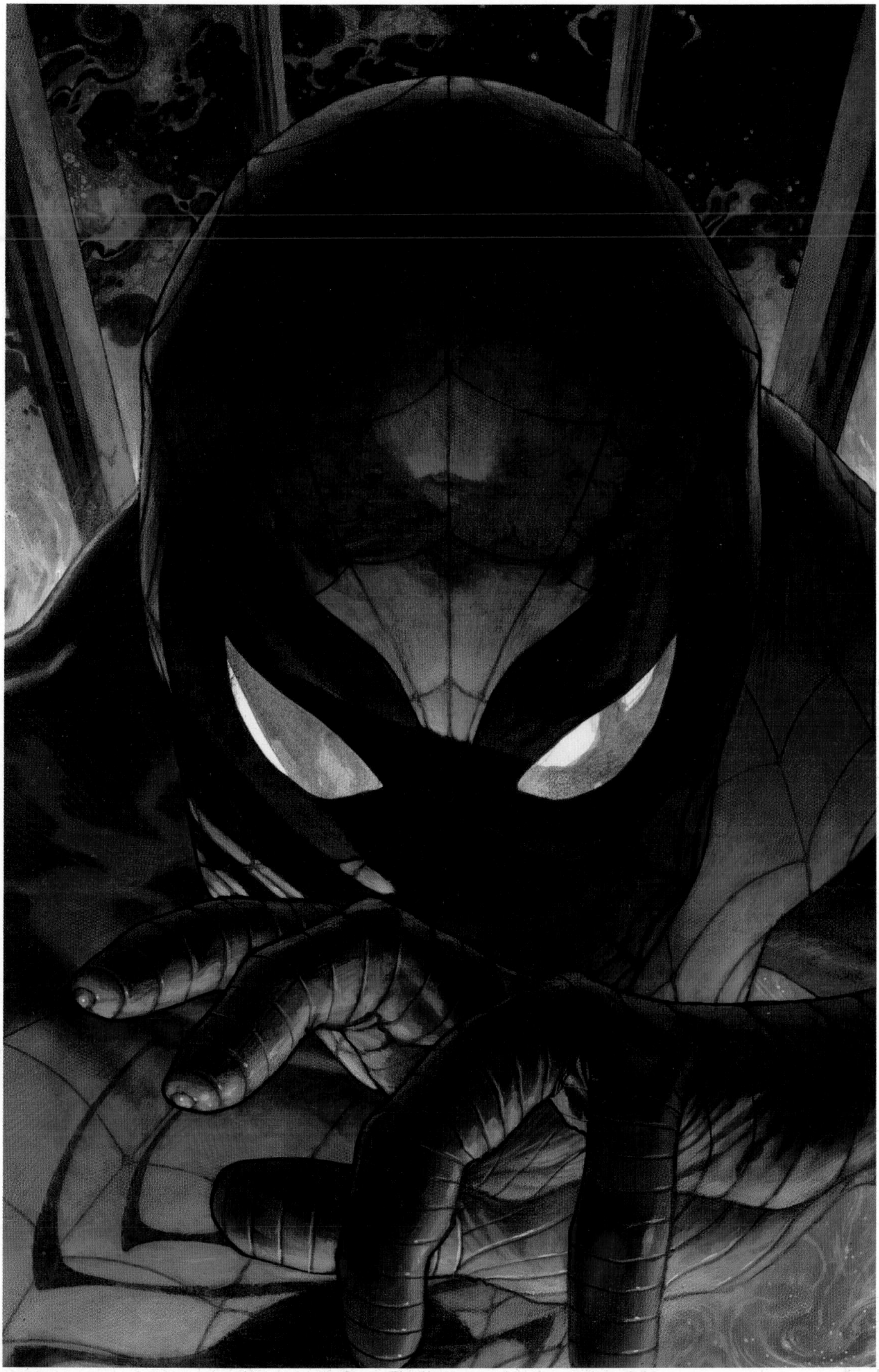

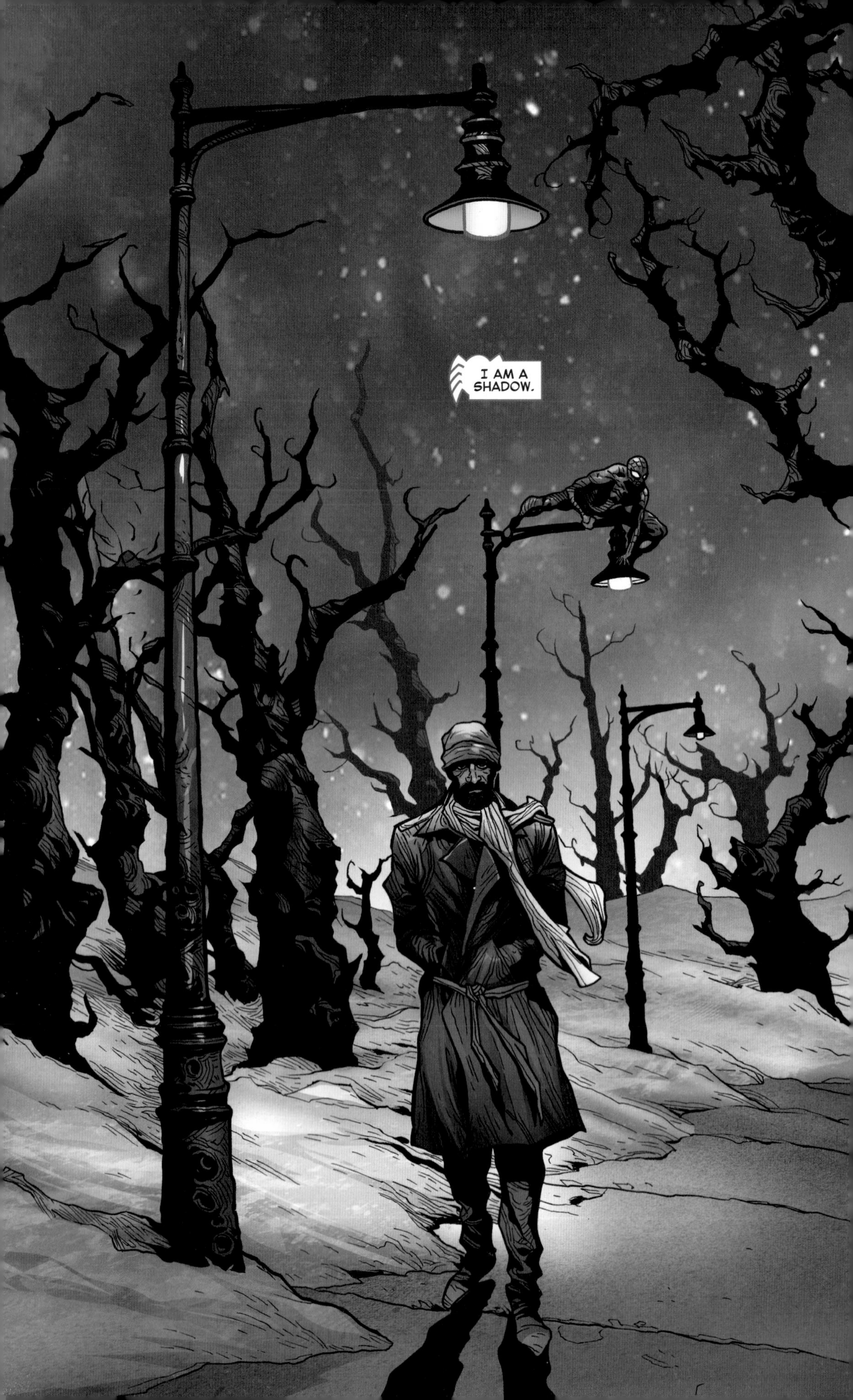
I AM A SHADOW.

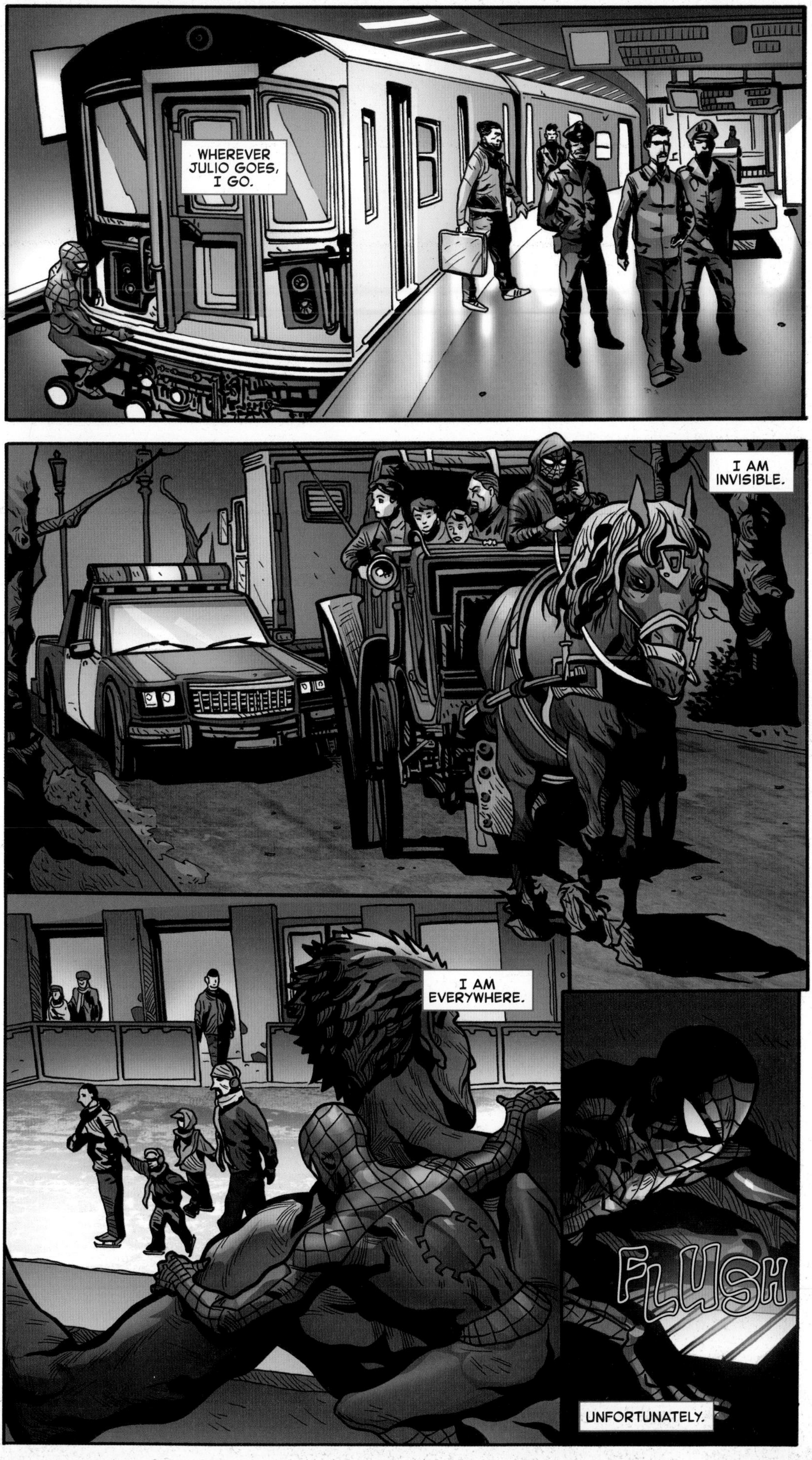
WHEREVER JULIO GOES, I GO.
I AM INVISIBLE.
I AM EVERYWHERE.
FLUSH
UNFORTUNATELY.

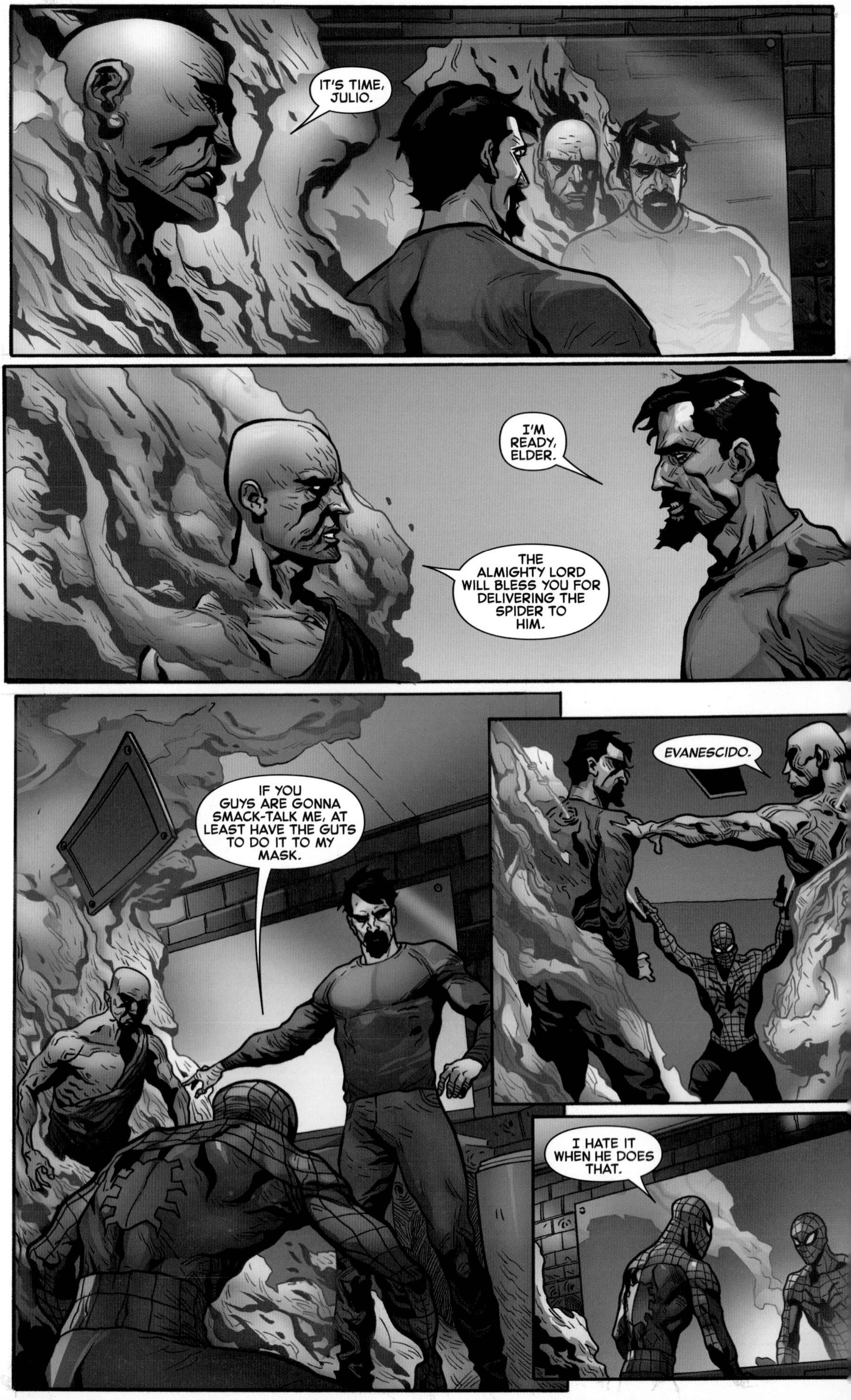
IT'S TIME, JULIO.
I'M READY, ELDER.
THE ALMIGHTY LORD WILL BLESS YOU FOR DELIVERING THE SPIDER TO HIM.
IF YOU GUYS ARE GONNA SMACK-TALK ME, AT LEAST HAVE THE GUTS TO DO IT TO MY MASK.
EVANESCIDO.
I HATE IT WHEN HE DOES THAT.

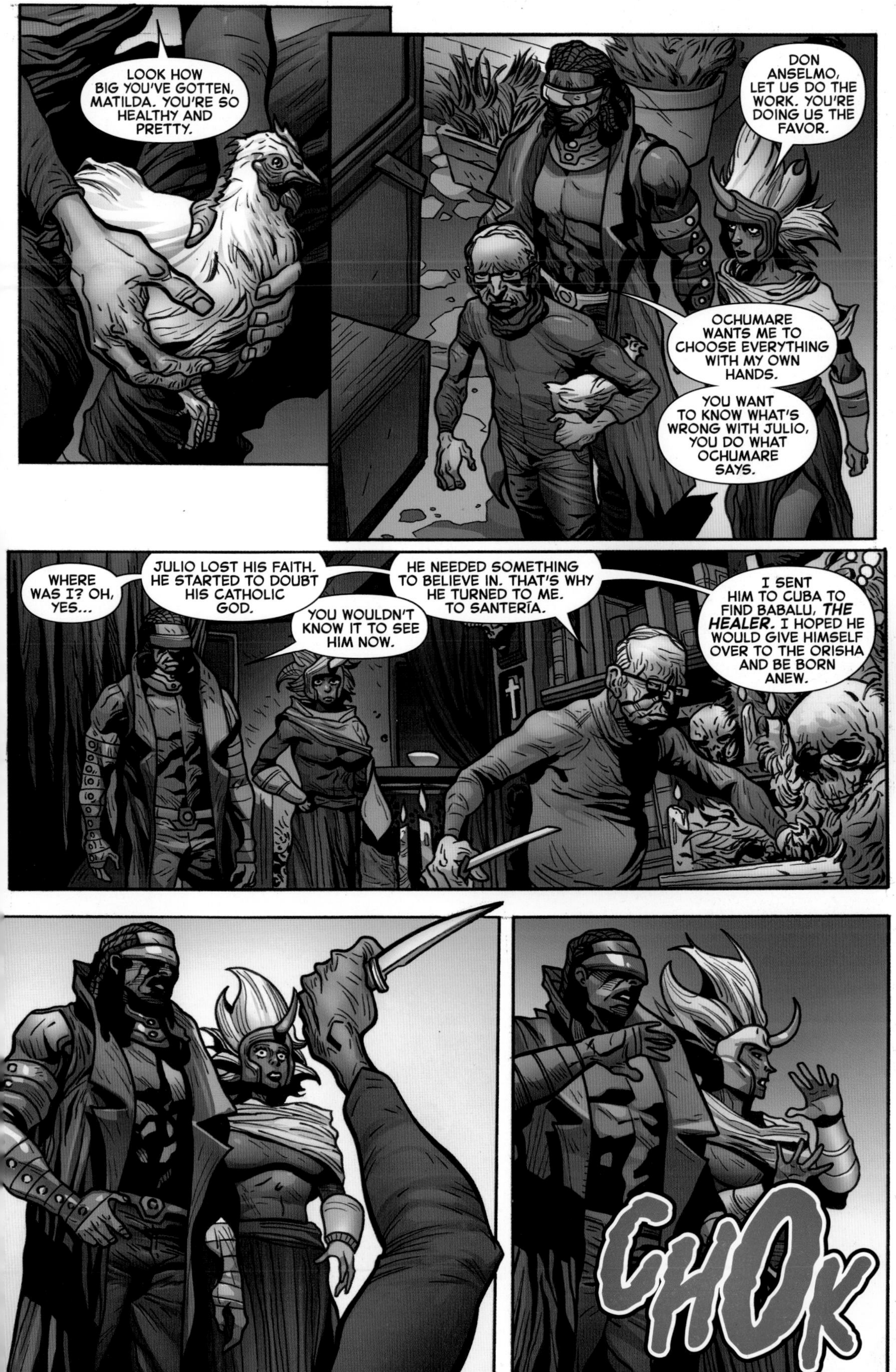
LOOK HOW BIG YOU'VE GOTTEN, MATILDA. YOU'RE SO HEALTHY AND PRETTY.
DON ANSELMO, LET US DO THE WORK. YOU'RE DOING US THE FAVOR.
OCHUMARE WANTS ME TO CHOOSE EVERYTHING WITH MY OWN HANDS.
YOU WANT TO KNOW WHAT'S WRONG WITH JULIO, YOU DO WHAT OCHUMARE SAYS.
WHERE WAS I? OH, YES...
JULIO LOST HIS FAITH. HE STARTED TO DOUBT HIS CATHOLIC GOD.
YOU WOULDN'T KNOW IT TO SEE HIM NOW.
HE NEEDED SOMETHING TO BELIEVE IN. THAT'S WHY HE TURNED TO ME. TO SANTERÍA.
I SENT HIM TO CUBA TO FIND BABALU, *THE HEALER.* I HOPED HE WOULD GIVE HIMSELF OVER TO THE ORISHA AND BE BORN ANEW.
CHOK

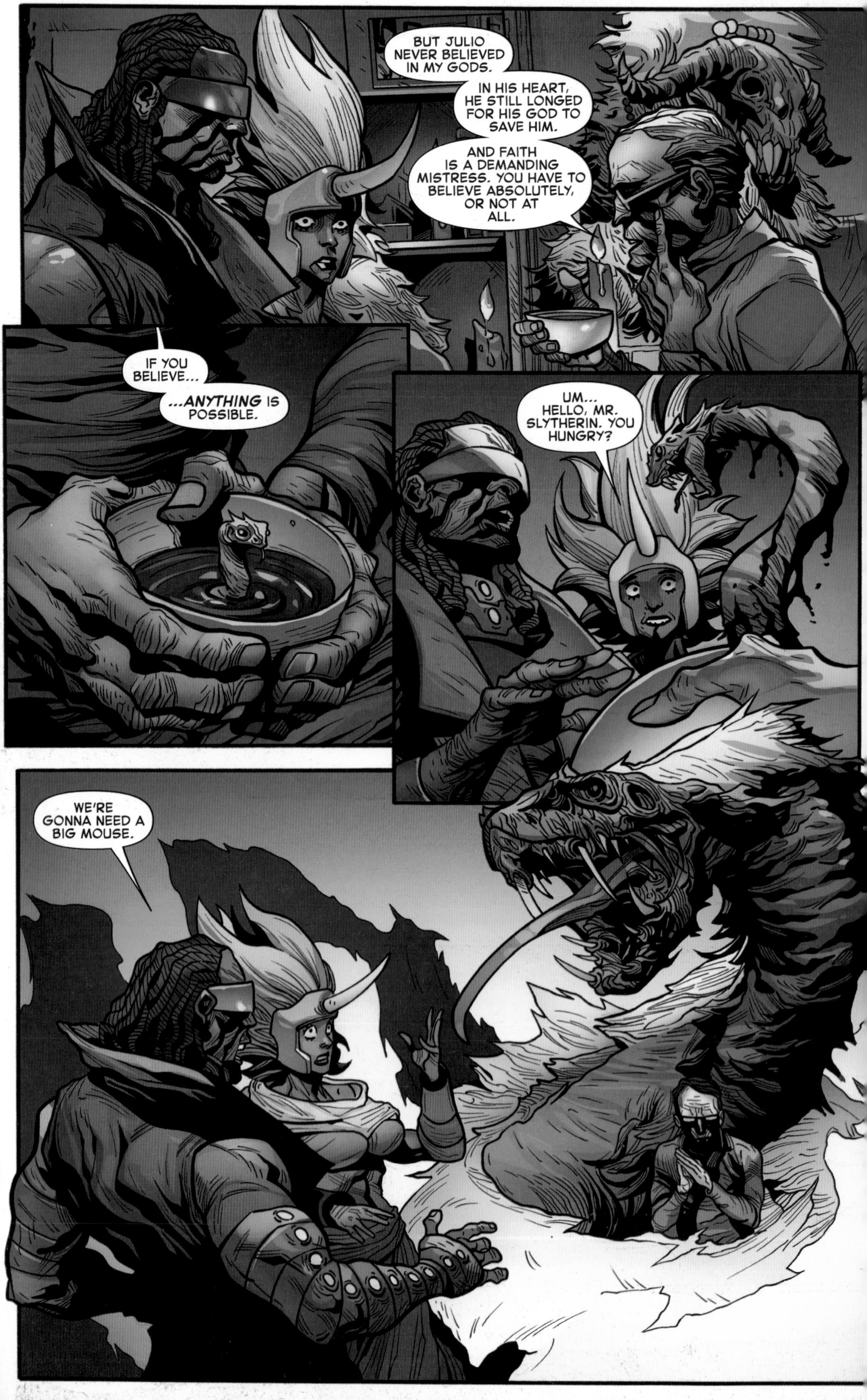
BUT JULIO NEVER BELIEVED IN MY GODS.
IN HIS HEART, HE STILL LONGED FOR HIS GOD TO SAVE HIM.
AND FAITH IS A DEMANDING MISTRESS. YOU HAVE TO BELIEVE ABSOLUTELY, OR NOT AT ALL.
IF YOU BELIEVE...
...*ANYTHING* IS POSSIBLE.
UM... HELLO, MR. SLYTHERIN. YOU HUNGRY?
WE'RE GONNA NEED A BIG MOUSE.

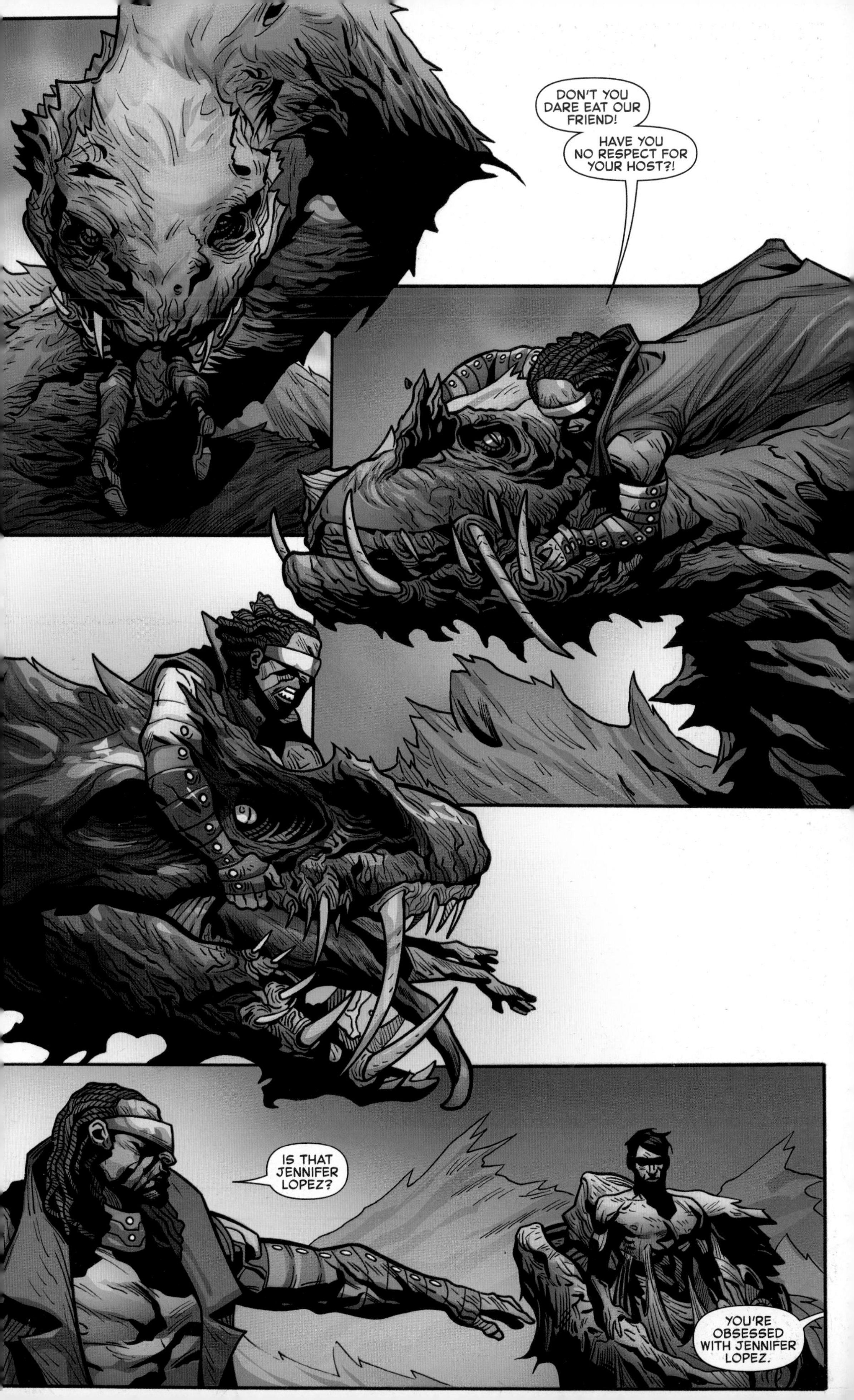
DON'T YOU DARE EAT OUR FRIEND!
HAVE YOU NO RESPECT FOR YOUR HOST?!
IS THAT JENNIFER LOPEZ?
YOU'RE OBSESSED WITH JENNIFER LOPEZ.

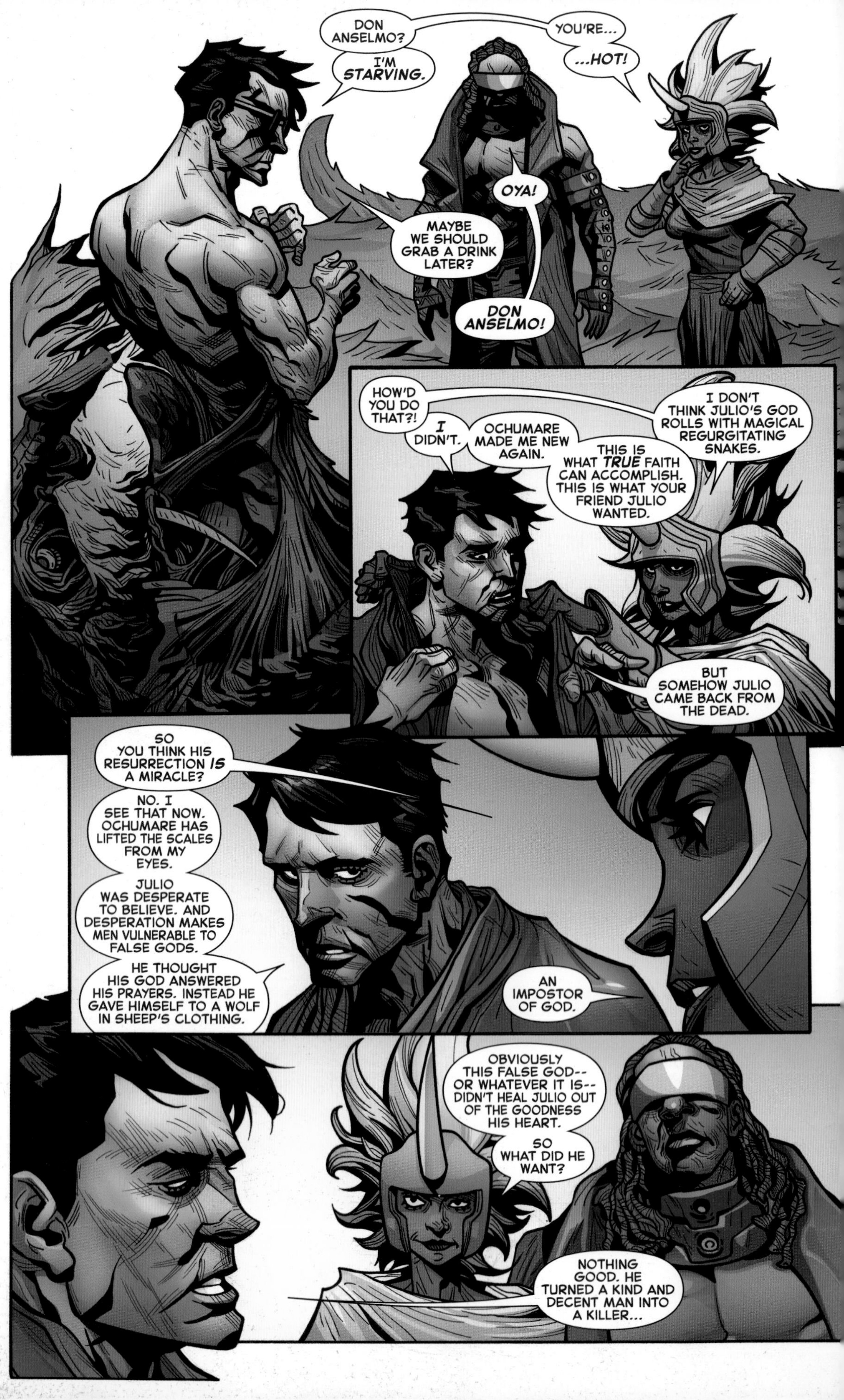
DON ANSELMO?
YOU'RE...
...HOT!
I'M STARVING.
MAYBE WE SHOULD GRAB A DRINK LATER?
OYA!
DON ANSELMO!
HOW'D YOU DO THAT?!
I DON'T THINK JULIO'S GOD ROLLS WITH MAGICAL REGURGITATING SNAKES.
I DIDN'T.
OCHUMARE MADE ME NEW AGAIN.
THIS IS WHAT TRUE FAITH CAN ACCOMPLISH. THIS IS WHAT YOUR FRIEND JULIO WANTED.
BUT SOMEHOW JULIO CAME BACK FROM THE DEAD.
SO YOU THINK HIS RESURRECTION IS A MIRACLE?
NO. I SEE THAT NOW. OCHUMARE HAS LIFTED THE SCALES FROM MY EYES.
JULIO WAS DESPERATE TO BELIEVE. AND DESPERATION MAKES MEN VULNERABLE TO FALSE GODS.
HE THOUGHT HIS GOD ANSWERED HIS PRAYERS. INSTEAD HE GAVE HIMSELF TO A WOLF IN SHEEP'S CLOTHING.
AN IMPOSTOR OF GOD.
OBVIOUSLY THIS FALSE GOD-- OR WHATEVER IT IS-- DIDN'T HEAL JULIO OUT OF THE GOODNESS HIS HEART.
SO WHAT DID HE WANT?
NOTHING GOOD. HE TURNED A KIND AND DECENT MAN INTO A KILLER...

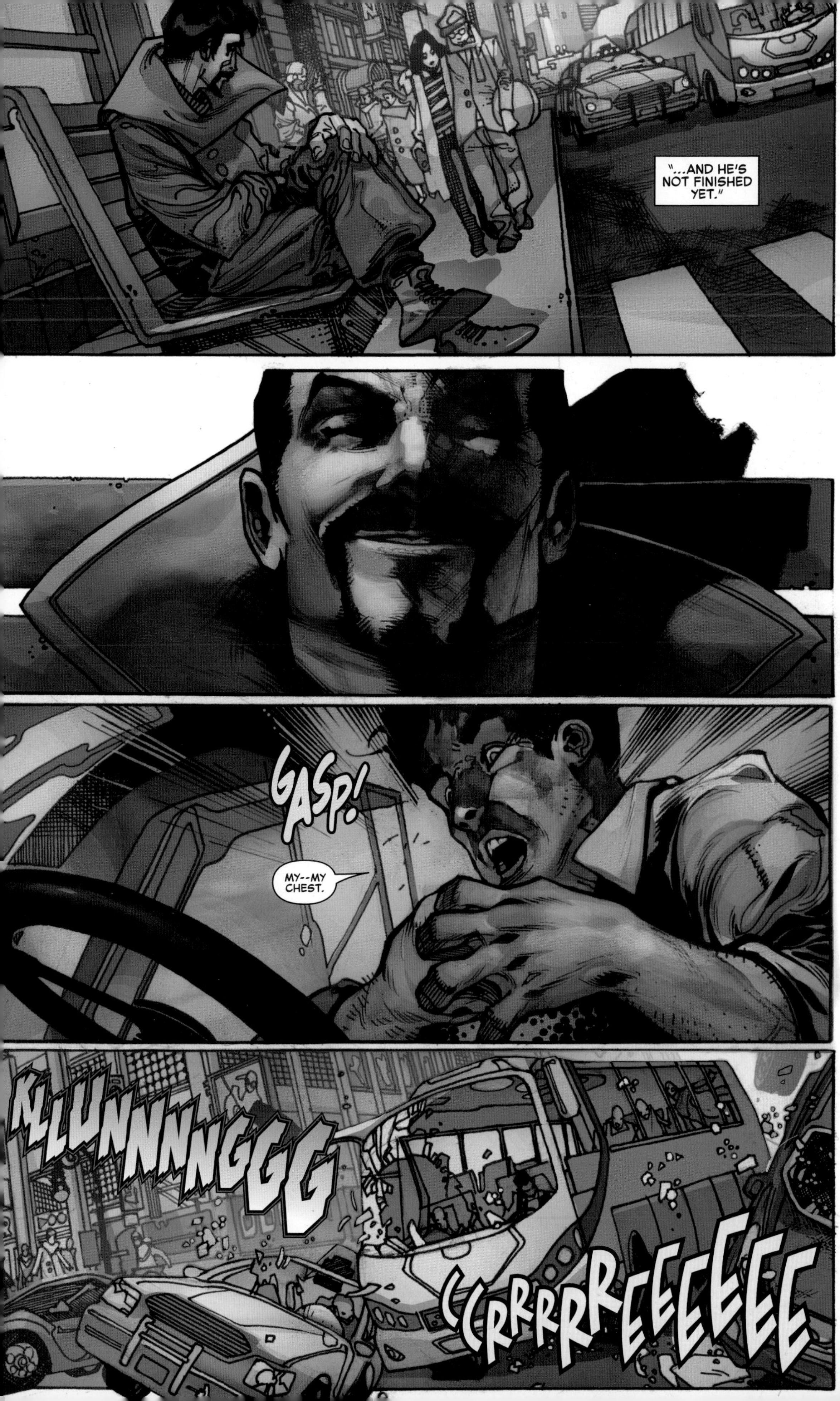
"...AND HE'S NOT FINISHED YET."
GASP!
MY--MY CHEST.
KLUNNNNGGG
CCRRRRREEEEEEEE

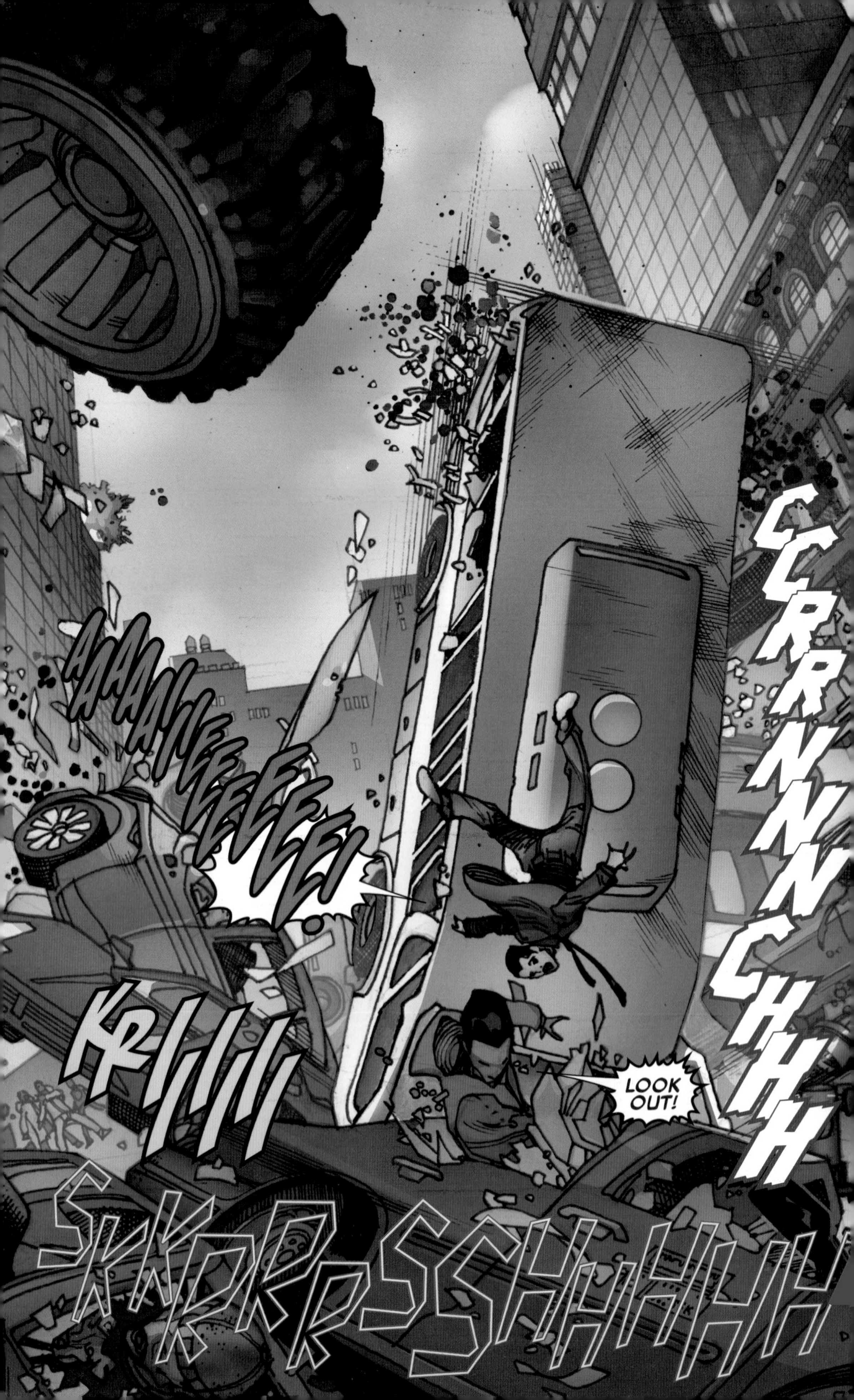
AAAAAIIEEEEEE!
CCCRRRNNNCHHHH
KRIIIIII
LOOK OUT!
SKKRRRSSHHHHHH

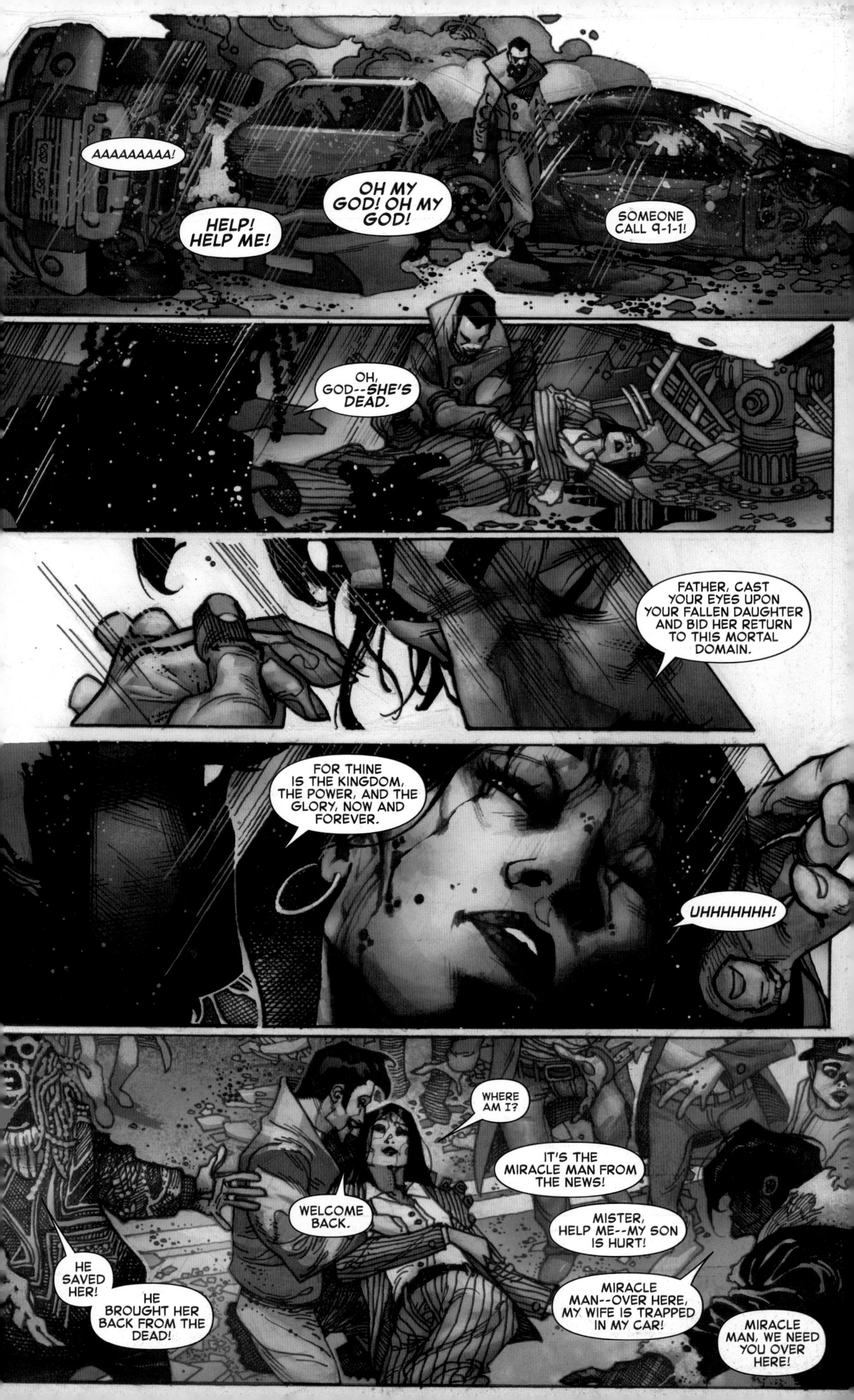
AAAAAAAAA!
HELP! HELP ME!
OH MY GOD! OH MY GOD!
SOMEONE CALL 9-1-1!
OH, GOD--SHE'S DEAD.
FATHER, CAST YOUR EYES UPON YOUR FALLEN DAUGHTER AND BID HER RETURN TO THIS MORTAL DOMAIN.
FOR THINE IS THE KINGDOM, THE POWER, AND THE GLORY, NOW AND FOREVER.
UHHHHHHH!
WHERE AM I?
WELCOME BACK.
IT'S THE MIRACLE MAN FROM THE NEWS!
MISTER, HELP ME--MY SON IS HURT!
HE SAVED HER!
HE BROUGHT HER BACK FROM THE DEAD!
MIRACLE MAN--OVER HERE, MY WIFE IS TRAPPED IN MY CAR!
MIRACLE MAN, WE NEED YOU OVER HERE!

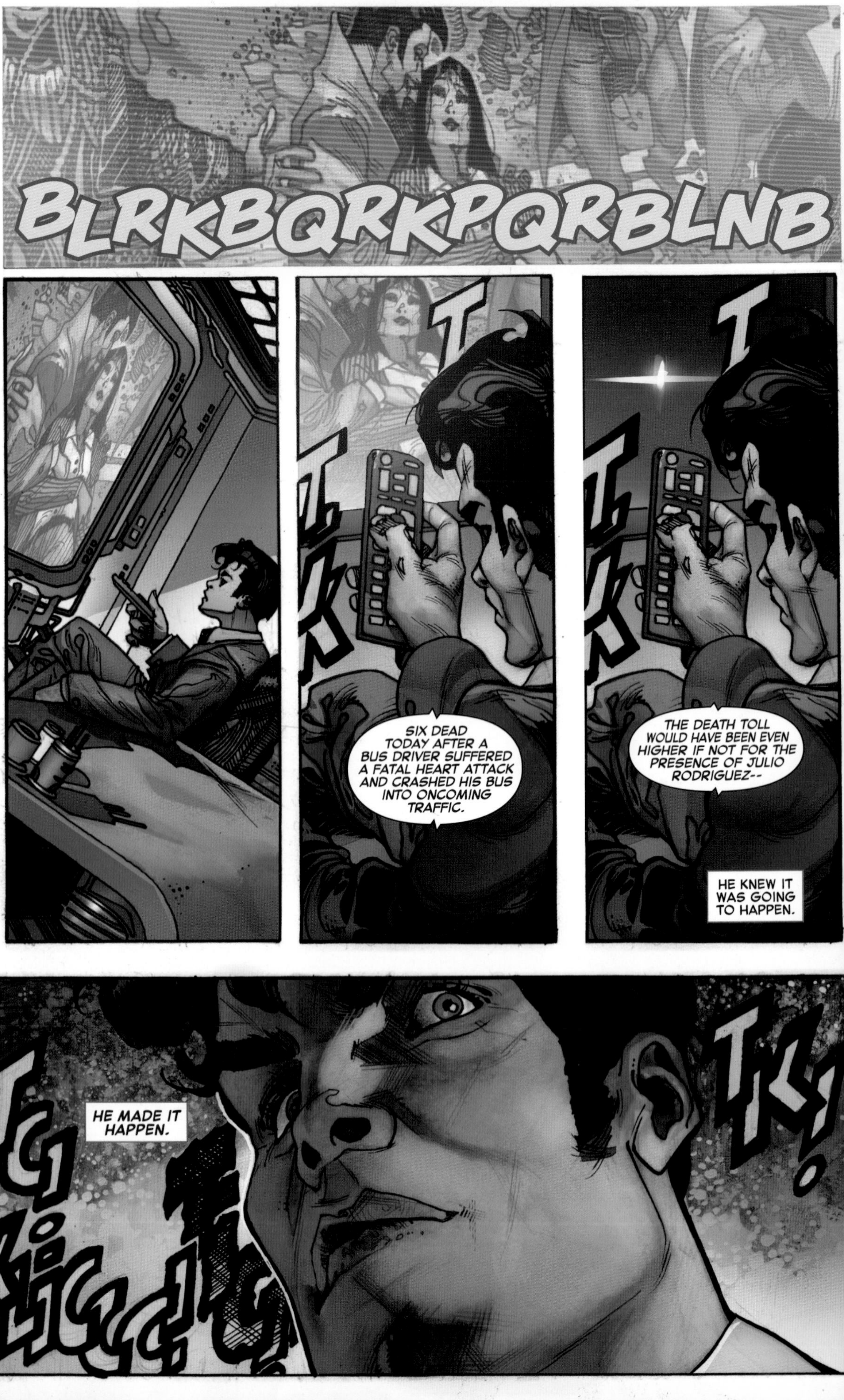
BLRKBQRKPQRBLNB
SIX DEAD TODAY AFTER A BUS DRIVER SUFFERED A FATAL HEART ATTACK AND CRASHED HIS BUS INTO ONCOMING TRAFFIC.
THE DEATH TOLL WOULD HAVE BEEN EVEN HIGHER IF NOT FOR THE PRESENCE OF JULIO RODRIGUEZ--
HE KNEW IT WAS GOING TO HAPPEN.
HE MADE IT HAPPEN.

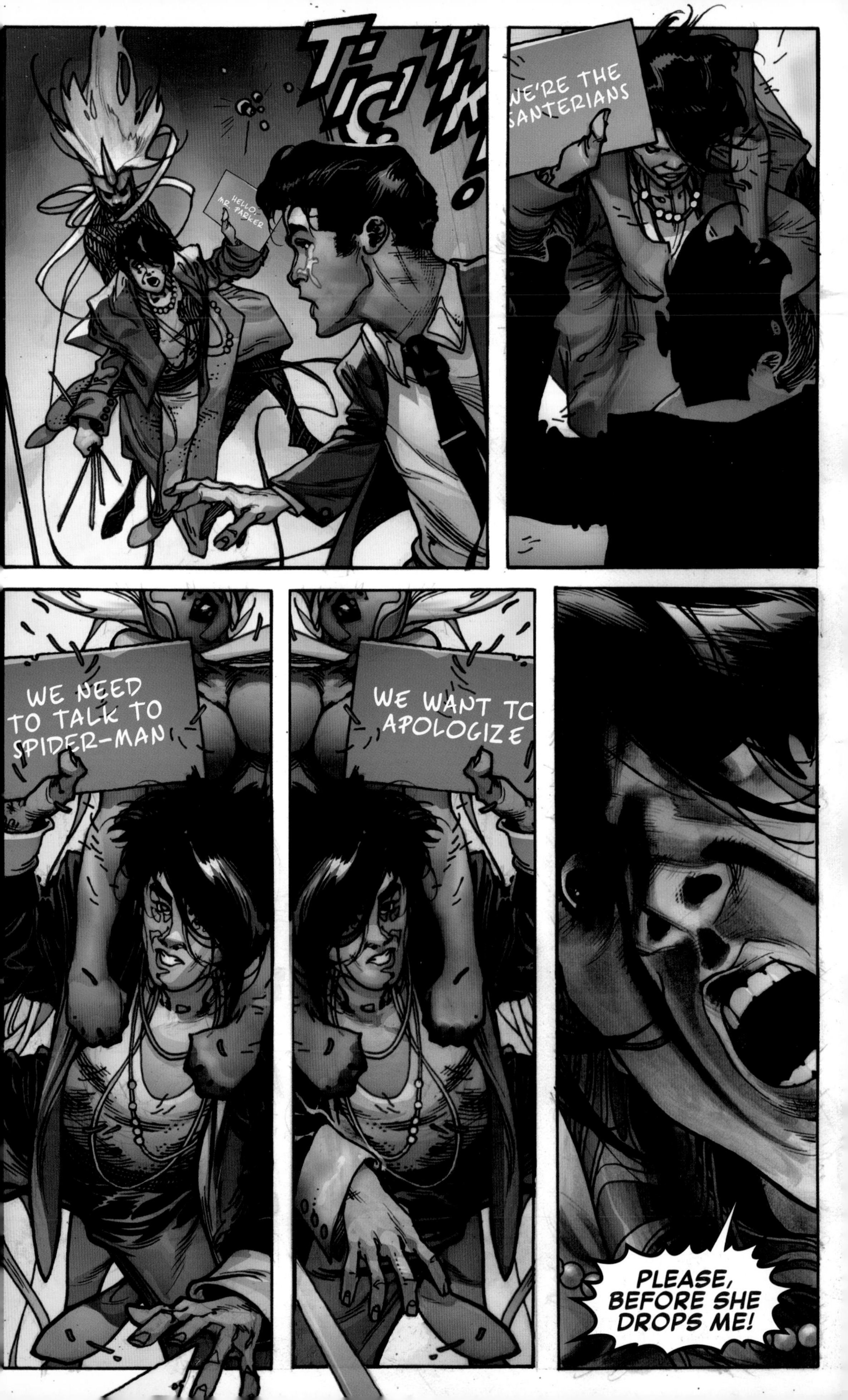
THOOOK!
HELLO, MR. PARKER
WE'RE THE SANTERIANS
WE NEED TO TALK TO SPIDER-MAN
WE WANT TO APOLOGIZE
PLEASE, BEFORE SHE DROPS ME!

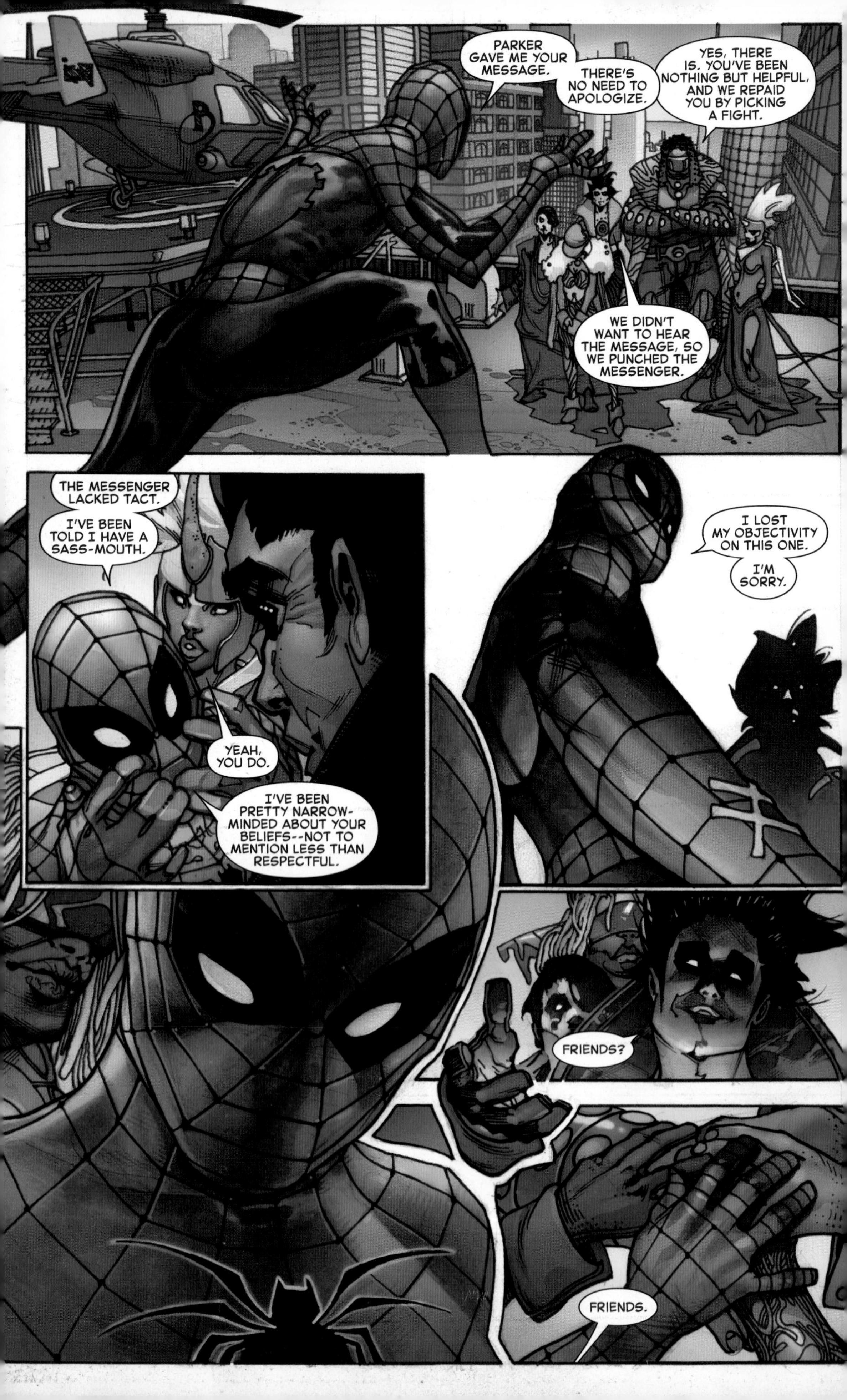
PARKER GAVE ME YOUR MESSAGE.
THERE'S NO NEED TO APOLOGIZE.
YES, THERE IS. YOU'VE BEEN NOTHING BUT HELPFUL, AND WE REPAID YOU BY PICKING A FIGHT.
WE DIDN'T WANT TO HEAR THE MESSAGE, SO WE PUNCHED THE MESSENGER.
THE MESSENGER LACKED TACT.
I'VE BEEN TOLD I HAVE A SASS-MOUTH.
YEAH, YOU DO.
I'VE BEEN PRETTY NARROW-MINDED ABOUT YOUR BELIEFS--NOT TO MENTION LESS THAN RESPECTFUL.
I LOST MY OBJECTIVITY ON THIS ONE.
I'M SORRY.
FRIENDS?
FRIENDS.

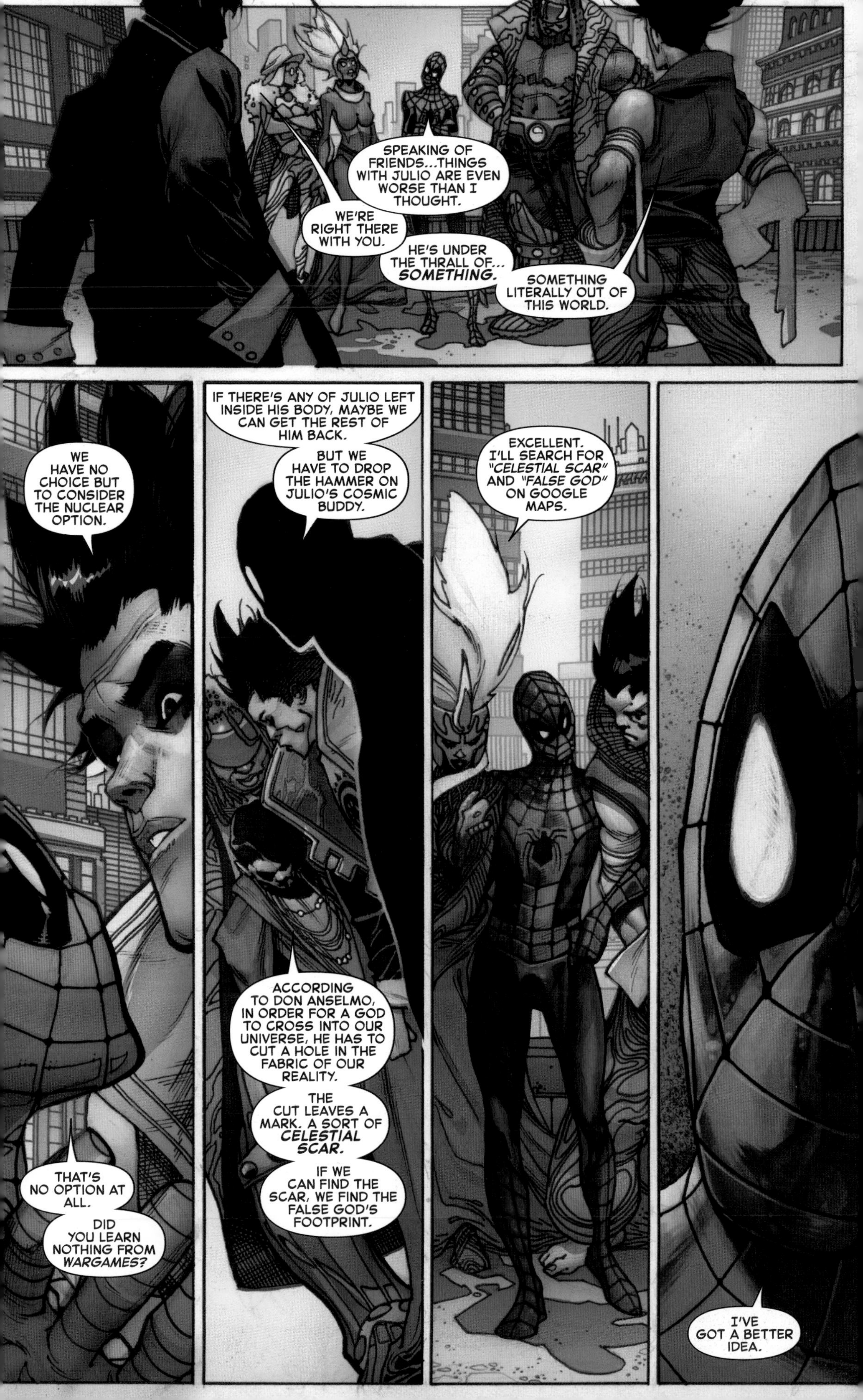
SPEAKING OF FRIENDS...THINGS WITH JULIO ARE EVEN WORSE THAN I THOUGHT.
WE'RE RIGHT THERE WITH YOU.
HE'S UNDER THE THRALL OF... SOMETHING.
SOMETHING LITERALLY OUT OF THIS WORLD.
WE HAVE NO CHOICE BUT TO CONSIDER THE NUCLEAR OPTION.
THAT'S NO OPTION AT ALL.
DID YOU LEARN NOTHING FROM WARGAMES?
IF THERE'S ANY OF JULIO LEFT INSIDE HIS BODY, MAYBE WE CAN GET THE REST OF HIM BACK.
BUT WE HAVE TO DROP THE HAMMER ON JULIO'S COSMIC BUDDY.
ACCORDING TO DON ANSELMO, IN ORDER FOR A GOD TO CROSS INTO OUR UNIVERSE, HE HAS TO CUT A HOLE IN THE FABRIC OF OUR REALITY.
THE CUT LEAVES A MARK. A SORT OF CELESTIAL SCAR.
IF WE CAN FIND THE SCAR, WE FIND THE FALSE GOD'S FOOTPRINT.
EXCELLENT. I'LL SEARCH FOR "CELESTIAL SCAR" AND "FALSE GOD" ON GOOGLE MAPS.
I'VE GOT A BETTER IDEA.

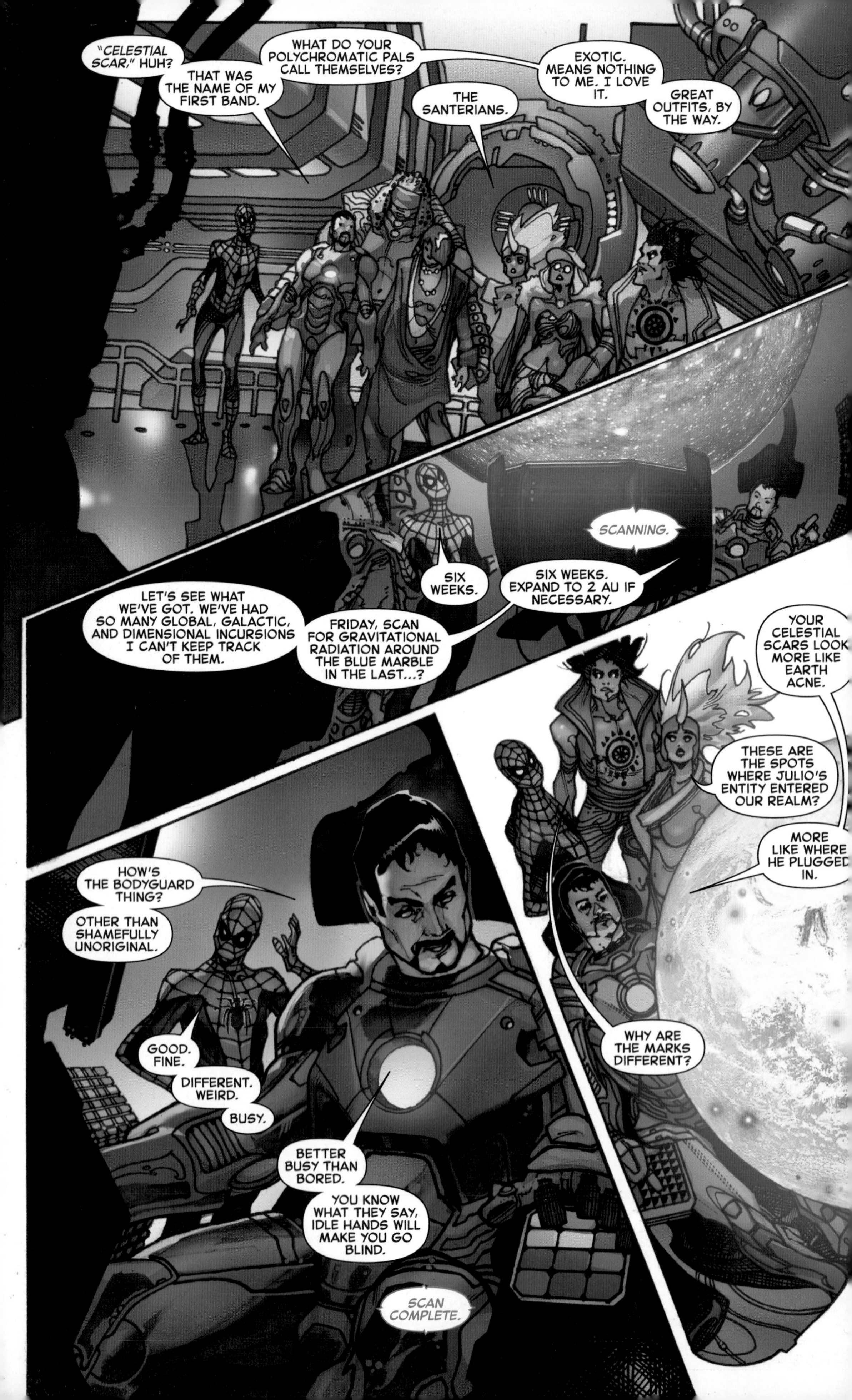
"CELESTIAL SCAR," HUH?
THAT WAS THE NAME OF MY FIRST BAND.
WHAT DO YOUR POLYCHROMATIC PALS CALL THEMSELVES?
THE SANTERIANS.
EXOTIC. MEANS NOTHING TO ME. I LOVE IT.
GREAT OUTFITS, BY THE WAY.
LET'S SEE WHAT WE'VE GOT. WE'VE HAD SO MANY GLOBAL, GALACTIC, AND DIMENSIONAL INCURSIONS I CAN'T KEEP TRACK OF THEM.
FRIDAY, SCAN FOR GRAVITATIONAL RADIATION AROUND THE BLUE MARBLE IN THE LAST...?
SIX WEEKS.
SIX WEEKS. EXPAND TO 2 AU IF NECESSARY.
SCANNING.
HOW'S THE BODYGUARD THING?
OTHER THAN SHAMEFULLY UNORIGINAL.
GOOD. FINE.
DIFFERENT. WEIRD.
BUSY.
BETTER BUSY THAN BORED.
YOU KNOW WHAT THEY SAY, IDLE HANDS WILL MAKE YOU GO BLIND.
SCAN COMPLETE.
YOUR CELESTIAL SCARS LOOK MORE LIKE EARTH ACNE.
THESE ARE THE SPOTS WHERE JULIO'S ENTITY ENTERED OUR REALM?
MORE LIKE WHERE HE PLUGGED IN.
WHY ARE THE MARKS DIFFERENT?

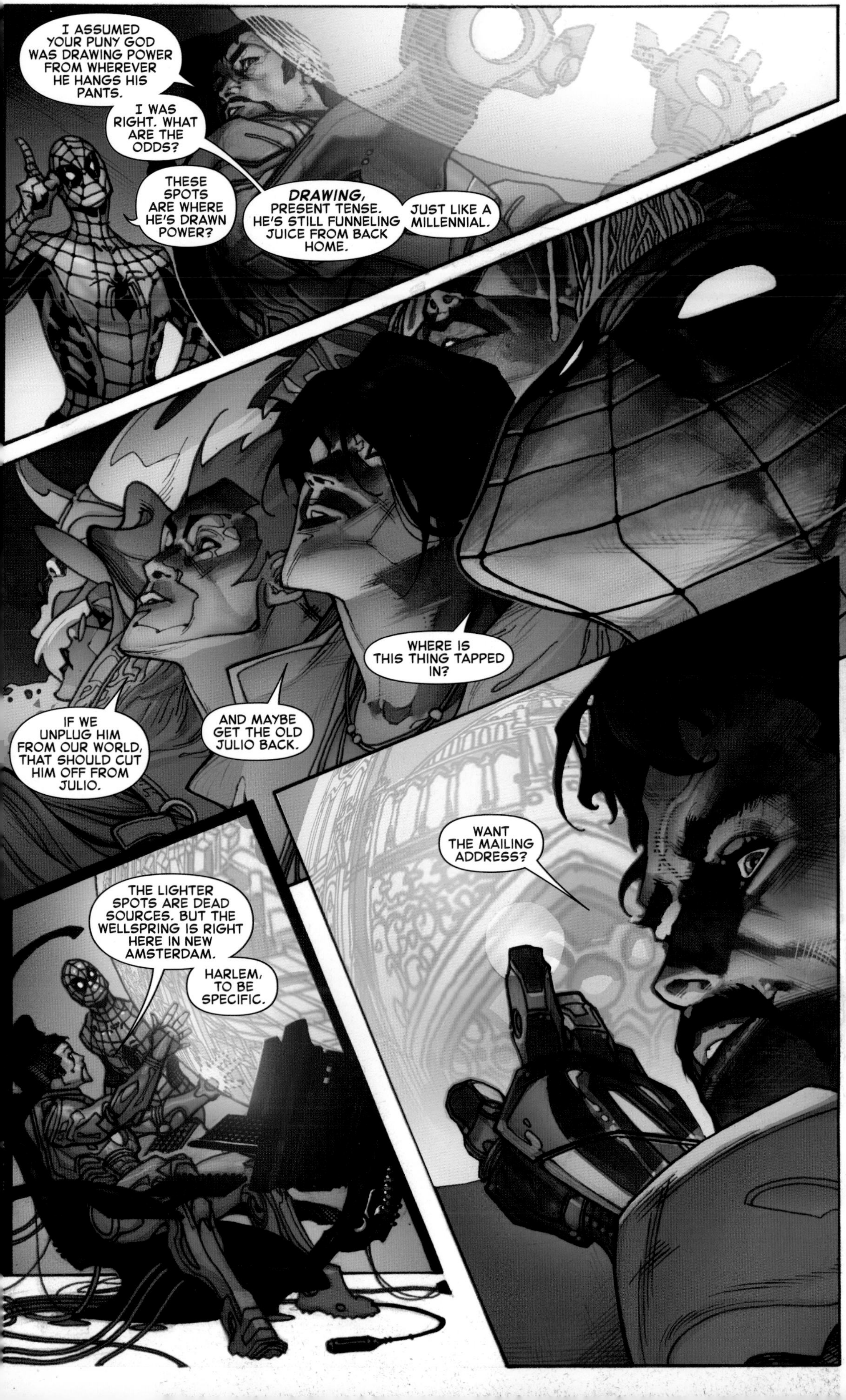
I ASSUMED YOUR PUNY GOD WAS DRAWING POWER FROM WHEREVER HE HANGS HIS PANTS.
I WAS RIGHT. WHAT ARE THE ODDS?
THESE SPOTS ARE WHERE HE'S DRAWN POWER?
DRAWING, PRESENT TENSE. HE'S STILL FUNNELING JUICE FROM BACK HOME.
JUST LIKE A MILLENNIAL.
WHERE IS THIS THING TAPPED IN?
IF WE UNPLUG HIM FROM OUR WORLD, THAT SHOULD CUT HIM OFF FROM JULIO.
AND MAYBE GET THE OLD JULIO BACK.
WANT THE MAILING ADDRESS?
THE LIGHTER SPOTS ARE DEAD SOURCES. BUT THE WELLSPRING IS RIGHT HERE IN NEW AMSTERDAM.
HARLEM, TO BE SPECIFIC.

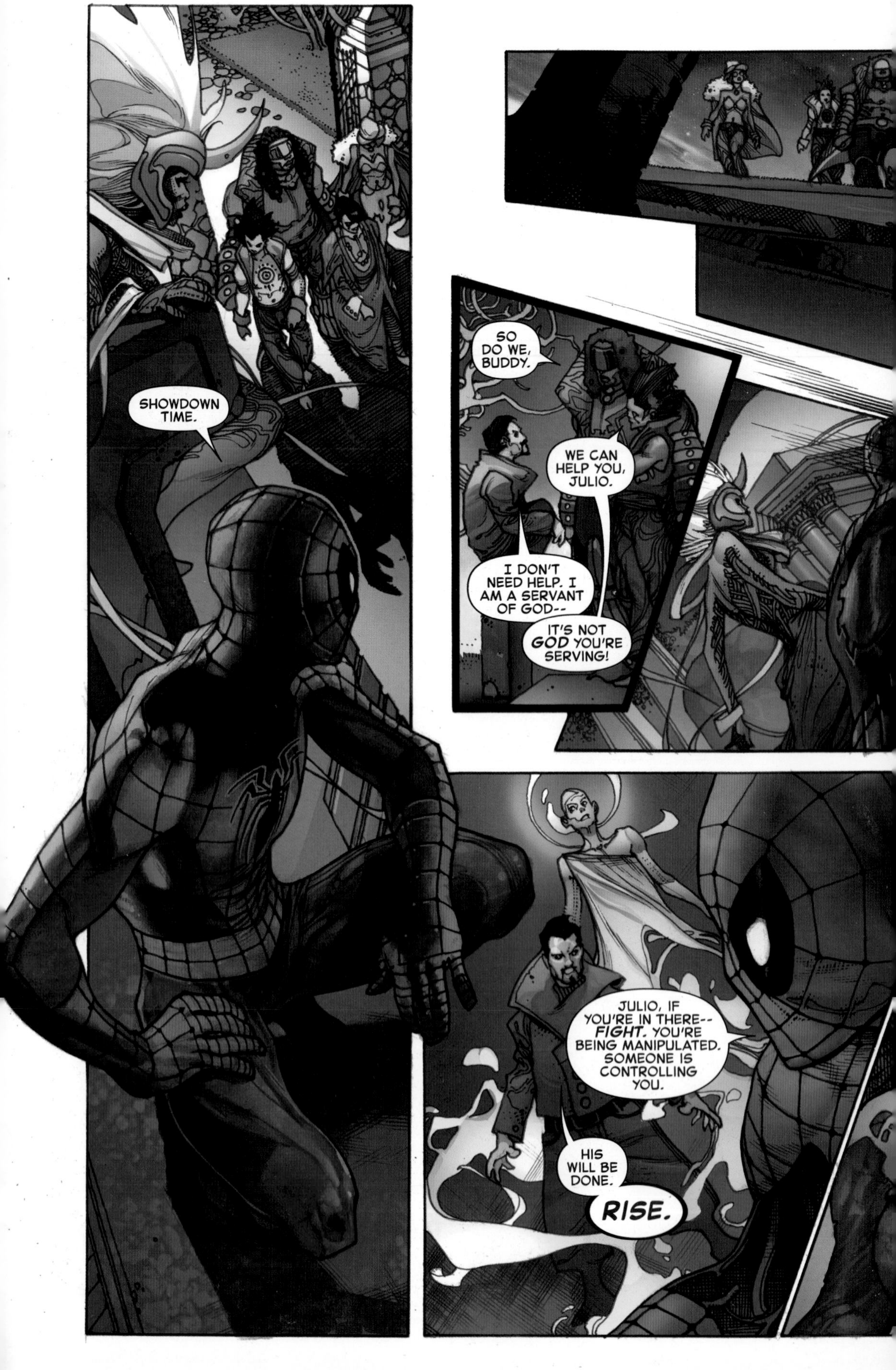
SHOWDOWN TIME.
SO DO WE, BUDDY.
WE CAN HELP YOU, JULIO.
I DON'T NEED HELP. I AM A SERVANT OF GOD--
IT'S NOT GOD YOU'RE SERVING!
JULIO, IF YOU'RE IN THERE-- FIGHT. YOU'RE BEING MANIPULATED. SOMEONE IS CONTROLLING YOU.
HIS WILL BE DONE.
RISE.

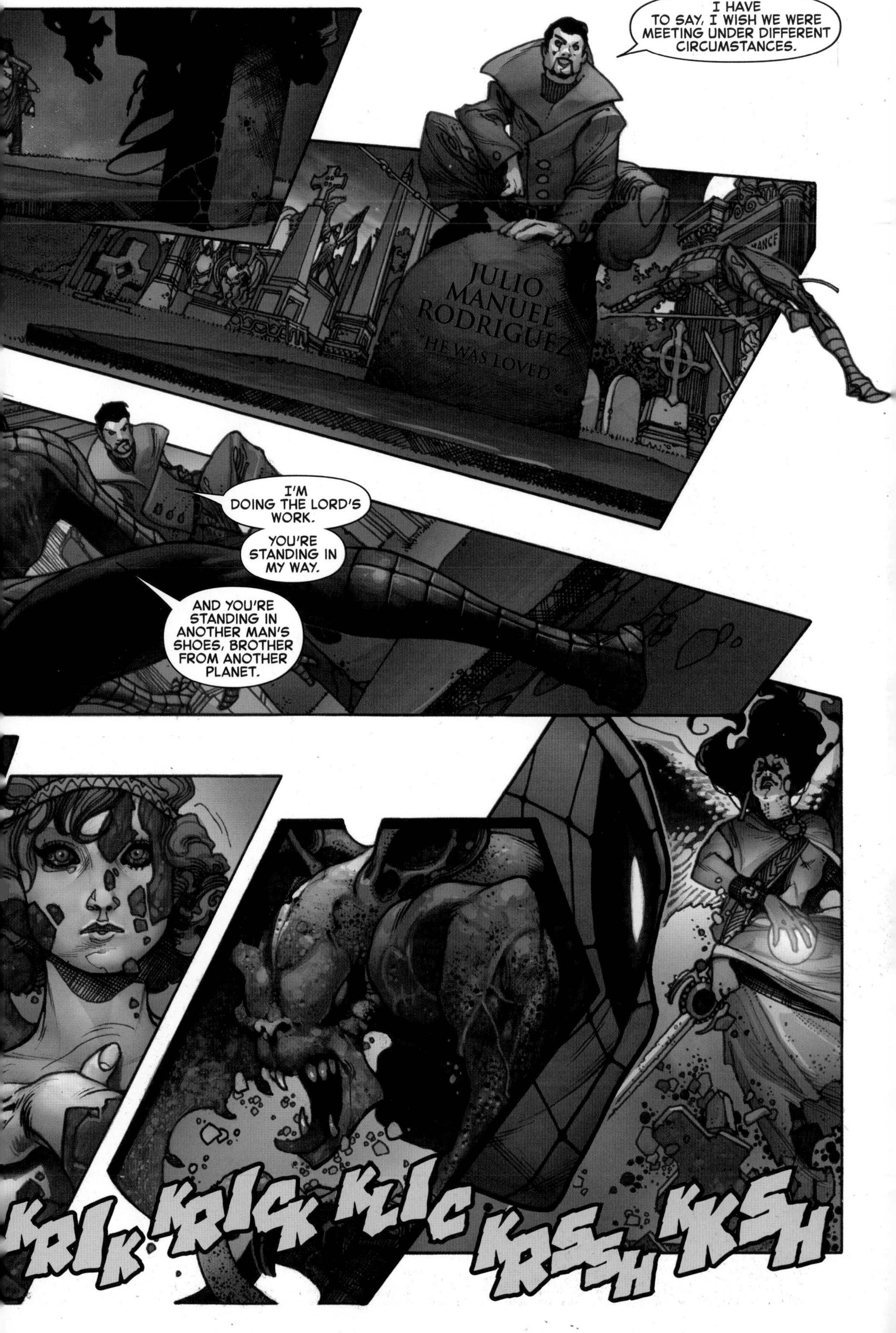
RIGHT ON TIME.
I HAVE TO SAY, I WISH WE WERE MEETING UNDER DIFFERENT CIRCUMSTANCES.
JULIO MANUEL RODRIGUEZ "HE WAS LOVED"
I'M DOING THE LORD'S WORK.
YOU'RE STANDING IN MY WAY.
AND YOU'RE STANDING IN ANOTHER MAN'S SHOES, BROTHER FROM ANOTHER PLANET.
KRIK KRICK KLIC KRSSH KKSH

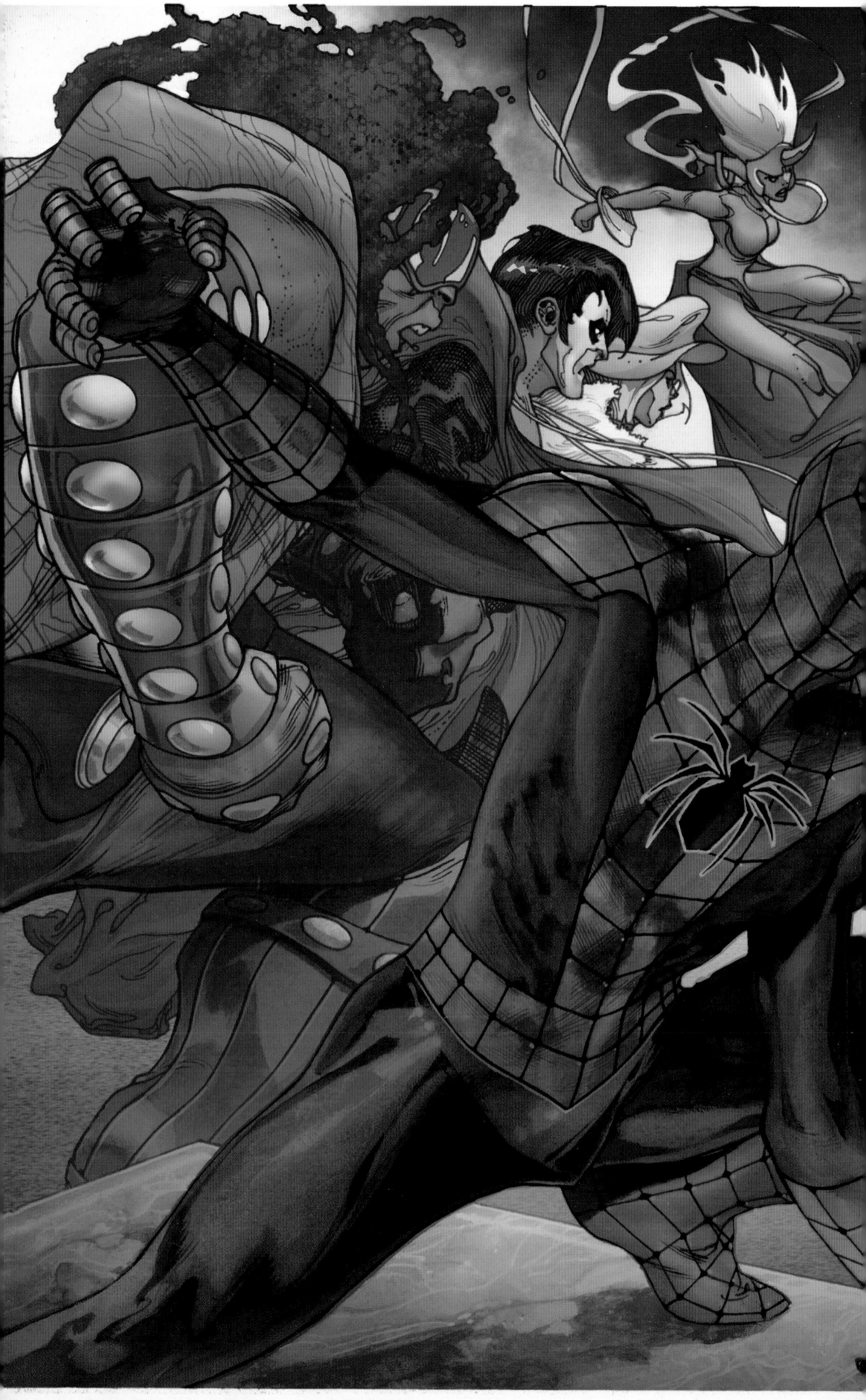

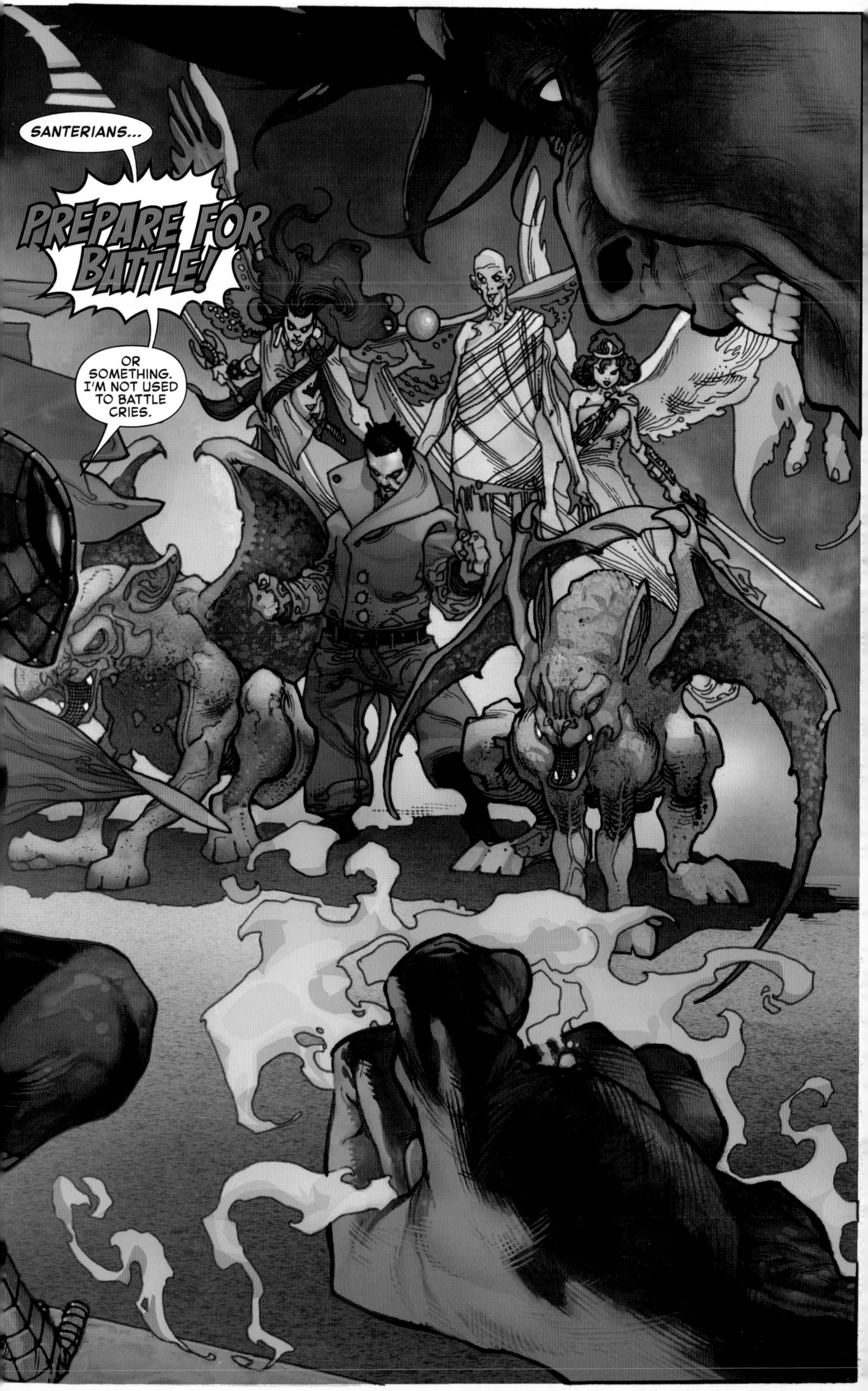
SANTERIANS...
PREPARE FOR BATTLE!
OR SOMETHING. I'M NOT USED TO BATTLE CRIES.

MARVEL GRAPHIC NOVEL AMAZING SPIDER-MAN VOL 5 #1.6

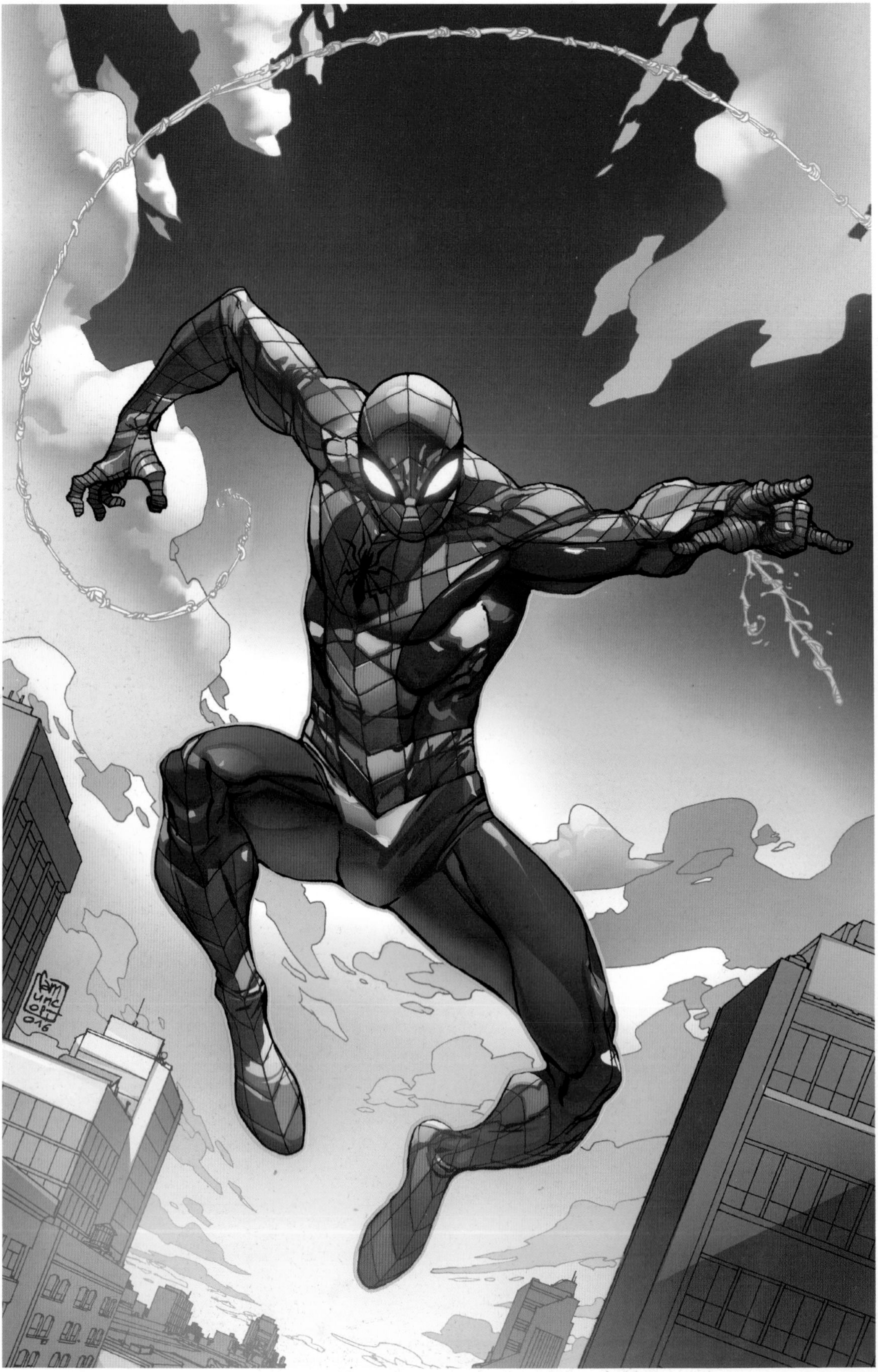

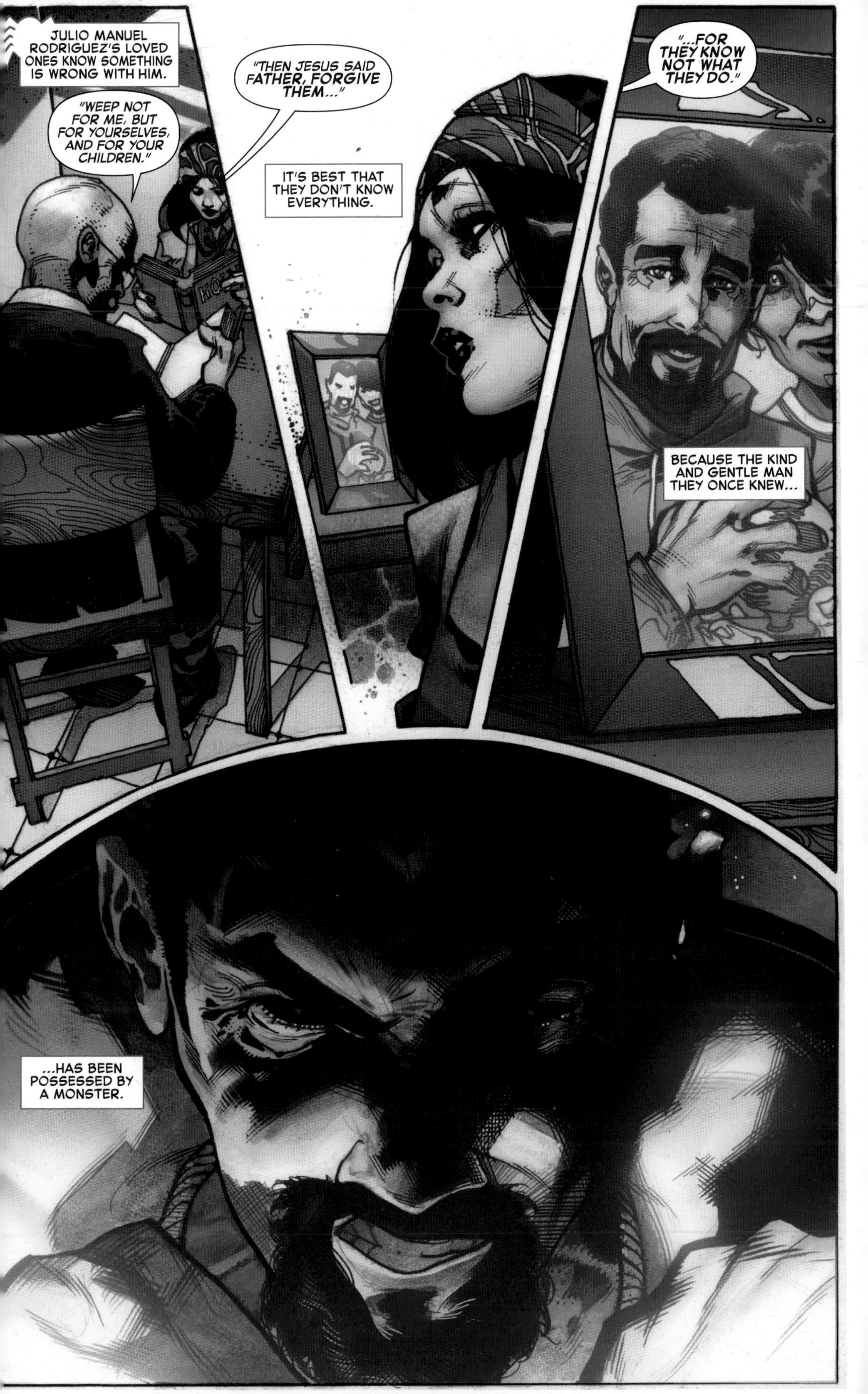
JULIO MANUEL RODRIGUEZ'S LOVED ONES KNOW SOMETHING IS WRONG WITH HIM.
"WEEP NOT FOR ME, BUT FOR YOURSELVES, AND FOR YOUR CHILDREN."
"THEN JESUS SAID FATHER, FORGIVE THEM..."
IT'S BEST THAT THEY DON'T KNOW EVERYTHING.
"...FOR THEY KNOW NOT WHAT THEY DO."
BECAUSE THE KIND AND GENTLE MAN THEY ONCE KNEW...
...HAS BEEN POSSESSED BY A MONSTER.

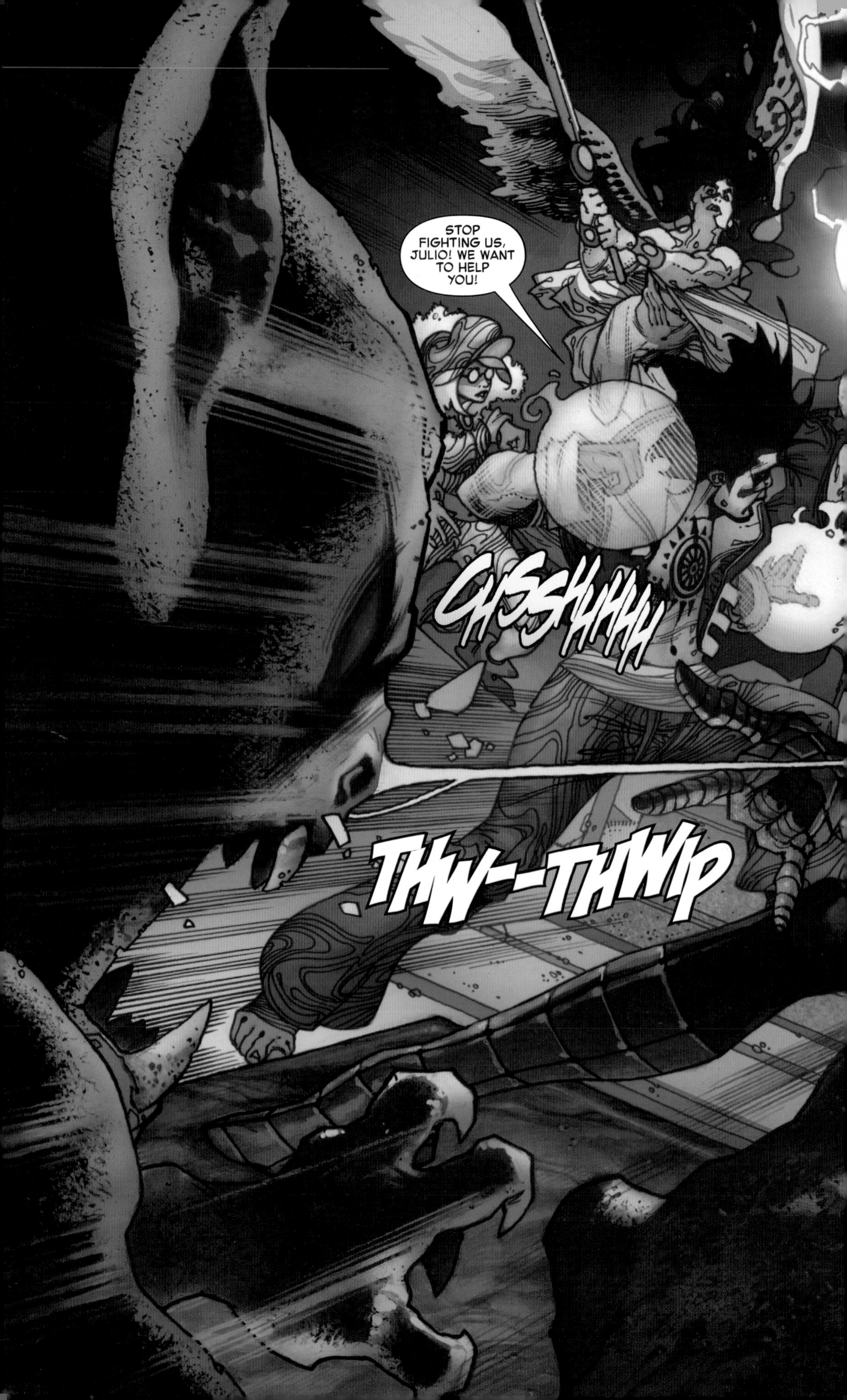
STOP FIGHTING US, JULIO! WE WANT TO HELP YOU!
CHSSHHHH
THW--THWIP

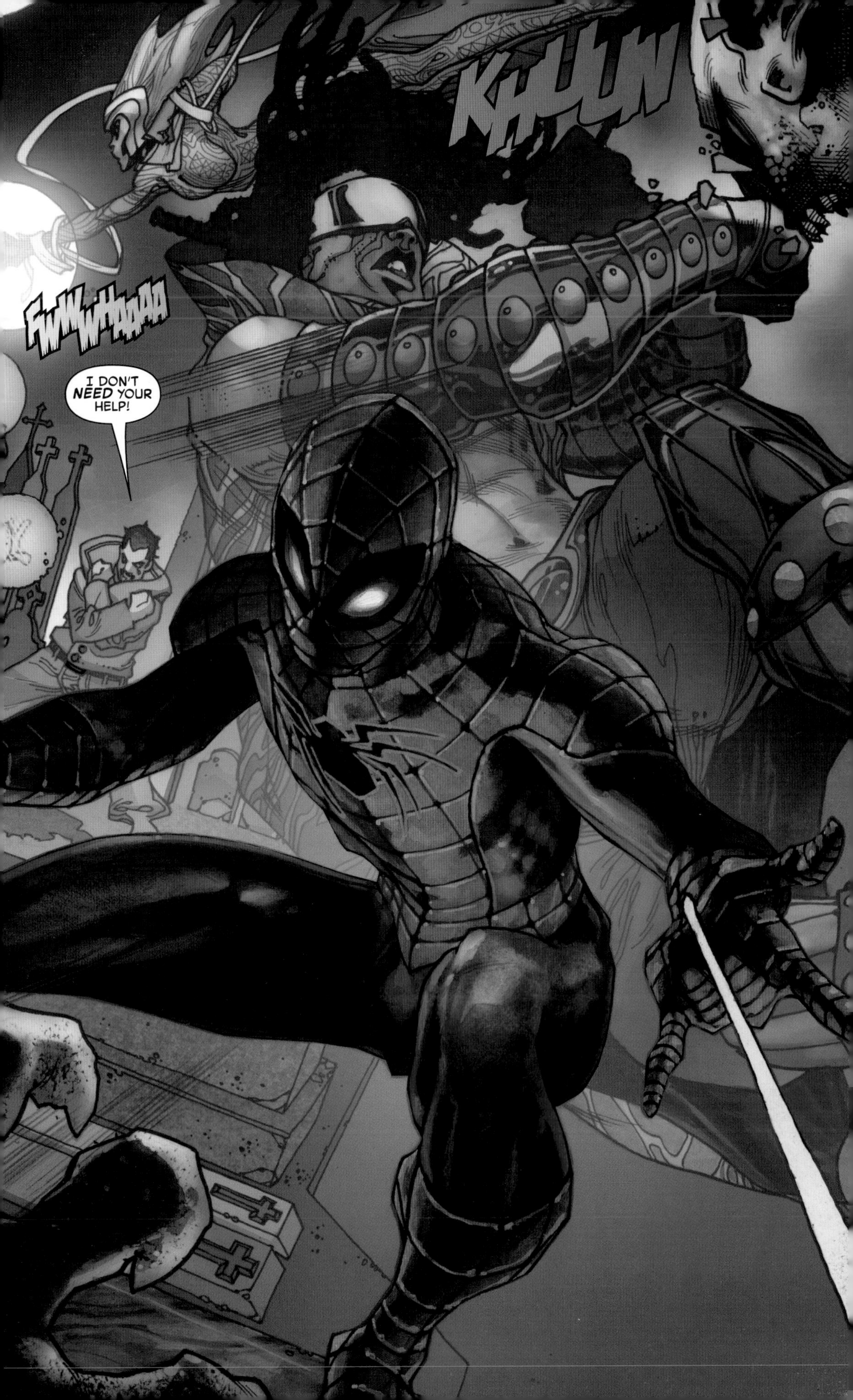
KHUUN
FWWWHAAAA
I DON'T NEED YOUR HELP!

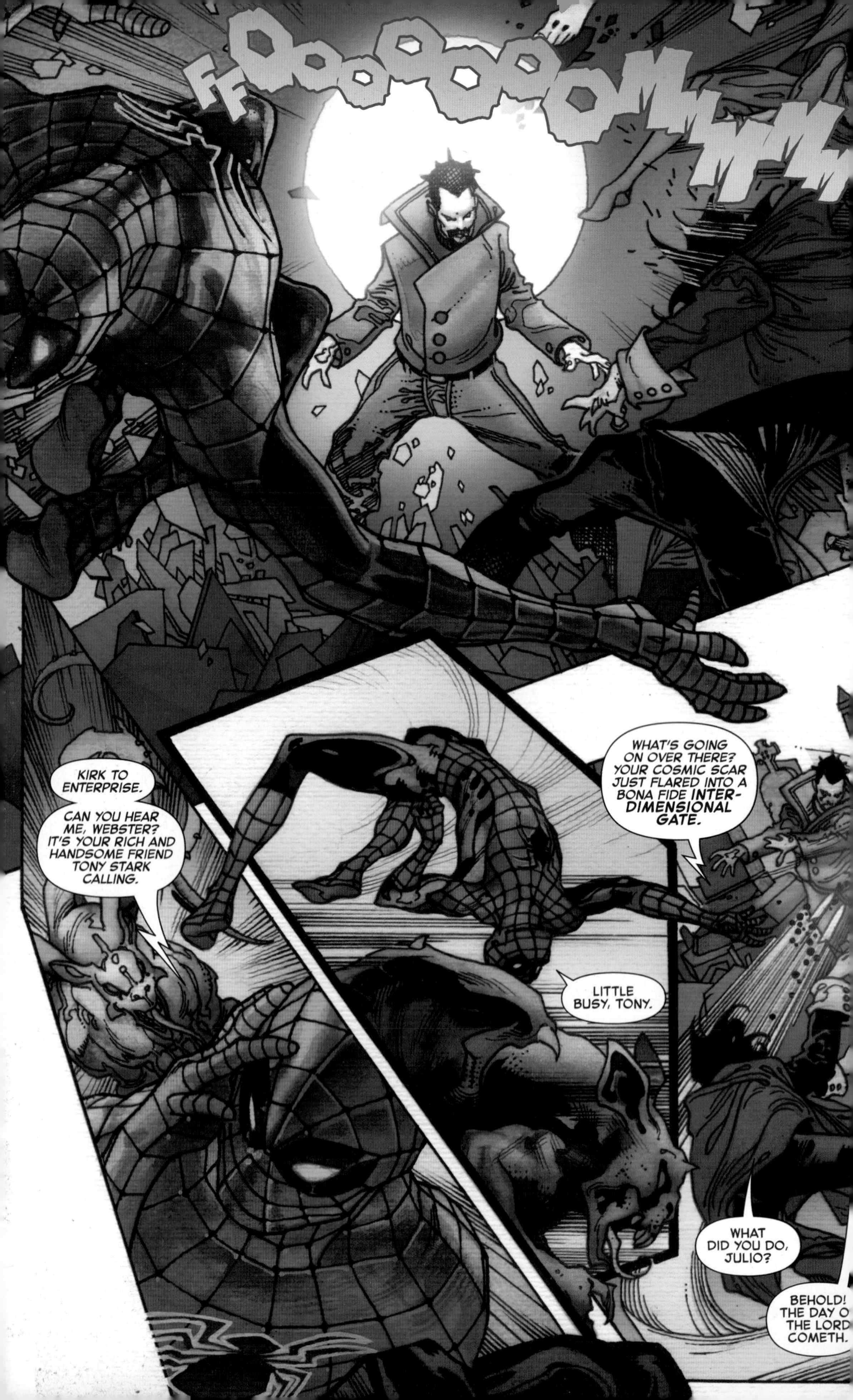
FFOOOOOOOOOMMMMM
KIRK TO ENTERPRISE.
CAN YOU HEAR ME, WEBSTER? IT'S YOUR RICH AND HANDSOME FRIEND TONY STARK CALLING.
WHAT'S GOING ON OVER THERE? YOUR COSMIC SCAR JUST FLARED INTO A BONA FIDE INTER-DIMENSIONAL GATE.
LITTLE BUSY, TONY.
WHAT DID YOU DO, JULIO?
BEHOLD! THE DAY O THE LORD COMETH.

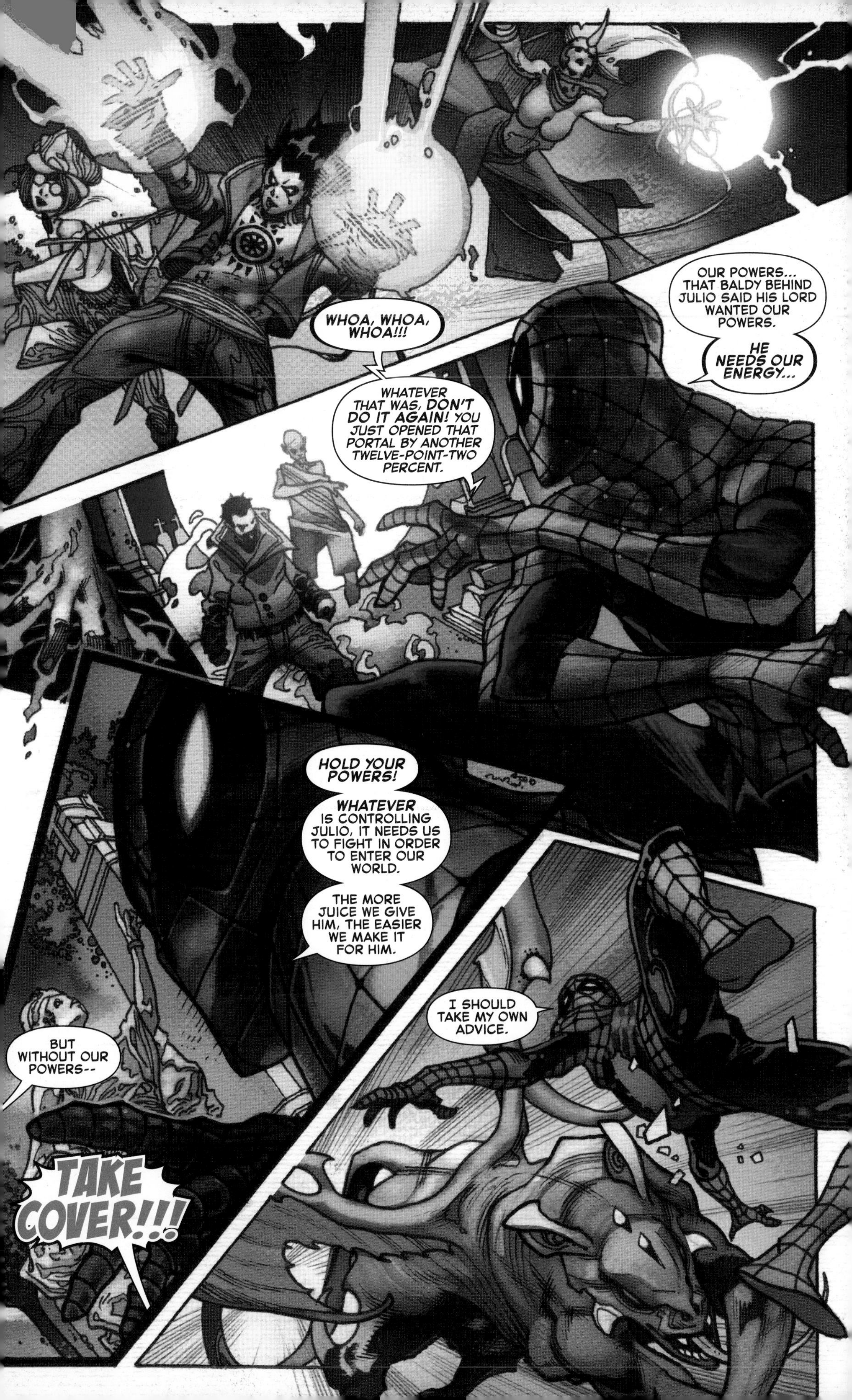
WHOA, WHOA, WHOA!!!
OUR POWERS... THAT BALDY BEHIND JULIO SAID HIS LORD WANTED OUR POWERS.
HE NEEDS OUR ENERGY...
WHATEVER THAT WAS, DON'T DO IT AGAIN! YOU JUST OPENED THAT PORTAL BY ANOTHER TWELVE-POINT-TWO PERCENT.
HOLD YOUR POWERS!
WHATEVER IS CONTROLLING JULIO, IT NEEDS US TO FIGHT IN ORDER TO ENTER OUR WORLD.
THE MORE JUICE WE GIVE HIM, THE EASIER WE MAKE IT FOR HIM.
BUT WITHOUT OUR POWERS--
TAKE COVER!!!
I SHOULD TAKE MY OWN ADVICE.

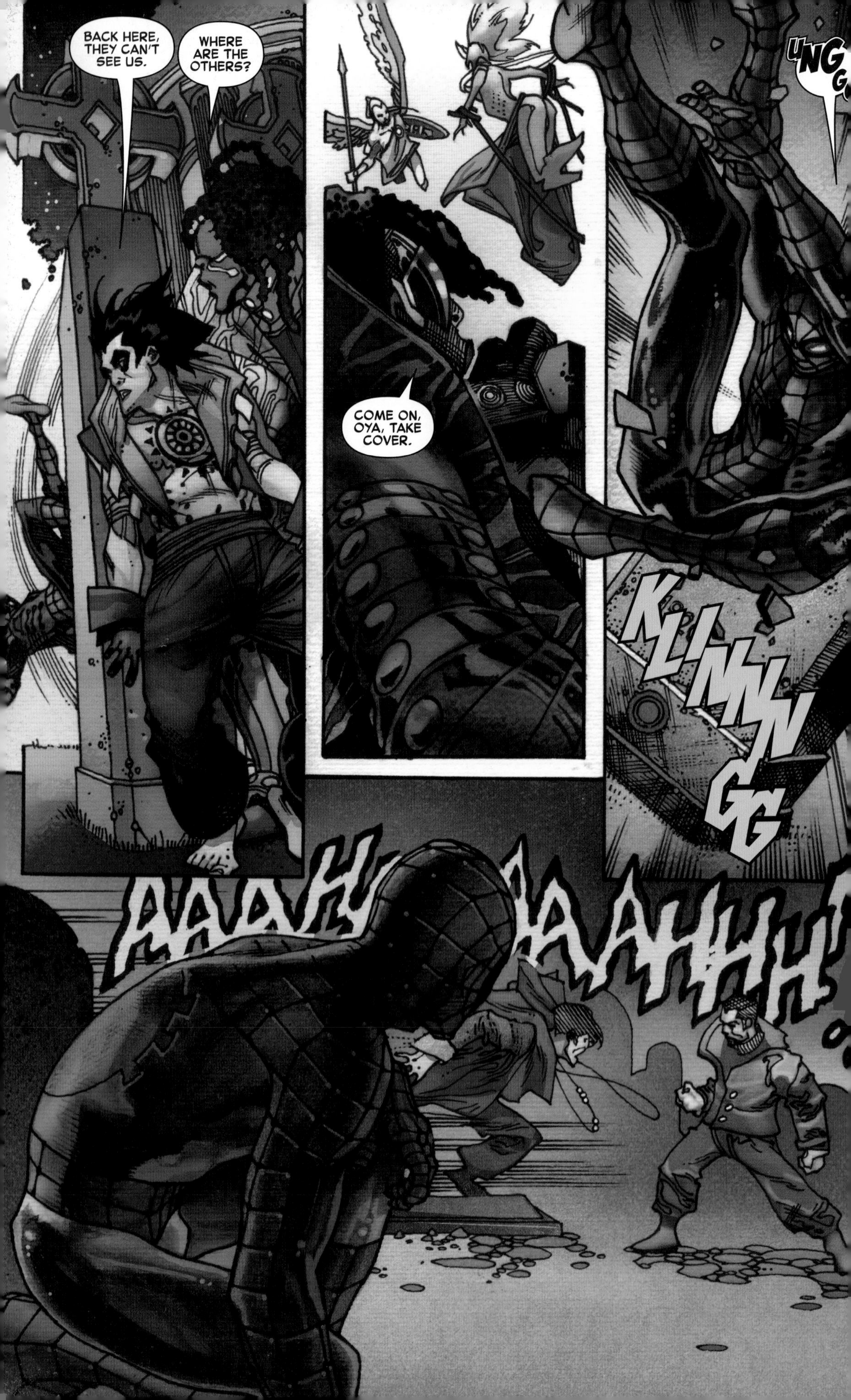
BACK HERE, THEY CAN'T SEE US.
WHERE ARE THE OTHERS?
COME ON, OYA, TAKE COVER.
UNG
KLIMMNGG
AAAHHAAAHHH!

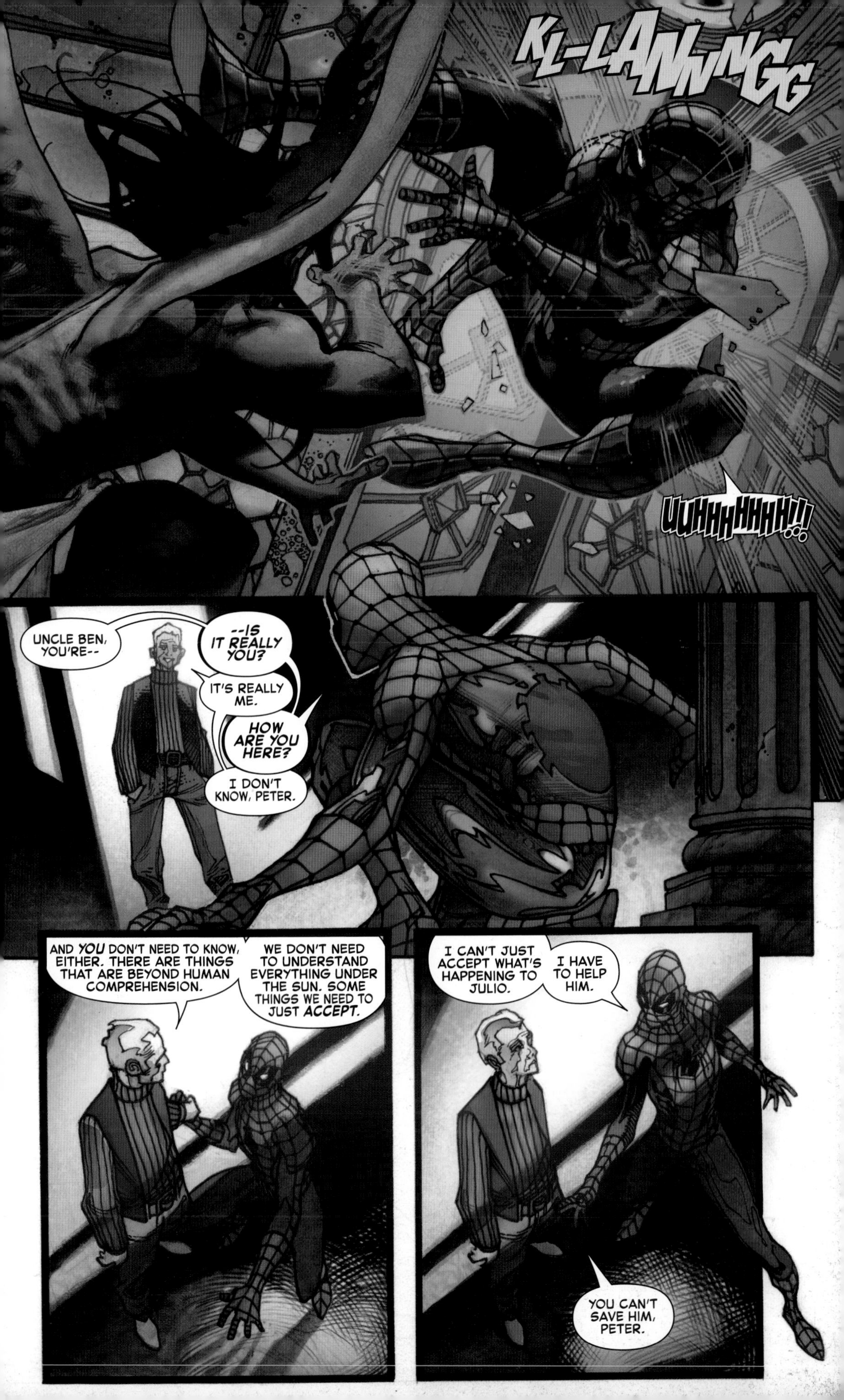
KL-LANNNGG
UUHHHHHHH!!!
UNCLE BEN, YOU'RE--
--IS IT REALLY YOU?
IT'S REALLY ME.
HOW ARE YOU HERE?
I DON'T KNOW, PETER.
AND YOU DON'T NEED TO KNOW, EITHER. THERE ARE THINGS THAT ARE BEYOND HUMAN COMPREHENSION.
WE DON'T NEED TO UNDERSTAND EVERYTHING UNDER THE SUN. SOME THINGS WE NEED TO JUST ACCEPT.
I CAN'T JUST ACCEPT WHAT'S HAPPENING TO JULIO.
I HAVE TO HELP HIM.
YOU CAN'T SAVE HIM, PETER.

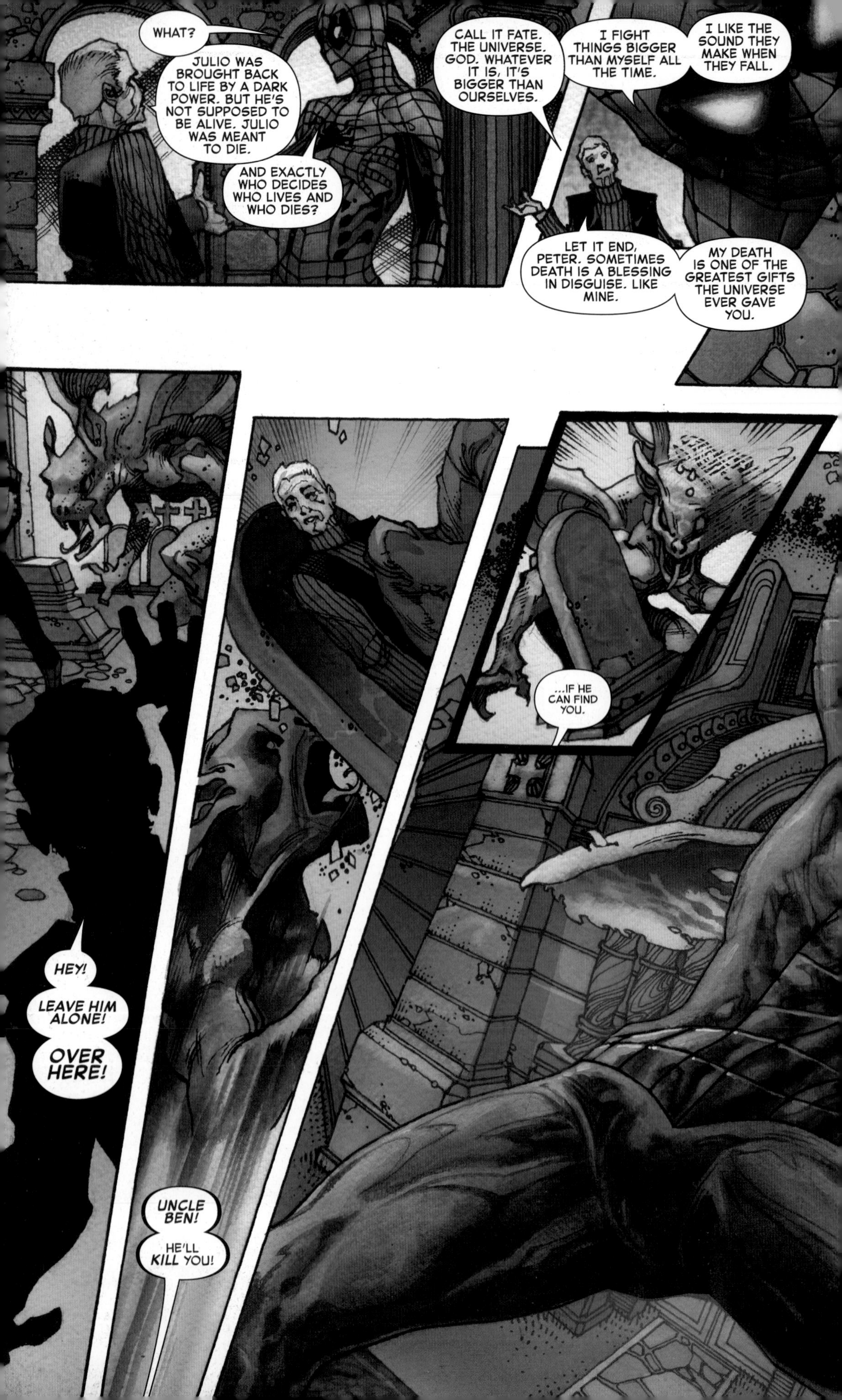
WHAT?
JULIO WAS BROUGHT BACK TO LIFE BY A DARK POWER. BUT HE'S NOT SUPPOSED TO BE ALIVE. JULIO WAS MEANT TO DIE.
AND EXACTLY WHO DECIDES WHO LIVES AND WHO DIES?
CALL IT FATE. THE UNIVERSE. GOD. WHATEVER IT IS, IT'S BIGGER THAN OURSELVES.
I FIGHT THINGS BIGGER THAN MYSELF ALL THE TIME.
I LIKE THE SOUND THEY MAKE WHEN THEY FALL.
LET IT END, PETER. SOMETIMES DEATH IS A BLESSING IN DISGUISE. LIKE MINE.
MY DEATH IS ONE OF THE GREATEST GIFTS THE UNIVERSE EVER GAVE YOU.
HEY!
LEAVE HIM ALONE!
OVER HERE!
...IF HE CAN FIND YOU.
UNCLE BEN!
HE'LL KILL YOU!

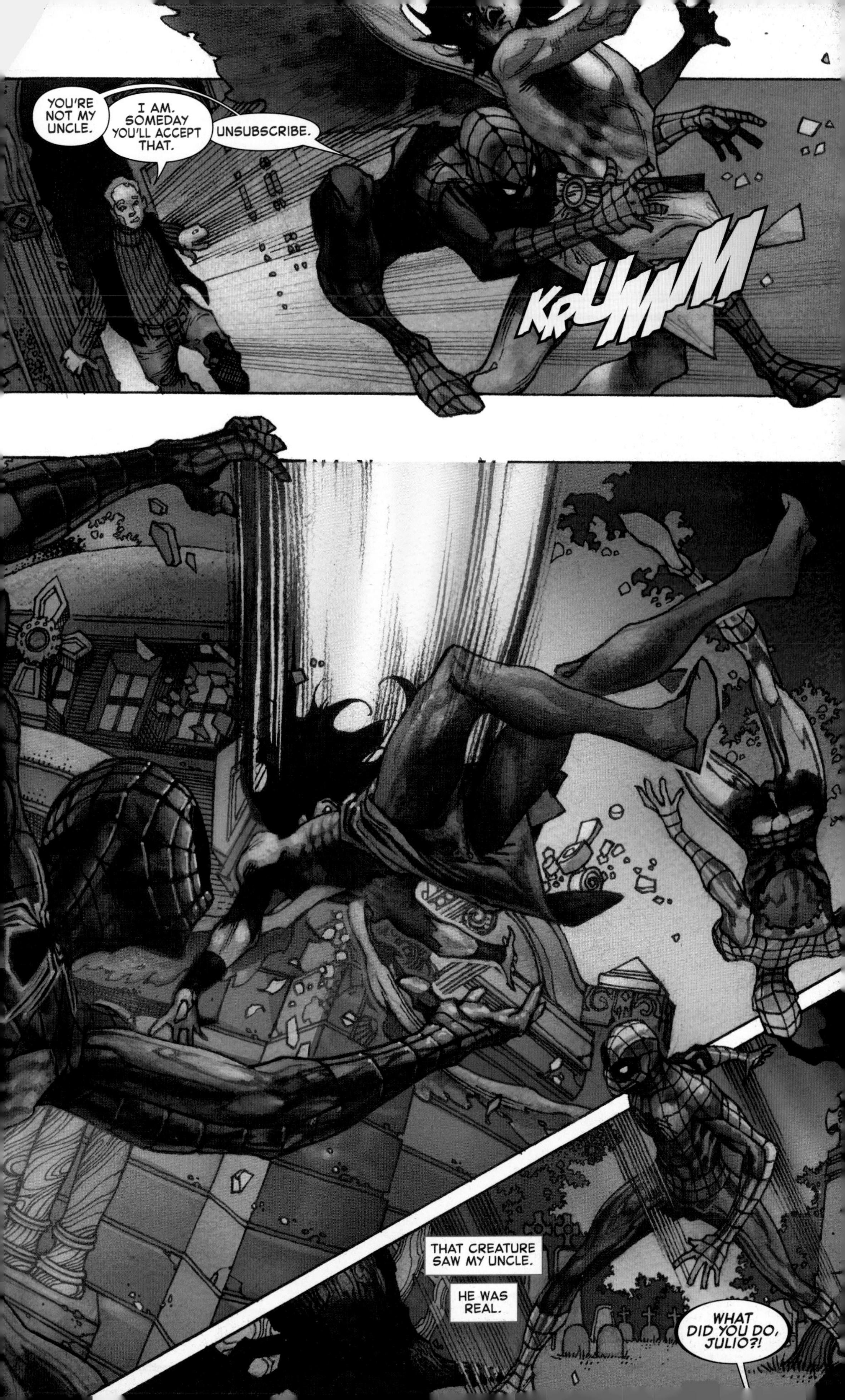
YOU'RE NOT MY UNCLE.
I AM. SOMEDAY YOU'LL ACCEPT THAT.
UNSUBSCRIBE.
KRUMMM
THAT CREATURE SAW MY UNCLE.
HE WAS REAL.
WHAT DID YOU DO, JULIO?!

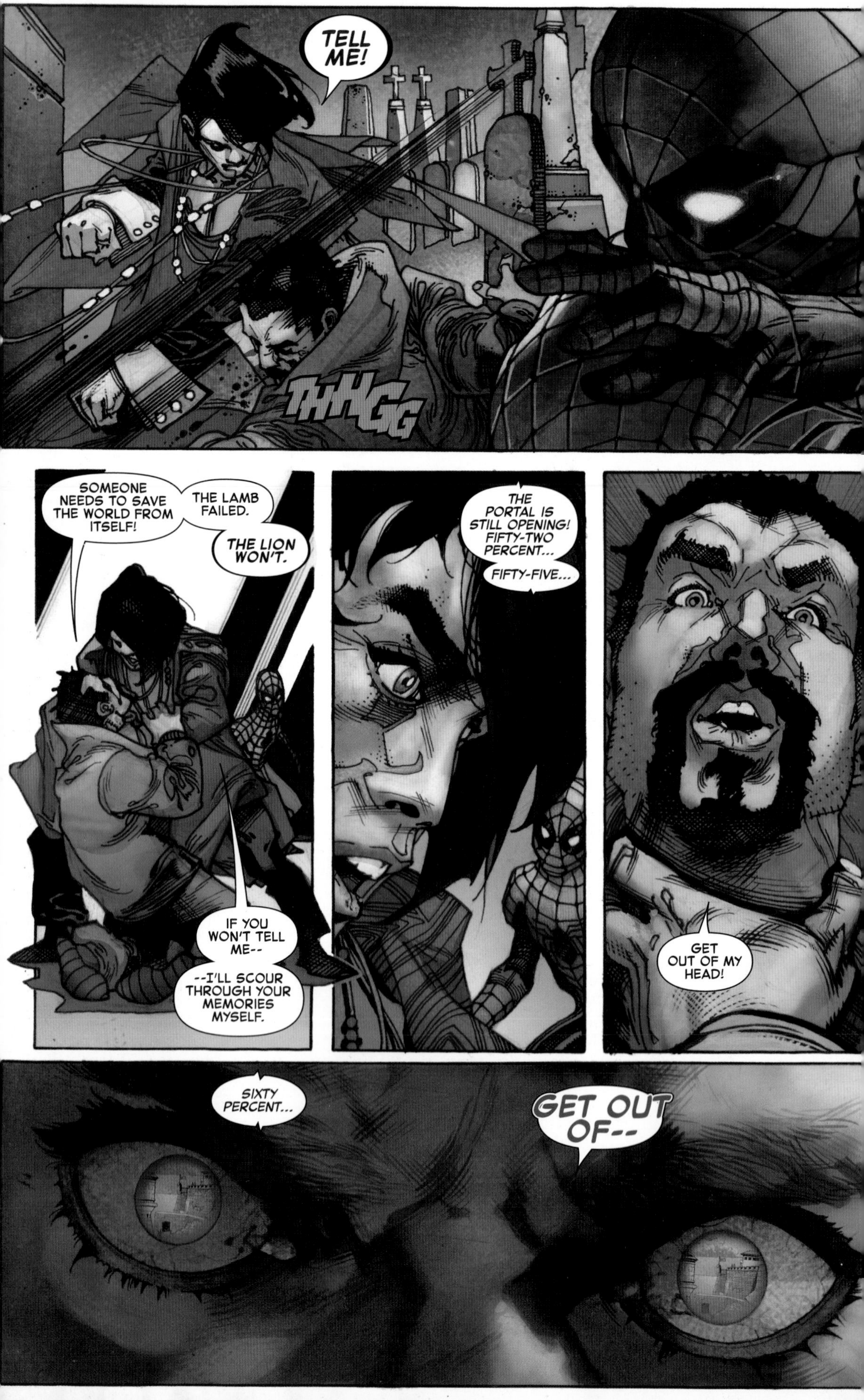
TELL ME!
THHGG
SOMEONE NEEDS TO SAVE THE WORLD FROM ITSELF!
THE LAMB FAILED.
THE LION WON'T.
IF YOU WON'T TELL ME--
--I'LL SCOUR THROUGH YOUR MEMORIES MYSELF.
THE PORTAL IS STILL OPENING! FIFTY-TWO PERCENT...
FIFTY-FIVE...
GET OUT OF MY HEAD!
SIXTY PERCENT...
GET OUT OF--

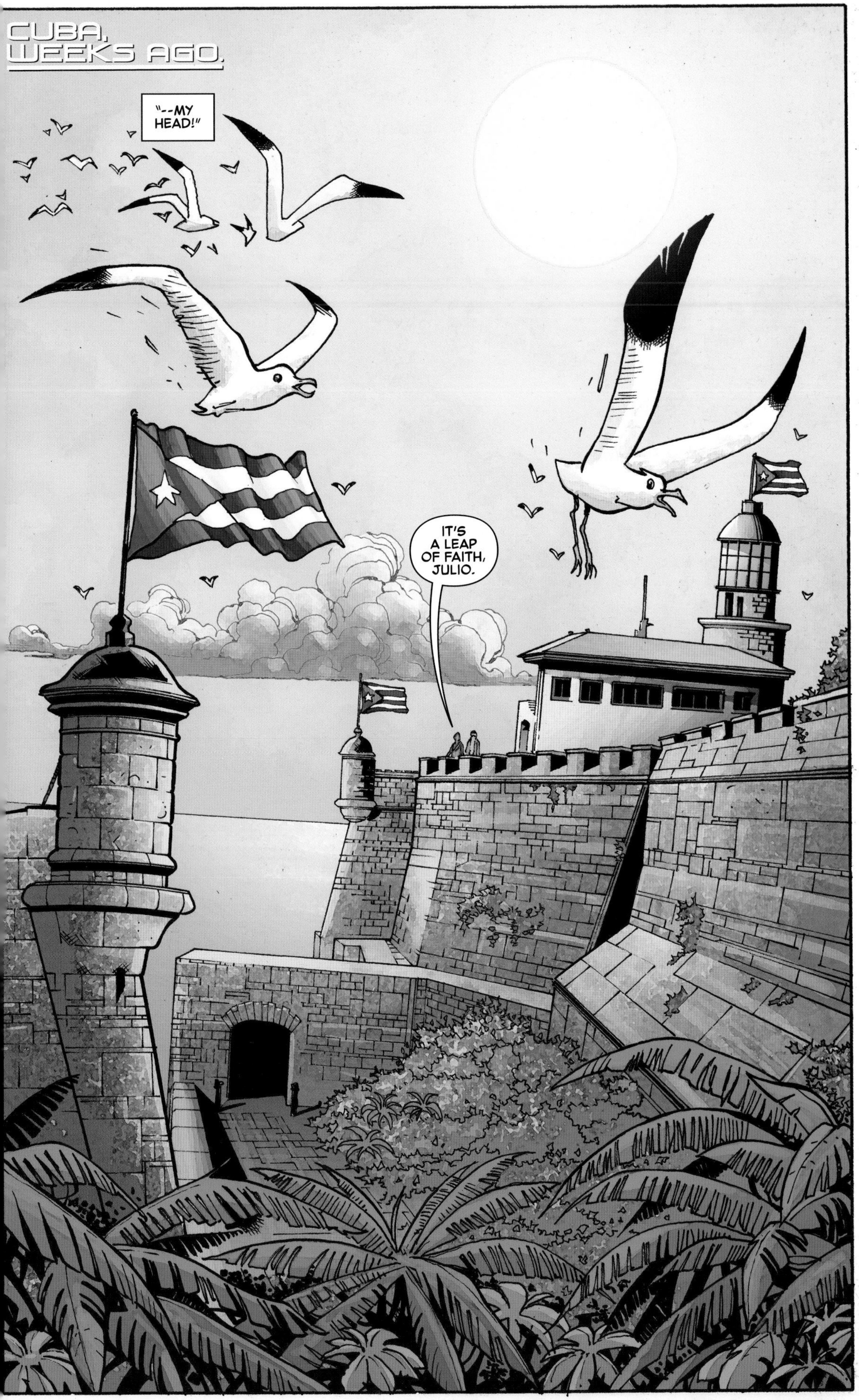
CUBA,
WEEKS AGO.
"--MY HEAD!"
IT'S A LEAP OF FAITH, JULIO.

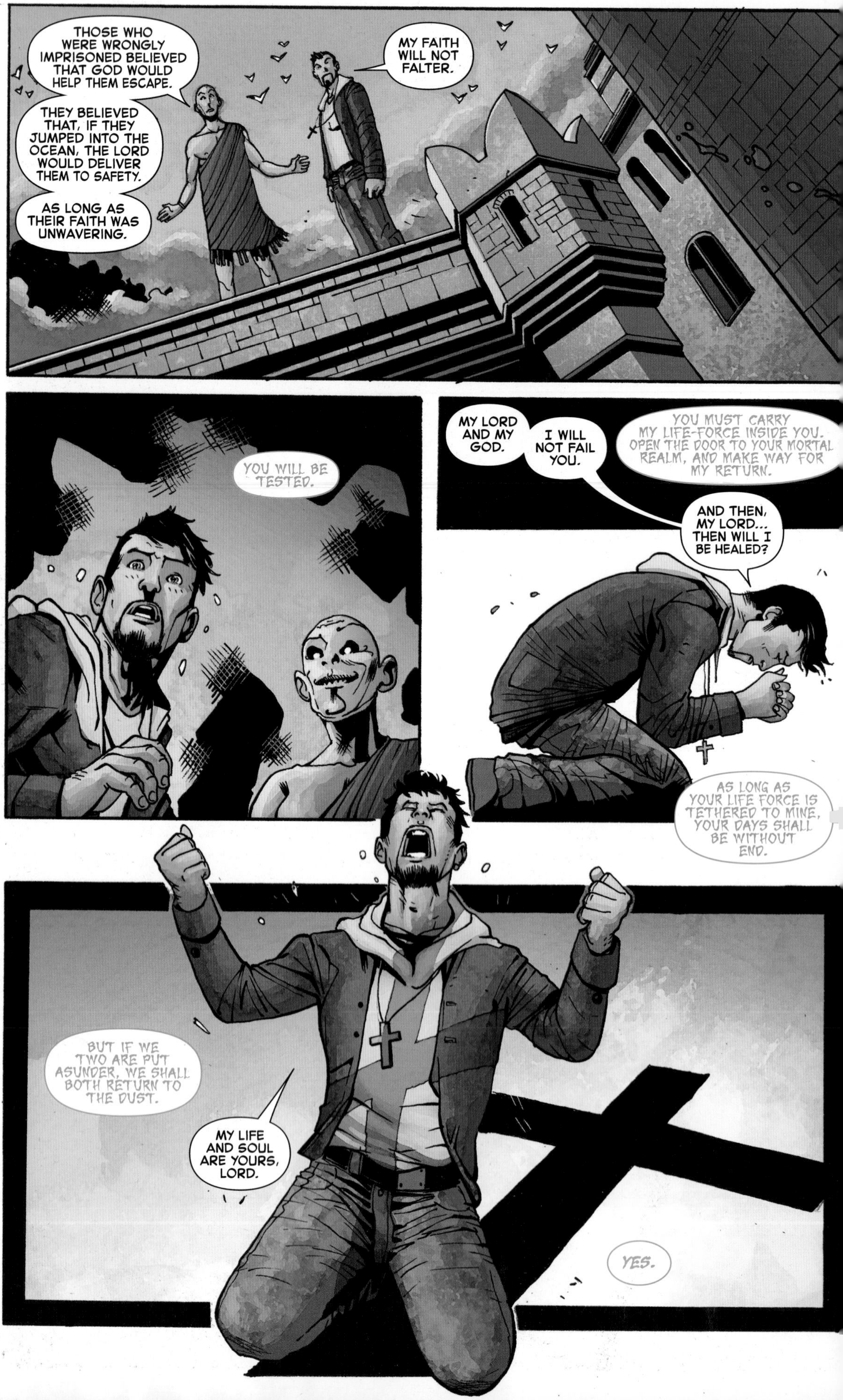
THOSE WHO WERE WRONGLY IMPRISONED BELIEVED THAT GOD WOULD HELP THEM ESCAPE.
THEY BELIEVED THAT, IF THEY JUMPED INTO THE OCEAN, THE LORD WOULD DELIVER THEM TO SAFETY.
AS LONG AS THEIR FAITH WAS UNWAVERING.
MY FAITH WILL NOT FALTER.
YOU WILL BE TESTED.
MY LORD AND MY GOD.
I WILL NOT FAIL YOU.
YOU MUST CARRY MY LIFE-FORCE INSIDE YOU. OPEN THE DOOR TO YOUR MORTAL REALM, AND MAKE WAY FOR MY RETURN.
AND THEN, MY LORD... THEN WILL I BE HEALED?
AS LONG AS YOUR LIFE FORCE IS TETHERED TO MINE, YOUR DAYS SHALL BE WITHOUT END.
BUT IF WE TWO ARE PUT ASUNDER, WE SHALL BOTH RETURN TO THE DUST.
MY LIFE AND SOUL ARE YOURS, LORD.
YES.

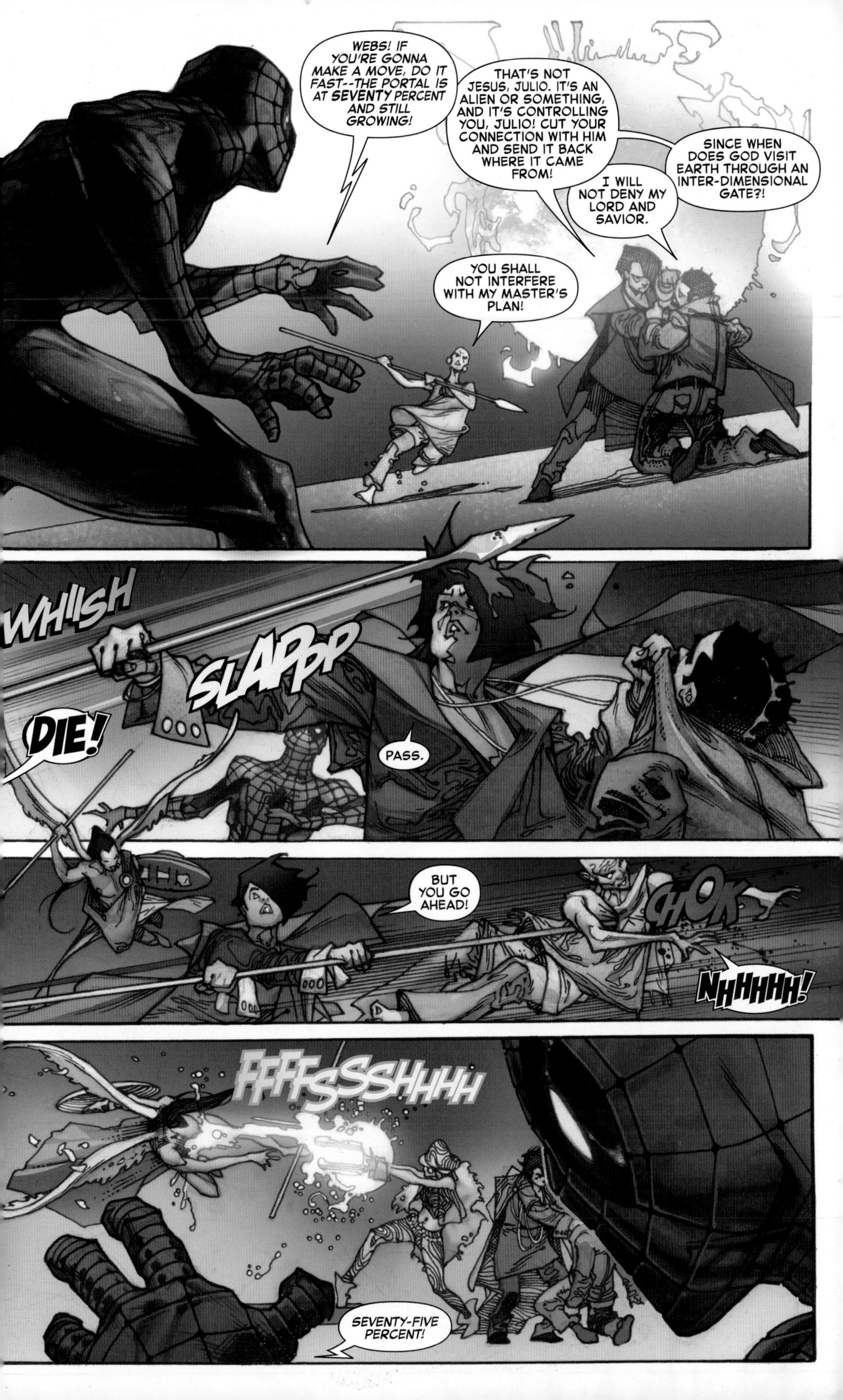

WEBS! IF YOU'RE GONNA MAKE A MOVE, DO IT FAST--THE PORTAL IS AT SEVENTY PERCENT AND STILL GROWING!
THAT'S NOT JESUS, JULIO. IT'S AN ALIEN OR SOMETHING, AND IT'S CONTROLLING YOU, JULIO! CUT YOUR CONNECTION WITH HIM AND SEND IT BACK WHERE IT CAME FROM!
SINCE WHEN DOES GOD VISIT EARTH THROUGH AN INTER-DIMENSIONAL GATE?!
I WILL NOT DENY MY LORD AND SAVIOR.
YOU SHALL NOT INTERFERE WITH MY MASTER'S PLAN!
WHIISH
SLAPPP
DIE!
PASS.
BUT YOU GO AHEAD!
CHOK
NHHHHH!
FFFFSSSHHHH
SEVENTY-FIVE PERCENT!

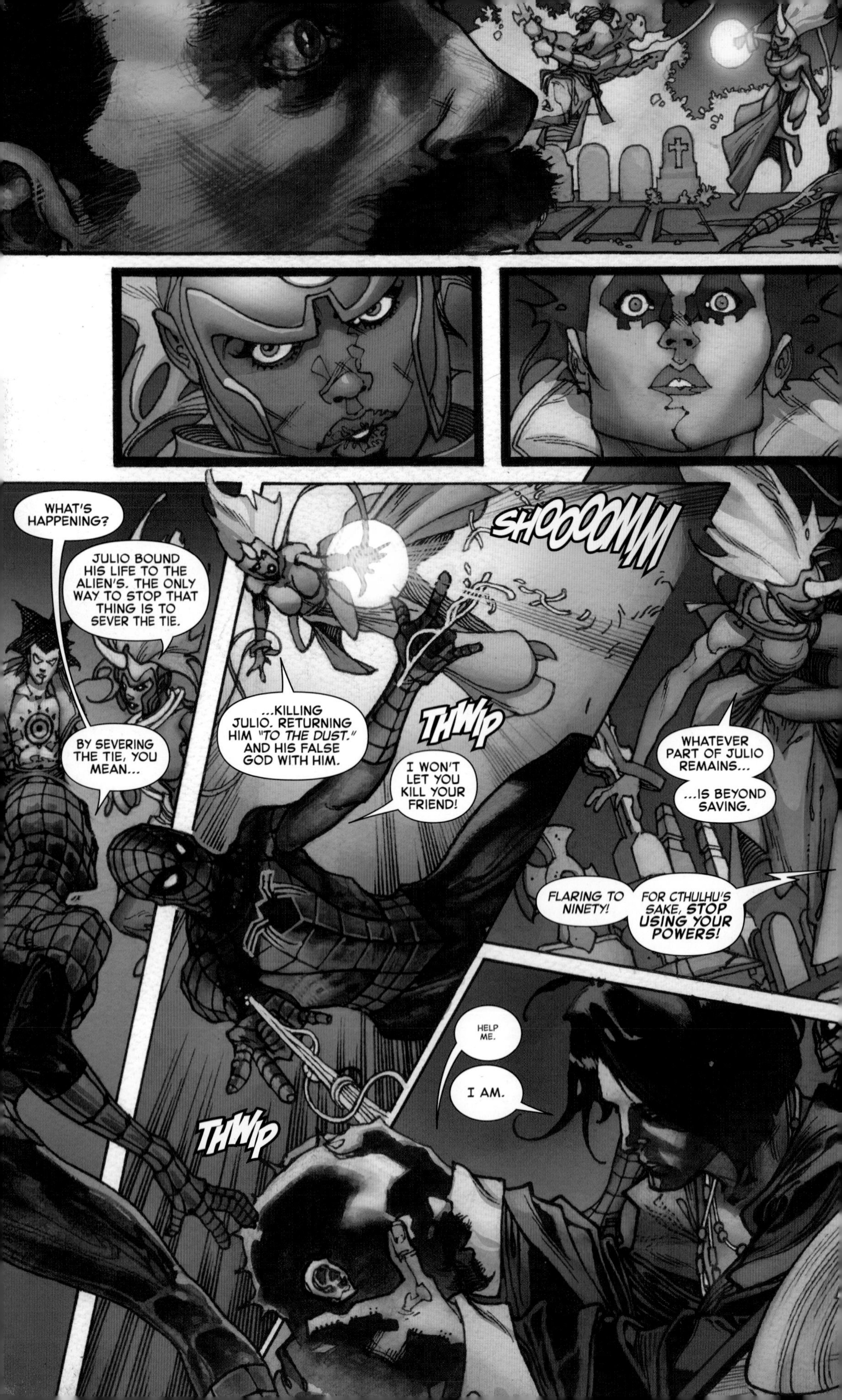

WHAT'S HAPPENING?
JULIO BOUND HIS LIFE TO THE ALIEN'S. THE ONLY WAY TO STOP THAT THING IS TO SEVER THE TIE.
BY SEVERING THE TIE, YOU MEAN...
...KILLING JULIO. RETURNING HIM "TO THE DUST." AND HIS FALSE GOD WITH HIM.
SHOOOOMM
THWIP
I WON'T LET YOU KILL YOUR FRIEND!
WHATEVER PART OF JULIO REMAINS...
...IS BEYOND SAVING.
FLARING TO NINETY!
FOR CTHULHU'S SAKE, STOP USING YOUR POWERS!
HELP ME.
I AM.
THWIP

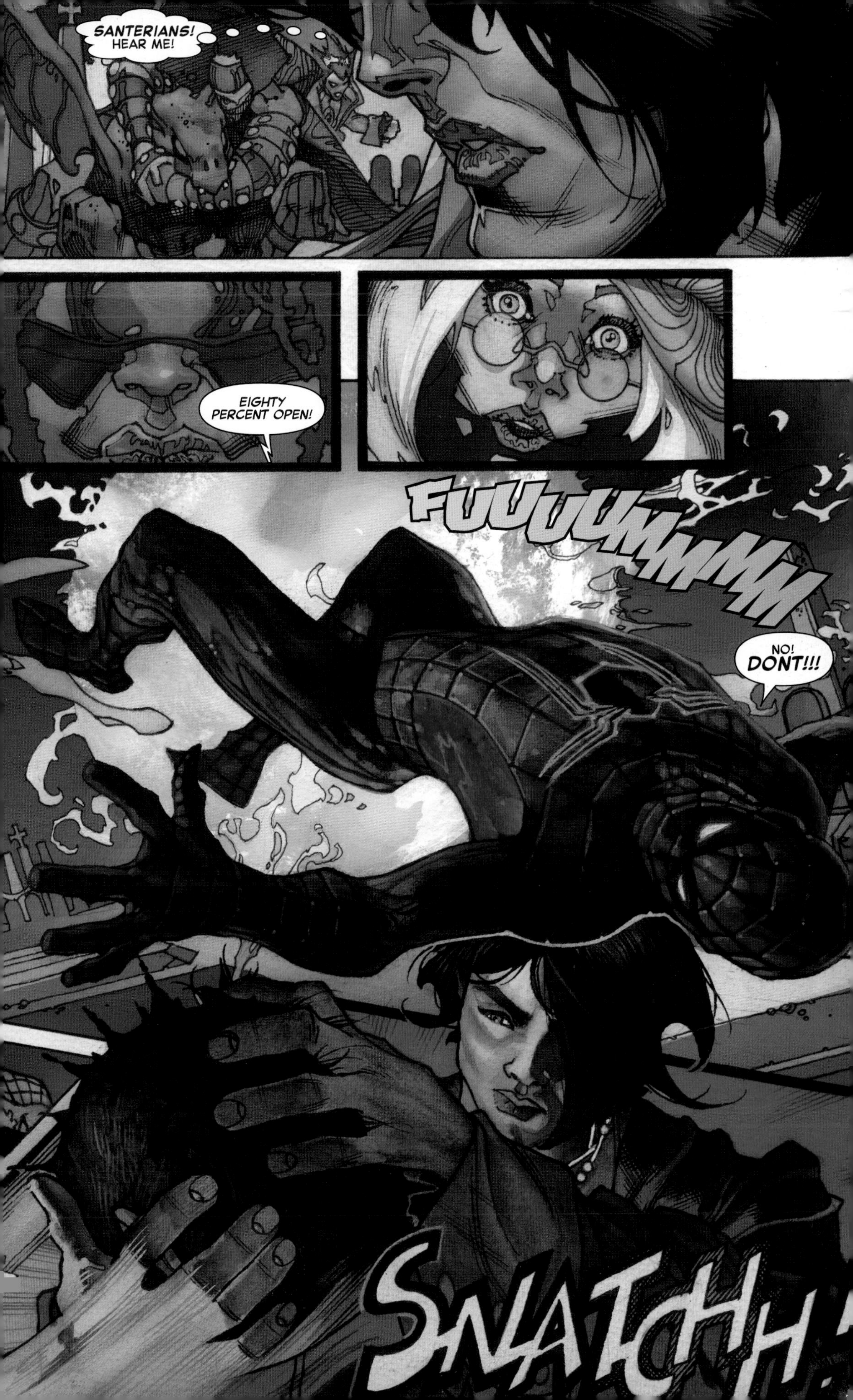
SANTERIANS! HEAR ME!
EIGHTY PERCENT OPEN!
FUUUUMMMMM
NO! DONT!!!
SNATCHH!

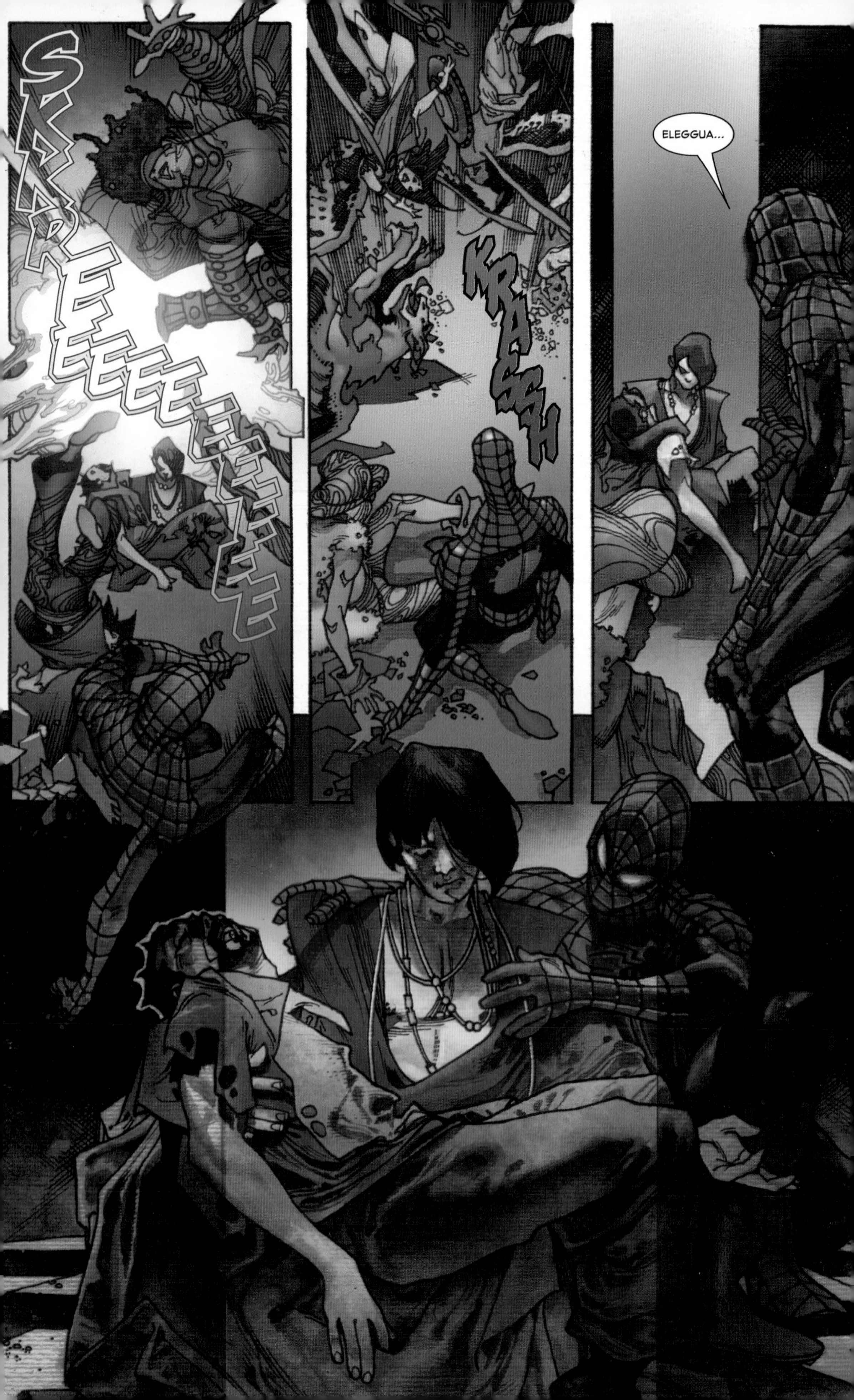
KRASSH
ELEGGUA...

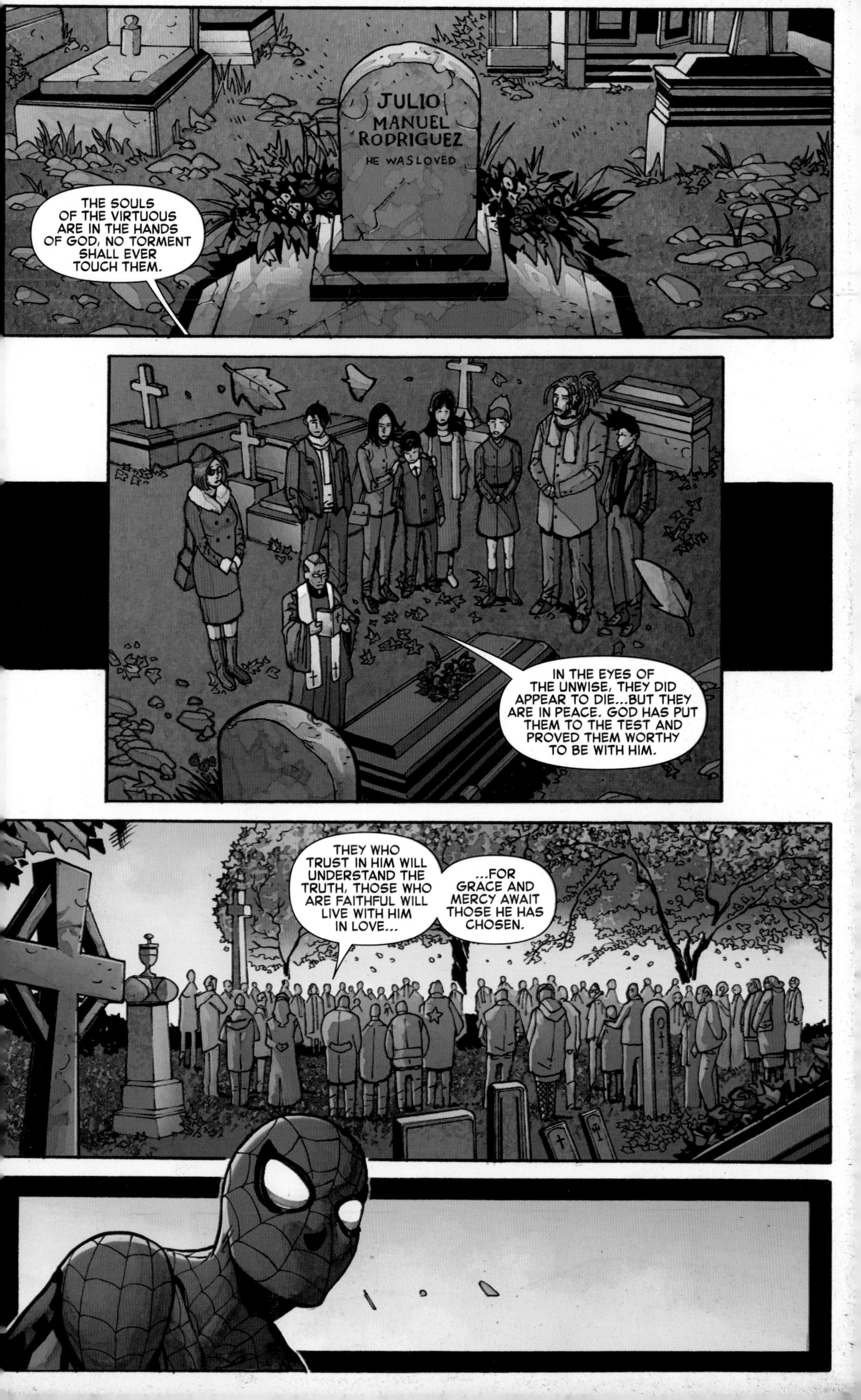
JULIO MANUEL RODRIGUEZ
HE WAS LOVED
THE SOULS OF THE VIRTUOUS ARE IN THE HANDS OF GOD, NO TORMENT SHALL EVER TOUCH THEM.
IN THE EYES OF THE UNWISE, THEY DID APPEAR TO DIE...BUT THEY ARE IN PEACE. GOD HAS PUT THEM TO THE TEST AND PROVED THEM WORTHY TO BE WITH HIM.
THEY WHO TRUST IN HIM WILL UNDERSTAND THE TRUTH, THOSE WHO ARE FAITHFUL WILL LIVE WITH HIM IN LOVE...
...FOR GRACE AND MERCY AWAIT THOSE HE HAS CHOSEN.

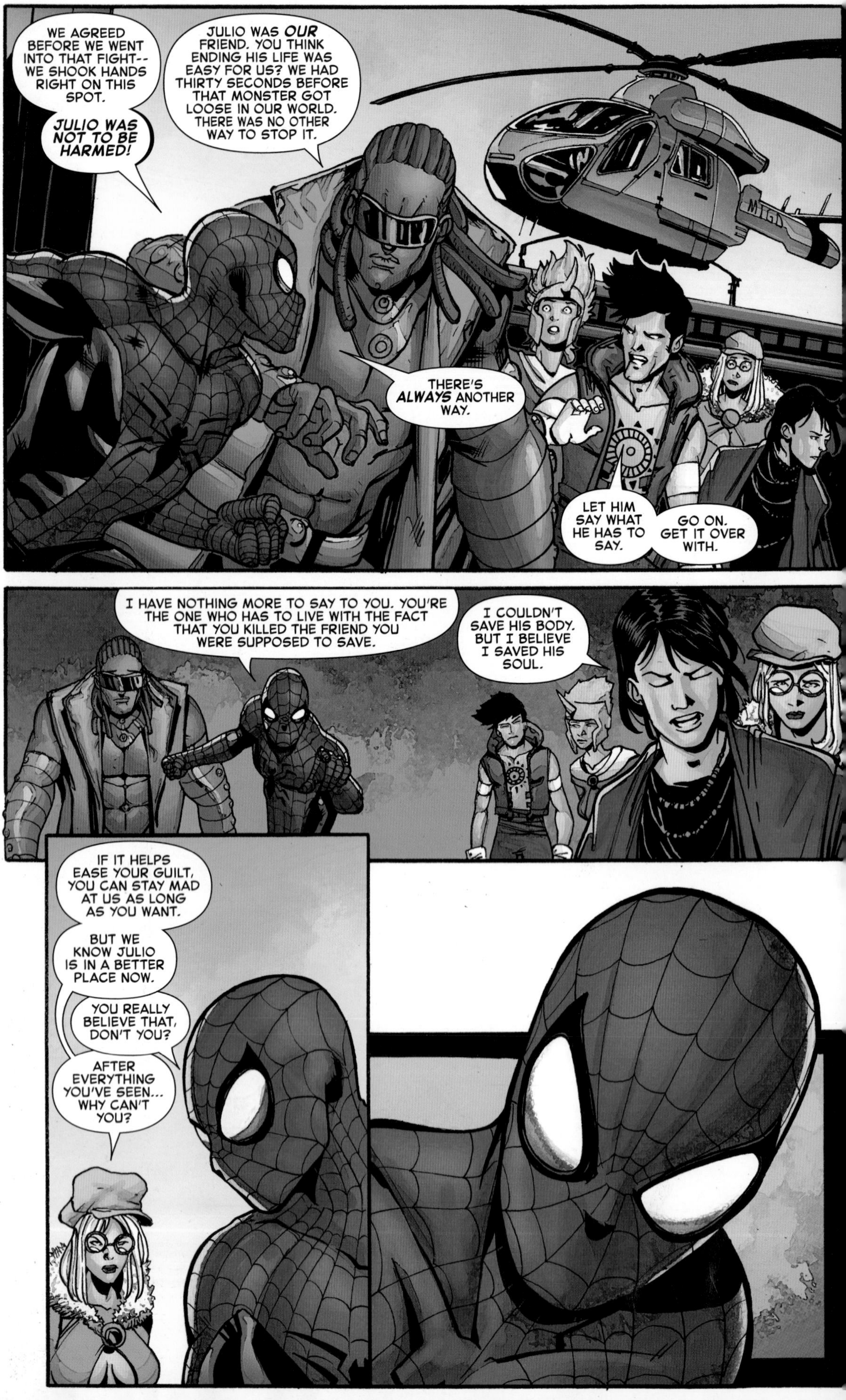
WE AGREED BEFORE WE WENT INTO THAT FIGHT-- WE SHOOK HANDS RIGHT ON THIS SPOT.
JULIO WAS NOT TO BE HARMED!
JULIO WAS OUR FRIEND. YOU THINK ENDING HIS LIFE WAS EASY FOR US? WE HAD THIRTY SECONDS BEFORE THAT MONSTER GOT LOOSE IN OUR WORLD. THERE WAS NO OTHER WAY TO STOP IT.
THERE'S ALWAYS ANOTHER WAY.
LET HIM SAY WHAT HE HAS TO SAY.
GO ON. GET IT OVER WITH.
I HAVE NOTHING MORE TO SAY TO YOU. YOU'RE THE ONE WHO HAS TO LIVE WITH THE FACT THAT YOU KILLED THE FRIEND YOU WERE SUPPOSED TO SAVE.
I COULDN'T SAVE HIS BODY. BUT I BELIEVE I SAVED HIS SOUL.
IF IT HELPS EASE YOUR GUILT, YOU CAN STAY MAD AT US AS LONG AS YOU WANT.
BUT WE KNOW JULIO IS IN A BETTER PLACE NOW.
YOU REALLY BELIEVE THAT, DON'T YOU?
AFTER EVERYTHING YOU'VE SEEN... WHY CAN'T YOU?

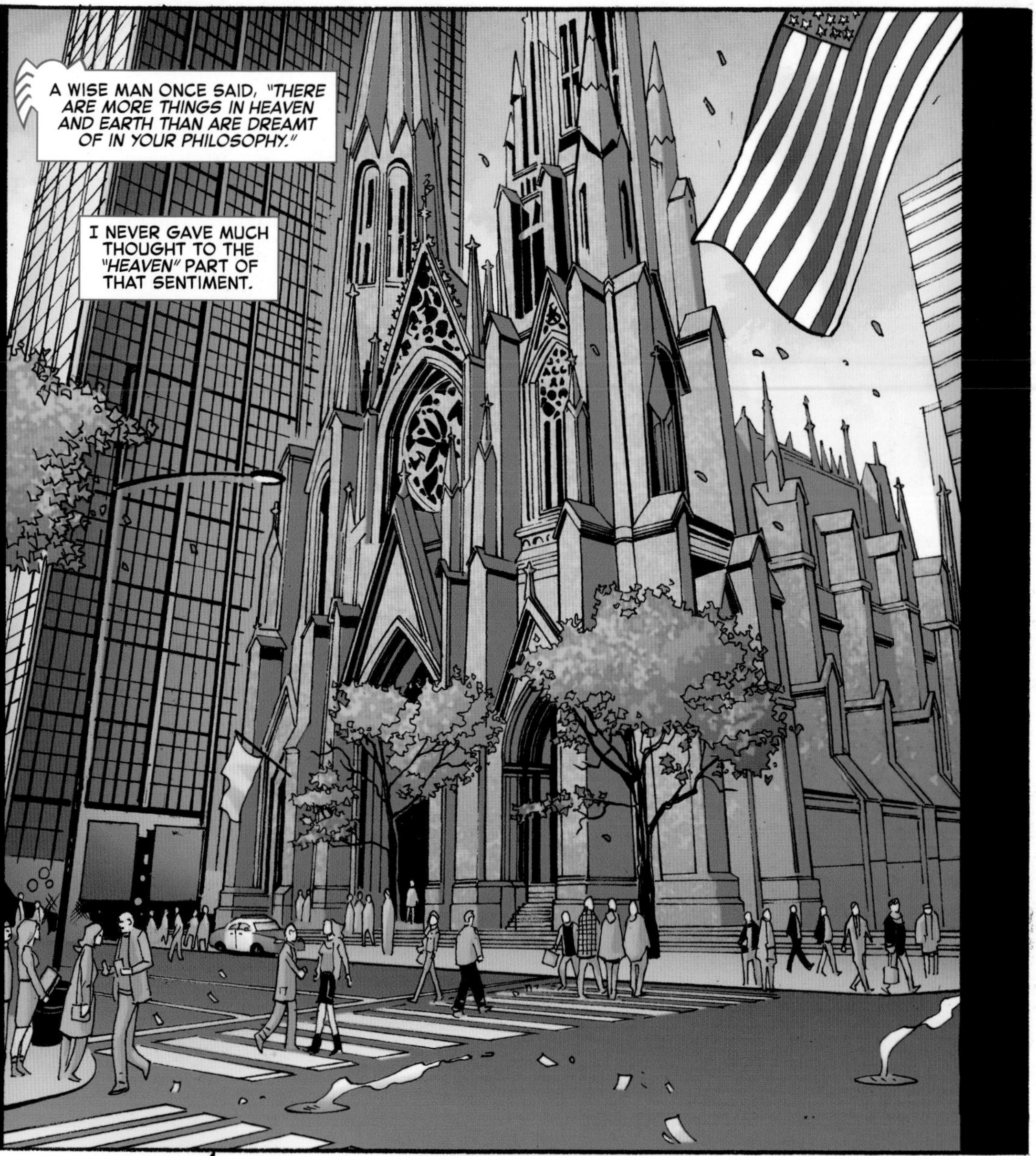
A WISE MAN ONCE SAID, "THERE ARE MORE THINGS IN HEAVEN AND EARTH THAN ARE DREAMT OF IN YOUR PHILOSOPHY."
I NEVER GAVE MUCH THOUGHT TO THE "HEAVEN" PART OF THAT SENTIMENT.

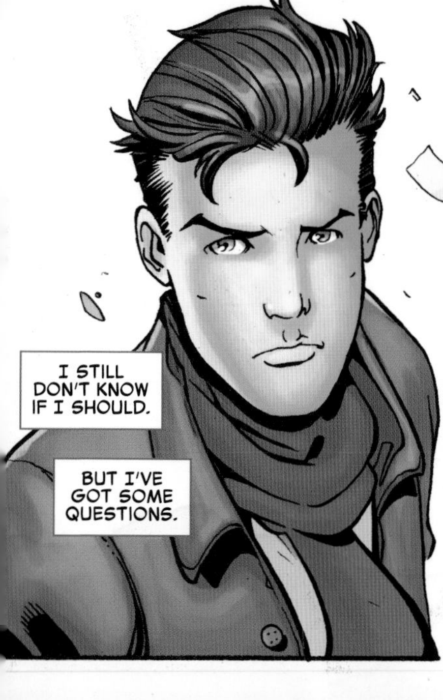
I STILL DON'T KNOW IF I SHOULD.
BUT I'VE GOT SOME QUESTIONS.

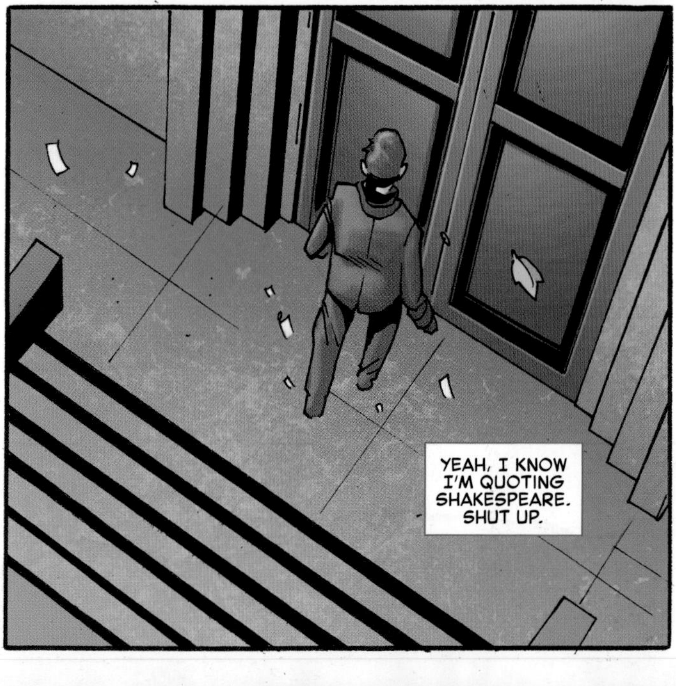
YEAH, I KNOW I'M QUOTING SHAKESPEARE. SHUT UP.

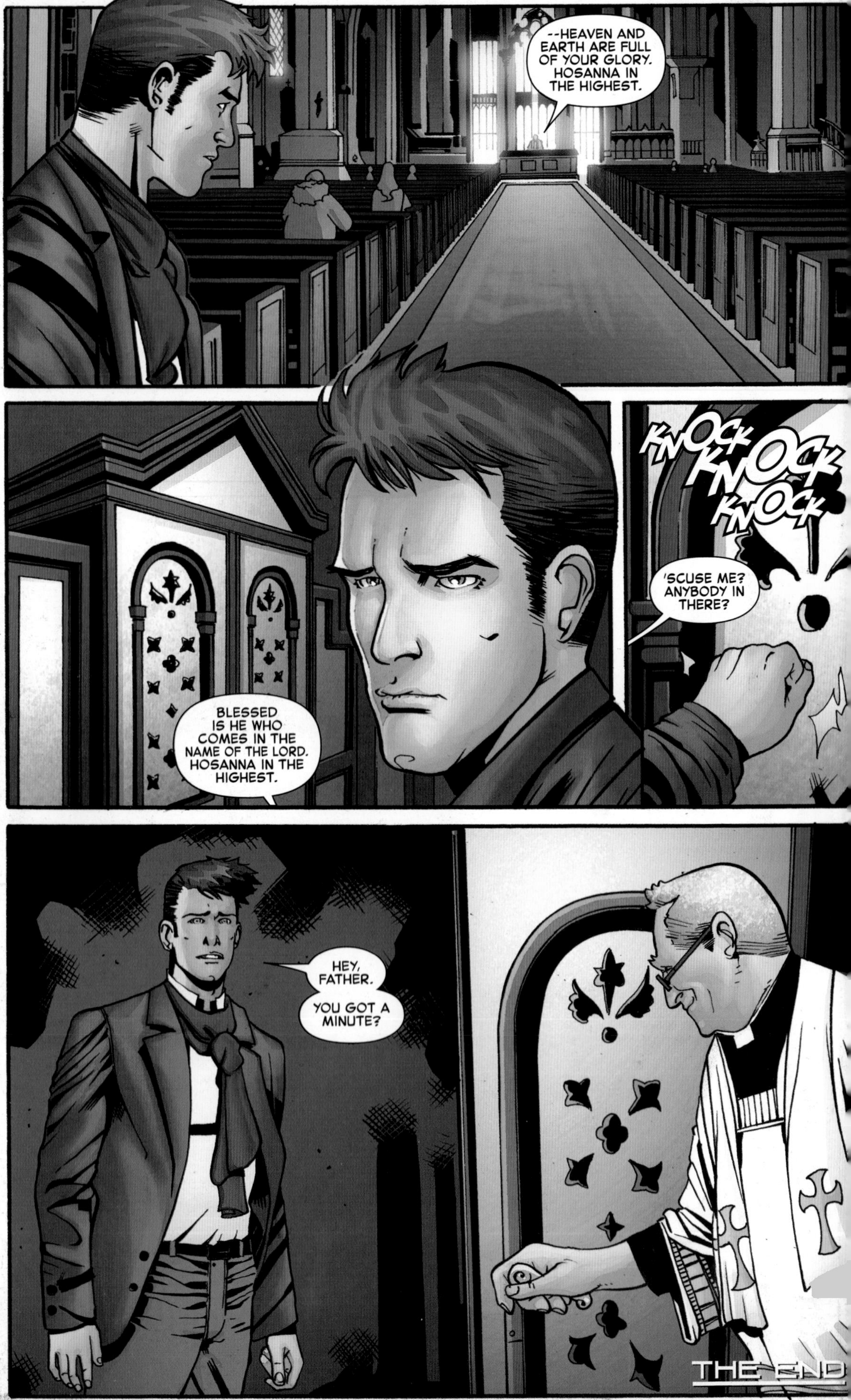
--HEAVEN AND EARTH ARE FULL OF YOUR GLORY. HOSANNA IN THE HIGHEST.
BLESSED IS HE WHO COMES IN THE NAME OF THE LORD. HOSANNA IN THE HIGHEST.
KNOCK KNOCK KNOCK
'SCUSE ME? ANYBODY IN THERE?
HEY, FATHER.
YOU GOT A MINUTE?
THE END

The AMAZING SPIDER-MAN
Variant Covers

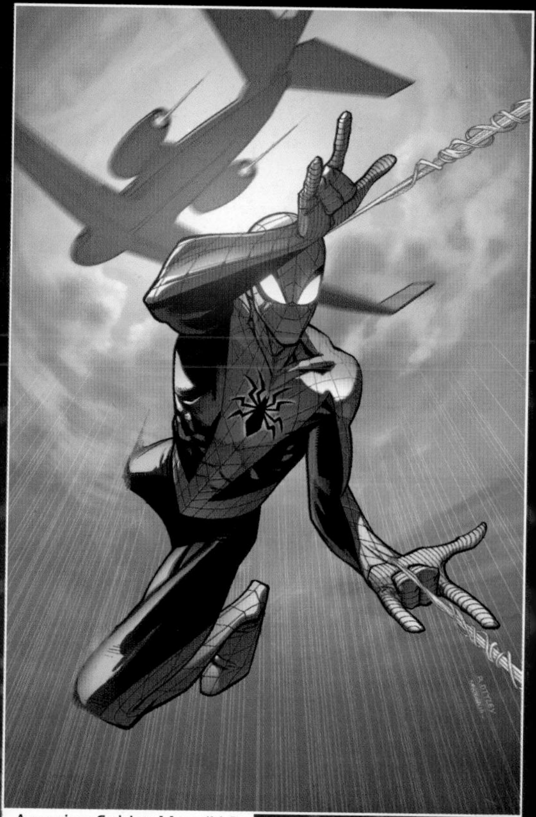

Amazing Spider-Man #1.2
by Ryan Ottley

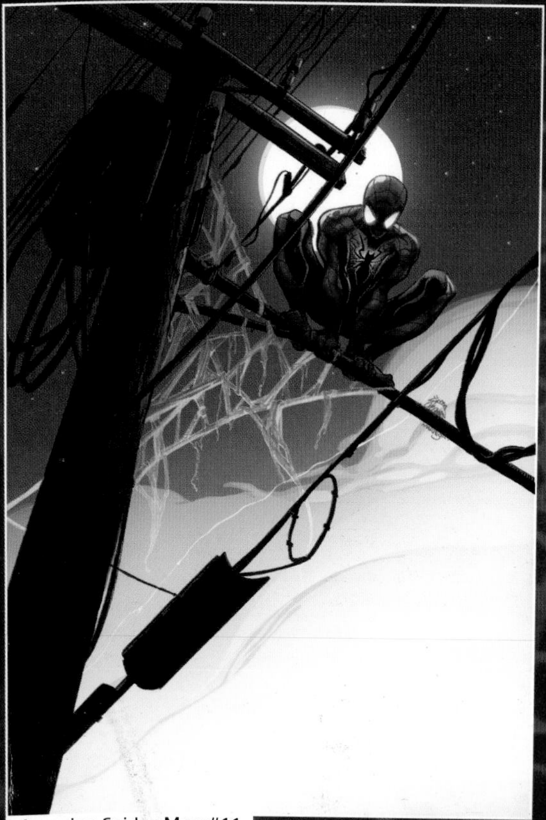

Amazing Spider-Man #1.1
by Ryan Stegman

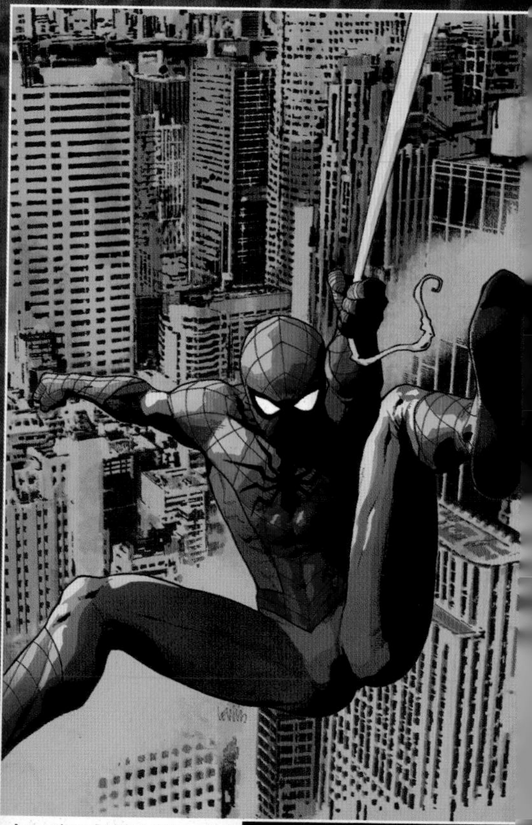

Amazing Spider-Man #1.3
by Leinil Yu

Amazing Spider-Man #1.5
by Simone Bianchi

Amazing Spider-Man #1.4
by Francesco Francavilla

Amazing Spider-Man #1.6
by Simone Bianchi